T0378046

The Socio-Cultural, Ethnic and Historic Foundations of Kenya's Electoral Violence

Kenya's 2007 General Election results announcement precipitated the worst ethnic conflict in the country's history; 1,133 people were killed, while 600,000 were internally displaced. Within 2 months, the incumbent and the challenger had agreed to a power-sharing agreement and a Government of National Unity.

This book investigates the role of socio-cultural origins of ethnic conflict during electoral periods in Kenya beginning with the multi-party era of democratization and the first multi-party elections of 1992, illustrating how ethnic groups construct their interests and cooperate (or fail to) based on shared traits. The author demonstrates that socio-cultural traditions have led to the collaboration (and frequent conflict) between the Kikuyu and Kalenjin that has dominated power and politics in independent Kenya. The author goes onto evaluate the possibility of peace for future elections.

This book will be of interest to scholars of African democracy, Kenyan history and politics, and ethnic conflict.

Stephen M. Magu is Assistant Professor of Political Science at Hampton University, USA.

Routledge African Studies

For a full list of available titles please visit: www.routledge.com/African-Studies/book-series/AFRSTUD

18 Sexual Violence in Conflict and Post-Conflict Societies
International Agendas and African Contexts
Edited by Doris Buss, Joanne Lebert, Blair Rutherford, Donna Sharkey and Obijiofor Aginam

19 Land Reforms and Natural Resource Conflicts in Africa
New Development Paradigms in the Era of Global Liberalization
Edited by Tukumbi Lumumba-Kasongo

20 Cultural Entrepreneurship in Africa
Edited by Ute Röschenthaler and Dorothea Schulz

21 The New African Diaspora in the United States
Edited by Toyin Falola and Adebayo Oyebade

22 Human Rights, Race, and Resistance in Africa and the African Diaspora
Edited by Toyin Falola and Cacee Hoyer

23 Inclusive Growth in Africa
Policies, Practice, and Lessons Learnt
Edited by Steve Kayizzi-Mugerwa, Abebe Shimeles, Angela Lusigi and Ahmed Moummi

24 Africa in Black Liberal Activism
Malcolm X, Stokely Carmichael & Walter Rodney
Tunde Adeleke

25 Global Africans
Race, Ethnicity and Shifting Identities
Edited by Toyin Falola and Cacee Hoyer

26 The Socio-Cultural, Ethnic and Historic Foundations of Kenya's Electoral Violence
Democracy on Fire
Stephen M. Magu

The Socio-Cultural, Ethnic and Historic Foundations of Kenya's Electoral Violence

Democracy on fire

Stephen M. Magu

LONDON AND NEW YORK

First published 2018
by Routledge
2 Park Square, Milton Park, Abingdon, Oxon OX14 4RN

and by Routledge
711 Third Avenue, New York, NY 10017

Routledge is an imprint of the Taylor & Francis Group, an informa business

British Library Cataloguing-in-Publication Data
A catalogue record for this book is available from the British Library

Library of Congress Cataloging-in-Publication Data
Names: Magu, Stephen M., author.
Title: The socio-cultural, ethnic and historic foundations of Kenya's electoral violence: democracy on fire/Stephen M. Magu.
Other titles: Routledge African studies; 26.
Description: New York: Routledge, 2018. | Series: Routledge African studies; 26 | Includes bibliographical references and index.
Identifiers: LCCN 2017049539 | ISBN 9780815350651 (hardback) | ISBN 9781351142441 (e-book)
Subjects: LCSH: Elections–Kenya. | Political violence–Kenya–History. | Kenya–Ethnic relations–Political aspects. | Kenya–Politics and government–1978–2002. | Kenya–Politics and government–2002–
Classification: LCC JQ2947.A95 M34 2018 | DDC 324.96762–dc23
LC record available at https://lccn.loc.gov/2017049539

ISBN: 978-0-815-35065-1 (hbk)
ISBN: 978-1-351-14244-1 (ebk)

Typeset in Times
by Apex CoVantage, LLC

Contents

Preamble

Shortly after the announcement of the results of the general election in December 2007, Kenya, a country once considered the bastion of peace in a tumultuous East Africa, was on fire, in a Rwanda-esque-type ethnic conflagration, with different communities appearing intent on exterminating the perceived enemy community, based on age-old land grievances, interspersed with genuine electoral malfeasance protests. Of course, the tensions had been simmering for long: 10 and 15 years previously, right before and after elections, the conflicts over land and domination of government especially by one ethnic group caused other ethnic groups to chafe. Ethnic conflict was to be expected; other than perhaps Tanzania, it is nigh impossible to find one African democracy that has not been racked by some sort of ethnic-driven electoral violence, including those countries thought to be ethnically homogeneous. *Like Somalia.*

The overriding questions, of course, were, What had gone wrong with this former island of tranquility, and why were Kenyans butchering each other in what threatened to re-create the tragedy of Rwanda of 1994? After all, Kenya was a former British colony, a staunch ally of the US, the North Atlantic Treaty Organization, and its Western partners against the Soviet Union and the Warsaw Pact during the Cold War and now was perhaps a reluctant partner in the global war on terror. Western powers, after taking a lot of heat over hand-wringing in Rwanda in 1994, were not about to let Kenya go *Rwanda*. The solution was going to be a rapid attempt at containing the violence, using everything from coercion to compellence – and the result was the later much-disparaged '*nusu-mkate*' (half-loaf) coalition government, the consequence of a rapidly, internationally negotiated arrangement.

The coalition government was formally known as the Government of National Unity (GNU); it ushered in a 5-year power-sharing government between the president, Mwai Kibaki, and his eternal nemesis (or the grand enemy of *Kibaki's people*), Raila Amolo Odinga. GNU would decidedly pacify the raging conflict, even as international development partners and major powers threatened dire consequences, sanctions and, possibly, invocation of the doctrine of the Responsibility to Protect (R2P) to the principals, if the fighting did not abate and Kenya was allowed to go the Rwanda or Somalia way. The principals decided it was foolhardy to play "chicken" and relented; multilateral diplomacy had won the day, and the concept of international R2P had won.

The factors underlying the genesis of the post-election violence are of special interest. Was it an issue of rigging (ballot stuffing and/or stolen election) results, threatening to overshadow decades of peace in practically the only non-socialist country in the East African region? Was it the work of unemployed youth, paid off by wealthy politicians to harass ethnic groups that were perceived to be different and to not have voted for the candidate in the predominant community in certain areas? Was it decades of pre-colonial, colonial and post-colonial tribal animosity, now fueled by a process that inherently favors numbers (which are then driven by ethnic identity/identification) boiling over, threatening to devastate the country? Or was it *the* shot across the bow, the template for future elections in Kenya and the dispute/conflict resolution, one that would pave the way for similar governments in Zimbabwe and perhaps the Ivory Coast? More important, what was the primary cause of the violence?

This monograph examines the circumstances preceding, surrounding and following the post-election violence in Kenya, beginning with a brief history of Kenya's tribal animosities, election violence during other elections (1988, 1992, 1997), the relatively peaceful 2002 elections and the lead-up to the 2007 election violence. It looks briefly at the post-conflict conditions, including the negotiated peace, the 2010 promulgation of a new constitution and the pacific 2013 elections. One of the outcomes of the 2007 post-election violence was the call to establish a national (or international) mechanism to prosecute the perpetrators and those bearing the greatest responsibility for the post-election violence. Failure to establish a local mechanism led to the referral of six individuals to the International Criminal Court (ICC). Under these conditions, Kenya promulgated the new constitution and held elections in 2013. In perhaps one of the great ironies of Kenyan politics, Uhuru Kenyatta and William Ruto, subject to ICC cases, were elected.

The history of Kenya's electoral (and ethnic) violence is complex; it is, however, rooted in the control of resources: land, government and the economy. It's about numbers, strategy, alliances and coalitions. Thus, in this monograph, each chapter examines the effect of ethnicity on prior violent electoral conflict. The running theme shows that even with democratization, ethnic violence *need* not happen. In fact, some communities that have generated and been targets of the violent conflict have gone on to cooperate, and to dominate government, producing between them all the presidents the country has had.

Introduction

In the summer of 2016, I had a conversation with a 70-year old Kenyan woman, for whom I have the utmost respect. This woman was born in 1946 (official records indicate that she was born in 1950). She lived through the sunset years of British colonial rule in Kenya, had first-hand knowledge of and possible interaction with the Mau Mau (as a harmless "runner" [messenger]) and recalled the unprecedented feat by the then-25-year-old Kenyan, Kisoi Munyao of raising the flag of the newly independent country on Mount Kenya at midnight of 11 December 1963, broadcast over radio, as Kenya became independent of the British Empire. She lived through the dawn of the new republic, as land was allocated, education became available to the new citizens and the new president pledged to fight poverty, ignorance and disease. As democracy's space shrank, she lived through the one-party state, index-finger-wagging practice designed to show membership and allegiance to Kenya African National Union (KANU) and enjoyed the political space after the second wave of democratization that brought about multi-party politics in Kenya. While she managed to acquire a sixth-grade education – she did not start school until she was 14, her memory is keen, and the license to embellish doesn't seem to be in her *bailiwick*.

Her accounts of events during and after colonization are quite believable because she recounts stories of raids by the "*Ngaati*", the colonial administration Home Guards, Kenyan (police) officers hired to assist the minority colonialists rule over the majority black population. She also recalls sometimes taking food to the forest but is not clear if she ever saw any Mau Mau freedom fighters (or, if you ask the British, terrorists). She also clearly recounts the "*kiugu*", shelters (unfit for animals) where the colonists held hundreds, often thousands, of civilians rounded up in an attempt to deny the Mau Mau support by the local populations. She also happens to be my mother, and I generally tend to believe nearly everything she tells me.

The political debate moved to the upcoming (in less than nine months) 2017 elections. She affirmed that "most people" were planning to vote for "*kamwana*" – the 55-year-old incumbent president, Uhuru Muigai Kenyatta, the son of the first president of independent Kenya, Johnston "Jomo" Kamau wa Ngengi "Kenyatta", and his expected running mate, William Samoei arap Ruto, the current vice president, who is also expected to run for president in 2022. The outcome of the 2017 election seemed pretty set; barring a Trumpesque upset, the Jubilee government, despite its political scandals, was expected to easily cruise to a second five-year term.

Will the Kikuyu people support William Ruto, when (not if), he decides to run for the highest office in the land? Yes, absolutely. Um, not so fast, counters a 43-year-old man. "William Ruto will not gain any support", he contends, particularly if Peter Kenneth, former member of parliament for Gatanga Constituency and a presidential aspirant in 2013, runs for office. One of the Kikuyu politicians from Kiambu had intimated as much, literally letting the cat out of the bag. My interest, though, was in why the Kikuyu have never supported Raila Odinga, or his father, Jaramogi Oginga Odinga, since the latter split from KANU in 1966 to form the Kenya Peoples' Union (KPU), and his son, Raila Odinga, began running for president, every election (except 2002), beginning 1992.

"What if Raila Odinga promises to build a Level 5 Hospital in North Kinangop" (about 10 miles from the Soapbox of the discussion) or upgrades the Engineer-Kirima-Naivasha Road, which, despite 30 years of Kikuyu presidencies, has never been tarmacked, and the section between Kirima and Naivasha, last paved in 1959? She still was not changing her mind. For reference, the Kirima-Naivasha Road is the major outlet for Nyandarua District, which provides the majority of Nairobi's dietary needs including fresh milk, potatoes and fresh vegetables. It reminded me of the proposition in politics that people regularly vote against their interests as regularly as the sun rises.

In the case of politics in Kenya, and the foundational reason that the Kikuyu will not now, or ever, (pledge to) support a Luo candidate for president yet have allied themselves with different groups including, at present, the Kalenjin peoples, has nothing to do with politics and everything to do with cultural norms and beliefs: circumcision. But, more on this later. The issue of politics in Kenya, the "political rivalry" between the Kikuyu and the Luo and the unshakeable support for the(ir) respective presidential candidates, voting as a bloc and only in very few instances splitting their votes, is well known in the Kenyan circles. Despite the bloc voting, within the ethnic group, the vote is sometimes split; for example, in 1992, the Kikuyu votes were split between Mwai Kibaki of the Democratic Party and Kenneth Matiba of the Forum for the Restoration of Democracy (FORD); even then, the split followed largely an ethnic/clan basis among the Kikuyus.

The creation of the most valid inter-group alliances then is not necessarily based on shared ideology. There are no Democrats or Republicans, liberals or conservatives. There are only members of ethnic groups vying for political office, creating coalitions that will get them elected into office. In fact, ideology is one of the least important determinants of how individuals cast their votes. Thus, despite the fact that one presidential candidate might be more inclined to have a more progressive development agenda, ethnic sensitivities have in the past have influenced, and are likely to continue to, the coalitions that are built by different ethnic groups in Kenya and the propensity of the groups to resort to violence the longer politics and democracy are based on ethnically driven voting.

Conversations such as those highlighted above go on every day, all over Kenya. For the first time in 2013, a presidential debate was held. While the current president's performance was not especially brilliant, it did not sink his prospects either. Yet, almost nationally (I daresay universally), it was agreed that the best debate performer, the "winner", was Peter Kenneth; he had national support by diverse groups of people, particularly the youth. So how did Uhuru Muigai Kenyatta end up in the State House, a place where he first arrived at, at the tender age of two, and spent the first 15 formative years as the son of the president? Much of it has to do with name recognition: his father, after all, was one of the most renowned freedom fighters; he had name recognition, a history of above-average political involvement and a US$10 billion fortune behind his bid. Peter Kenneth, for all his charm, charisma, youth, progressive ideas and mixed heritage – literally, Kenya's (second) Obama – did not have a prayer.

Kenya's democracy is intensely ethnic in nature. Pre-colonial and immediate, post-colonial considerations play an outsized role in its current political dispensations. The absence of a national identity and the overriding fidelity to ethnic identity make democracy an almost necessarily ethnic proposition. The memories of past injustices and grievances are long, and the social and cultural traditions and beliefs about leadership deep. The allegiance to the "nation" of Kenya is superficial, and it is easy to see how, despite all the best of British intents to have a unitary nation, it is more accurate to view Kenya as a nation of 43-plus tribes, generally thought to be peaceful and a beacon of what a modern capitalist-democratic African nation could be.

Island of peace or well-managed simmering conflicts?

"Kenya, the island of peace in the volatile Great Lakes region of Africa . . ."[1] So begins an article by Jacqueline Klopp and Prisca Kamungi, discussing the impact of the 2007 post-election violence. This view of Kenya is repeated over and over again; Kenya "an island of peace", a place of "tranquility", a country that offered the template on how to be both ethnically divided and avoid the conflicts that have plagued Africa, particularly since the fall of the Berlin Wall and the collapse of the Soviet Union.[2]

How did the once bastion of political stability, surrounded by years and spaces of inter- and intra-state violence, so quickly descend into mayhem and tribal killings and threaten to descend quickly into Rwanda/Somalia? Was it a consequence of stolen elections? Or was it a culmination of many years of social, political and economic marginalization of some of the communities? Did the political scores needing settling go back all the way to the beginning of multi-party democracy? Did it go further back, to the 1982 coup and the subsequent crackdown on some communities and their elites? Was it the final chapter in ethnic cleansing, one that had gone on for several election cycles? Was it a final score settlement between the Kikuyu community, sometimes intensely disliked, and the alliance of other communities? Did this go back to before independence, to the fight for political independence from British colonial rule, or did go even further back, when Kenya consisted of disparate ethnic groups, not bound by any sense of common national heritage?

Many scholars have advanced theories and reasons for the rapid and deadly descent into political violence following the 2007 elections in Kenya. The sources and explanation of the violence, in 2007 and during other times, are as numerous and complex as is Kenya. Some Kenyan scholars have attributed the violence to the first independent Kenya's president, and his general disdain for Odinga and the Luo community, and the assassination of some of the leading figures from the community. Others have traced the violence back to a consequence of the British colonial policy that dispossessed the numerous Kikuyus, forcing them to relocate to the Rift Valley, thus setting up the template for clashes over ownership of land in the province. Some have attributed some of the conflicts to electoral outcomes, while others have pointed to a perceived Kikuyu sense of superiority that brings intense hatred for the group. What is clear is that the Kikuyus have always been targeted but that they have also dominated government and business more than all the other communities in Kenya.

The post-election violence in Kenya leveraged traditional aspects (e.g., the causes of the violence, based on ethnic identity and a history of political and economic grievances), state-sponsored tools (national identity cards, which clearly listed the individual and their place of birth, often closely associated with ethnic identity) and utilized modern technologies (e.g., the role of the Internet – social media, rapid communication using text messages[3] – and FM radio, much as was the case in Rwanda 13 years previously) to leverage and spread ethnically driven sentiment, using these to coordinate attacks and revenge attacks and to plan new ones. The results of the violence altered the ethnic composition of many areas of the country, particularly in the western parts of the Rift Valley Highlands, whose makeup had been changing already, following the 1992 and 1997 attacks. In particular, according to Human Rights Watch (HRW), the 2007 attacks

> dramatically altered the ethnic makeup of many parts of Kenya. Scores of communities across the Rift Valley, including most of Eldoret itself, are no longer home to any Kikuyu residents. The rural areas outside of Naivasha, Nakuru, and Molo are similarly emptying of Kikuyu while Kalenjin and Luo are leaving the urban areas. In Central Province, few non-Kikuyu remain. The slums of Mathare, Kibera and others in Nairobi have been carved into enclaves where vigilantes from one ethnic group or another patrol "their" areas.[4]

Scholarship on the post-election violence in Kenya generally tends to localize the problem to any of the myriad issues that plague nascent democracies – ballot-box stuffing, voter intimidation, disagreement with the results and lack of "credible" mechanisms to address the election outcomes, the sense of a "rigged system" against certain ethnic groups, the idea that it was another group's "turn to eat" and a host of other conditions peculiar to Africa's multi-party democratic politics in ethnically divided countries. Yet, such scholarship fails to account for the historical conditions, ranging from the conditions before the advent of colonial rule, and what was considered ancestral homelands. Under colonial rule, the most fertile areas of the Kenya highlands were appropriated by the colonialists; upon independence, resettlement in these areas did not necessarily pay heed to the ancestral claims, pitting ethnic group against another.

Throughout its post-colonial history, the ethnic divisions flared up from time to time, and political intrigue and maneuvering continued; these included the demotion of Oginga Odinga from the vice presidential slot in 1969; the attempt by the "Kikuyu mafia" to bar the then vice president, Daniel Toroitich arap Moi, from ascending to the presidency on the death of Jomo Kenyatta in August 1978; the military coup d'état attempted by air force officers on 1 August 1982; the subsequent imprisonment of Raila Oginga, Jaramogi Oginga Odinga's son, and the virulent crackdown on pro-democracy forces in the early 1990s; and, ultimately, the first multi-party elections in almost three decades in 1992.

The advent of multi-party politics brought a different dimension to the politics of Kenya: one in which now pitted ethnic groups against other ethnic groups, with each coalition attempting to ascend to the highest office in the land. Surprisingly, Kenya's half-century of independence have been marked by four presidencies; Jomo Kenyatta (Kikuyu, 15 years), Daniel Arap Moi (Kalenjin, 24 years); Mwai Kibaki (Kikuyu, 10 years) and, currently, Uhuru Kenyatta (Kikuyu, 5 years). For the more than 40 other groups, this domination by one or two ethnic groups has been a source of constant chafing and ideas as diverse as a rotational presidency. Thus, multi-party democracy in Kenya has not taken on the notions of "deliberative decision-making"; rather, it has brought about much-resented domination by the major ethnic groups (the Kikuyu ethnic group is thought to compose 22 percent of Kenya's population). It was thus no surprise that the events of 2007 occurred. With the regular frequency of elections, post-election violence occurs in Kenya; except in 2007, it appeared that the level and intensity might exceed any previous levels.

Not another Rwanda

Kenya's flirtation with genocide and ethnic strife after the 2007 election was relatively short-lived; the combination of local business interests particularly by the elite class; the potential and actual losses already occurring in sectors such as agriculture and tourism, which have significant investments from the same; and the quick pressure brought to bear by international partners, coupled with the threats of sanctions, were sufficiently motivational enough to bring the parties to an agreement late in February 2008. In addition, the practical difficulties of ethnic conflict in Kenya can confound the entire enterprise: there are 43 ethnic groups, and some of them are rather numerous: who becomes an enemy, or a friend, and who allies with whom? Additionally, the ethnic groups not involved in the 2007 post-election violence may not have wanted to have their country destroyed by two ethnic groups. Thus, both internal and external pressure, and the fact that the country's leaders had no properties on the French Riviera, engendered the ultimate outcomes.

Structure

This book argues that Kenya's post-election violence in 2007 was merely a more intense version of what had been going on practically during every election in since the return of multi-party democracy in 1991. In attempts to influence elections, votes for certain candidates over others, or to control parliament and thus government, and enact legislation with little to no opposition, political actors in Kenya have utilized different strategies, including forcible removal of "foreigners" – people of different ethnic groups who might be persuaded to vote differently. As such, 2007 was not unique. It was simply a culmination of decades of political maneuvering that has had its history in the politics of Kenya, even before independence.

Chapter 1 considers the historical conditions in Kenya, touching on the pre-colonial societies and their relations with each other, and the (diverse) structure of the local (perhaps even ethnic groups') governments that existed before the colonial rule. This chapter focuses, especially, on the Kikuyu, the Kalenjin (these two were some of the earliest anti-colonial societies), and the conditions of leadership within the communities, questioning whether these conditions were (a) transferred onto the new leadership structure of the independent, unitary country; (b) illustrative of the problems with centralization of governmental administration and (c) of sufficient disagreement that they threatened the post-colonial administration; and (d) magnified further by British colonial policy in Kenya. It examines the genesis of the Kikuyu–Luo rivalry and how the seeds of future (reaction against the) domination were sown.

Chapter 2 traces the developments of the early years of the Republic, examining the death of the first president, the attempts by the Kikuyu ethnic group's elites (Kiambu mafia) to keep President Moi from power, especially through the "Change the Constitution" movement that aimed to change the succession structure, by replacing the vice president with the Speaker of the House as the next in line to temporarily assume the presidency for 90 days. This involved machinations such as framing the vice president with weapons trafficking. Ultimately, these proposals failed, and Moi became president, promising to *fuata nyayo* – that is, follow the footsteps of the late first president, Jomo Kenyatta, perhaps in order to calm the Kikuyu and consolidate his leadership. It covers the subsequent attempted coup and the consolidation of the one-party state, including the start of an intensely repressive regime that would see the rise of underground groups such as Mwakenya.

Chapter 3 examines the beginnings of the multi-party era: from the botched elections based on Kenya's unique version of democracy, dubbed "*Mlolongo*" (queue) elections ostensibly meant to illustrate that citizens had electoral choices, to the global geopolitical events that culminated with the fall of the Berlin Wall and the collapse of the Soviet Union. With the supremacy of the US now firmed, the latter events diminished the leverage that countries had, for example, by threatening to align with the Soviet Union. Thus, following internal and external pressure from internal agitation for multi-party democracy, and the unrelenting pressure from international partners, including donors, Kenya caved, repealed the infamous "section 2 A" of the constitution that had made Kenya a *de jure* one-party state and opened up democratic space. However, this opening up was also accompanied by some of the worst pre- and post-election violence that the country had experienced until then; almost 600 people were killed, and over half a million dispossessed, disenfranchised and displaced.

In Chapter 4, the beginnings of consolidation of democracy around Africa and particularly in Kenya is discussed. The discussion moves to incumbency, attempts at further constitutional reforms, the question of term limits and whether Moi would respect the will of the people, the need to win "by any means" and the problems of ethnic identity (splitting the vote). The third election held under the multi-party era is discussed, especially Moi's attempts to anoint his successor, incidentally, his successor's son, and the republic's fourth president. The attempted coronation followed an alliance with some of the opposition (Raila Odinga's National Democratic Party, NDP), at which the different political leaders angled for power and to be Moi's successor. The acrimonious alliances that included the merging and re-branding of KANU failed rather spectacularly, and subsequently, Raila split, joining with Kibaki to oppose Uhuru and KANU, and ultimately, Kibaki was elected with the biggest margin of electoral victories in the multi-party era. This chapter also examines the falling out over the "MOU" (memorandum of understanding) between Raila and Kibaki; the breaking point that was the constitutional review referendum in 2005, where the government failed to have the new constitution passed; and the setting up for the 2007 elections under different coalitions, aligned with their support or opposition to the constitution.

Chapter 5 examines the coming storm: the elections of 2007, the campaigns thereof (a continuation of the campaigns for/against the constitutional review) and the reformulation of the alliances based on ethnic identities. Although Kenya is generally thought to have 40-plus "tribes", there are three major classifications – Bantu, Nilotes and Cushites – and these are discussed in-depth, including the frequent alliances, such as KAMATUSA (Kalenjin, Maasai, Turkana and Samburu) and GEMA (Gikuyu, Embu and Meru Association, and sometimes the Akamba). These alliances would be re-constituted in 2007 and would be pitted against each other. The chapter further discusses the general societal and national conditions preceding the election. It starts by examining the culmination of the fall-out between Raila and Kibaki; it also looks at ethnic groups' alliances in the 2007 election: Kibaki, on one hand, and Uhuru Kenyatta/Raila Odinga, on the other. The chapter also discusses how the new administration pulled from the old playbook of using ethnicity to corral votes. The chapter then discusses the elections, the outcomes and the beginning of the bloodletting.

Chapter 6 examines the descent into conflict and the role of different shadowy groups, such as Mũngiki, Jeshi la Mama and Baghdad Boys, among others. It discusses the complexity of the conflict, given Kenya's numerous ethnic groups, and the general instability affecting other communities outside of the Luo/Kalenjin versus Kikuyu conflict. It briefly traces the efforts of national, regional and international mediators and their role in ending the conflict within two months, and setting up a government of national unity, otherwise widely and derisively known as "nusu mkate" in Kenya. The chapter discusses how, as part of the National Dialog and Reconciliation Act that introduced the Government of National Unity, different institutional changes were implemented: the Commission of Inquiry on Post-Election Violence (or the Waki Commission), the Truth Justice and Reconciliation Commission (TJRC) and the requirement for a special Election Violence Tribunal (which did not happen), thus culminating in the referral of six individuals to ICC. Specifically, the chapter has a wide-ranging discussion on TJRC and some of the issues that have led to the necessity for TJRC. It then examines the 2010 constitution, the changes, the successes, the 2013 elections and whether or not the president subsequently elected was a hero or villain, based on their indictment by ICC.

Chapter 7 not only reviews the contemporary Kenya and the ongoing opportunities and challenges for the pacific settlement of disputes but also reviews the question of democracy as an ongoing tyranny of numbers. It argues that despite the proclivity towards violence, the largest ethnic group commands 22 percent of the population, and given that winning candidates need 50 percent + 1 vote of all the votes cast (in the event of elections such as in 1992, where KANU won with 36 percent, a run-off between the two highest scoring candidates would be carried out until a candidate attained the threshold of 50 percent + 1). The chapter further examines whether the different ethnic groups can live together, whether the outcomes of 2010 and 2013 were simply the calm before the storm or whether the same situation might happen in 2017 during the presidential elections. It also examines whether the now-concluded trials at ICC sufficiently demonstrated global resolve in tackling genocide and related issues. The chapter discusses whether consociational democracy might be a more useful way to organize Kenya's politics, considering the failure of liberal democracy in ethnically divided states.

Chapter 8, the concluding chapter, reviews the key events in Kenya's history, the problems of conflict, the numbers of people affected by the conflict, and whether Kenya's political violence is especially outstanding, notwithstanding the foregoing discussions. It examines the strategies that have been used to contain conflict in Kenya, the success thereof (including, e.g., international institutions and Kenya's membership thereof – and, more recently, the gripes against these institutions) and the road map to peace. It especially reviews the "Kenyan Problem" with the Kikuyu people: their dominance of the entire country's landscape – political, economic and social – which leads to hostility from all other communities but also reviews the role of the British colonial policies (including appropriating land and relocating the capital to Nairobi, the area around which Kikuyus settled); it discusses British colonial policy of divide and rule and the Kikuyu reactions that paradoxically set them up as political, economic and business leaders, in addition to the significance of population. The chapter concludes by discussing the "two tribes thesis", which portends possibilities for Kenyans considering themselves as members of the haves and have-nots, rather than as members of ethnic groups.

The utility of ethnic identity in modern African states

In each of the chapters, the question of community (ethnic) relations is explored. This stems from the view that while literature on the development of modern states, be they democracies or autocracies or other models of governance, there is what might be thought of as erroneous assumption of a unitary, homogeneous state. These assumptions proceed to suggest that even in contested states, ideology, rather than identity, is the principal source of disagreement. Thus, analyses of what ails states – domestic audiences, their interests, their conflicts – are often premised on disagreements with this hypothesized unitary state. Having lived in Kenya for the majority of my life, it has occurred to me that western scholarship has not quite engaged with the issue of identity and its role in shaping the state.

Even though scholars *generally* acknowledge and pay some attention to the differences between nations, nation-states and states, the construction of identity, outside that of ideology (for example, Marxism, socialism or democratic capitalism) is the most critical aspect of the development of modern states in Africa. Whereas there were several nations in existence before the Berlin Conference, nations that carried out all the functions of a modern state, from war to diplomacy, elections of executives and representatives (village councils, councils of elders) and jurisprudence relating to all matters, from theft to murder to unwanted pregnancies, the imposition of European rule both magnified the difference between the "new, foreign" way of doing business and exploited the divided unity (unity, within the nation, division, within the larger, "national boundaries"), and the resulting state was perhaps the absolutely worst format of the first instance of central government that the African "nations" experienced (or endured). Thus, even after the granting of independence, the most useful form of government was that derived from the kin, the ethnic group.

Kenya's experience in the past one-and-a-half centuries has had as much to do with imperialism as with the group identity. The questions of who gets what, when and how[5] are inextricably interwoven with the concept of the African first as a member of their ethnic group and perhaps peripherally as a national of whatever colonial-era boundaries they find themselves finagled into. Perhaps the African state stood a chance at redemption, had the events of the 1990s and the second wave of democratization taken place as soon as independence. As it were global geopolitics and who was a commie or not was more important than whether there was an equitable sharing of resources.

As such, as was the case in Kenya, the government facilitated, or ignored corruption, cronyism, nepotism – and a myriad of other "isms" as long as the fundamental question of whether the government aligned with the United States, Western Europe, the North Atlantic Treaty Organization and its allies was answered in the affirmative. In the case of Kenya, the first years saw a systematic undertaking of a post-colonial government that perpetuated primarily the vices of colonialism, including dividing the nation ethnically. It thus behooves us to contemplate how the question of the tribe has had such a significant impact on the issue of government and continues to be the primary source of conflict and the primary method of organizing, even as the country makes strides towards democratization. Thus, the question of ethnic identity and ethnic implications of political decisions is dealt with in each chapter.

Notes

1 Jacqueline Klopp & Prisca Kamungi. "Violence and Elections: Will Kenya Collapse?" *World Policy Journal*, 24, No. 4 (Winter, 2007/2008): 11.
2 See, for example, Maupeu: "Kenyan democracy was viewed as the most successful in the region, particularly after the 2002 political transition" (Hevre Maupeu. "Revisiting Post-Election Violence." In Jérôme Lafargue, Ed. *The General Elections in Kenya, 2007*. (Dar es Salaam: Mkuki na Nyota Publishers, 2009): 187) and Kagwanja's description of Kenya as "one of Africa's most promising democracies" Peter Kagwanja. "Courting Genocide: Populism, Ethno-Nationalism and the Informalisation of Violence in Kenya's 2008 Post-Election Crisis." *Journal of Contemporary African Studies*, 27, No. 3, Kenya's Uncertain Democracy: The Electoral Crisis of 2008 (2009): 365.
3 Ofeibea Quist-Arcton. "Text Messages Used to Incite Violence in Kenya." 20 February 2008: n.p.
4 Human Rights Watch. "Ballots to Bullets: Organized Political Violence and Kenya's Crisis of Government." *Human Rights Watch* (March, 2008): 37.
5 Harold Laswell's well-quoted definition of Politics: "PoliticsIs WhoGetsWhat, When, How."

References

Human Rights Watch. "Ballots to Bullets: Organized Political Violence and Kenya's Crisis of Government." Human Rights Watch (March 2008). Accessed from: http://hrw.org/reports/2008/kenya0308/kenya0308web.pdf

Kagwanja, Peter. "Courting Genocide: Populism, Ethno-Nationalism and the Informalisation of Violence in Kenya's 2008 Post-Election Crisis." *Journal of Contemporary African Studies*, 27, No. 3, Kenya's Uncertain Democracy: The Electoral Crisis of 2008 (2009): 365–387. doi:10.1080/02589000903187024

Klopp, Jacqueline & Prisca Kamungi. "Violence and Elections: Will Kenya Collapse?" *World Policy Journal*, 24, No. 4 (2007): 11–18. Accessed from: www.jstor.org/stable/40210203

Maupeu, Hevre. "Revisiting Post-Election Violence." In Jérôme Lafargue, Ed. *The General Elections in Kenya, 2007*. Dar es Salaam: Mkuki na Nyota Publishers, 2009.

Quist-Arcton, Ofeibea. "Text Messages Used to Incite Violence in Kenya." 20 February 2008, 6:00 AM. Accessed on 11/17/2016 from: www.npr.org/templates/story/story.php?storyId=19188853

1 A brief history of Kenya

From colony to independence

Kenya's current political boundaries have existed in their present form for less than 100 years. Before 1895, Kenya was an amalgamation of individual, ethnically constituted "nations"; they were composed of peoples drawn together by language, history, cultural traditions and experiences and, for the most part, shared well-delineated spaces, perhaps other than the pastoral communities, but whose boundaries and expansive territories were well defined. True, there were occasional raids by neighboring communities, raids that took materiel – cattle, grain and women – perhaps all the vestiges of stuff victorious armies have aspired to, throughout the history of war. After the 1885 Berlin Conference, Kenya, as a colony, was claimed by the British, who formally declared it a colony in 1920. Kenya gained independence in 1963. British direct and indirect rule had lasted approximately 68 years.

Prior to the earliest missionary contact with the interior of East Africa, not much was written, or known, about modern-day Kenya. Missionaries and explorers such as Ludwig Krapf, H. M. Stanley and David Livingston, among others, penetrated the interior beginning in the 1840s. Dr. Krapf, a representative of the Church Missionary Society, landed in Mombasa in 1844.[1] The interactions between the peoples of the coast of Kenya, though, were well chronicled. Coastal Kenya had been in contact for thousands of years with the Arabs, Chinese, and Persians and, from the 15th century, Europeans of different nationalities. The connection between the interior of Kenya and the coast was primarily driven by trade: long-distance trade in ivory, cowrie shells and animal products, including hides, salt, cloves and other goods, is well chronicled, through such pre-colonial figures as Chief Kivoi of the Akamba people.

The earliest record of Kenya's formal experience with the British in any sort of organized manner was through the Imperial British East Africa Company (IBEA Coy). The connection between IBEA and the subsequent British declaration of an East African Protectorate, preceding the Kenya colony, are well articulated. For example, McDermott chronicles Sir William Mackinnon's views – Mackinnon was one of IBEAs founders – and the responsibilities of IBEA: "it was evident that neither could the Company [IBEA] fulfill its mandate as the pioneer of the country's Colonial policy."[2] In other places, the McDermott articulates the goals of the British government of expanding colonization, for example, through the

Royal Niger Company.[3] IBEA formally ceded control of territory and process on 11 April 1895. Part of the necessity for the declaration of a protectorate was due to the fact that the British, after granting IBEA, British South African Company (BSA) and the Royal Niger Company, charters, it had to "protect them from foreign encroachments"[4] and, in part, to follow the lead of other countries.

Much of the earliest colonization was carried out, in both British and German colonization, by these trading companies, granted trading charters, but also with an indirect mandate to facilitate greater economic and political control; their process and procedure of expanding their influence were not without incident. McDermott, for example, writes that

> the Chief Director of the [German East Africa] Company, on attempting to land at Pangani, was fired upon by the townspeople . . . the whole coast burst into a flame of rebellion against European authority, and the people even threatened to renounce their allegiance to the Sultan of Zanzibar[5]

as the sultan had been the party signing the German charter for the colonization of what would later become Deutsche Ostafrika, or German East Africa. For the part of the coastal Kenya that corresponds to the current Coast Province, the British largely left it to the authority of the sultan of Zanzibar (who controlled all of about 10 miles of the coastal strip). Ultimately, the sultan of Zanzibar, now no more than a figurehead, would cede control to the British to become part of British East Africa Protectorate and later, in 1920, the Kenya colony.

Present-day Kenya was thus primarily part of the British East Africa protectorate, territory that extended all the way westwards into Uganda. By June 1920 when the colony of Kenya was established and separated from the Uganda protectorate (11 June), Kenya's map extended far into Somalia and parts of modern-day Kenya's Rift Valley Province, west of Lake Rudolph, were part of Uganda. However, by 1926, Kenya's political boundaries looked much as they do today.[6] By 1920, the British had hived off approximately 6 million acres of land for white settlement, and an estimated 3.2 million acres had been occupied by 1920, against approximately 24 million acres for the natives,[7] Economic production in the agricultural sector primarily covered maize, sisal, wheat, beans and peas, coconuts, citrus and other fruits.[8]

The opening up of the interior of Kenya was facilitated by the Uganda Railway, whose construction began in 1895 in Mombasa. Lugard writes that the reason for Africa's previous lack of contact with the rest of the world was that "the world had not hitherto had urgent need for its products, and [because] its warlike tribes were able to repel unwelcome visitors armed but little better than themselves."[9] Lugard further writes that initially, the limit of control of (especially tropical territories, arising from the Berlin Act [or Conference] of 1885), was to coastal lands, although the French argued that administrative control of the territories – including the interior, not just the coast – was the only legitimate claim for colonial powers. Thus, the "necessity of securing the existence of sufficient authority, in the territories occupied, to ensure respect for acquired rights, and if necessary for freedom of commerce and transit"[10] necessitated British occupation of the interior of East Africa, in part to forestall German expansion from Tanganyika, or Deutsche Ostafrika.

Once the protectorate was established, the task of populating its expansive tracts of land began in earnest, as the figures highlighted in the 1920 Colonial Report show. Settlers and adventurers, drawn by "glowing descriptions of an expansive tract of country where the geniality of European summers prevailed perpetually, and where vast areas were occupied only by enormous herds of game"[11] began. The church was often complicit in colonization: Ross writes that "Bishop Tucker . . . suggested that European enterprise and even colonization might be found to be possible in these East African highlands."[12] Additional reasoning suggested that the occupation of these lands would ensure that slave trade, that morally abysmal practice, would never find support in these lands.

Arrival: strange pale men and long angry, puffing iron snakes

Such was the opening act of the future of Kenya; the coming of Europeans. Several instances and stories of predictions of the coming of the British are assiduously recorded; these feature leaders, prophets and medicine men such as Mugo wa Kibiru, Masaku, Mwenda Mwea, Syokimau and Kimnyole, the Nandi Orkoiyot, among others.[13] A Turkana diviner was recorded to have said, in 1875, "I have seen a great vulture, coming down from the sky, and scooping up the land of Turkana in its talons."[14] It appears that there was an expectation for the arrival of the European, predicted independently by different communities. Is it possible that since Lugard had appeared on the scene more than 30 years previously and the communities traded all the time, the knowledge was commonplace? What is clear is that none of the communities took any active steps to confront the coming of the Europeans, and the colonization process, although some interactions were marked by conniving and deception, was easy.

What were the conditions in Kenya before the coming of and occupation by Europeans? Nasong'o and Ayot write that "in pre-colonial Kenyan societies, clusters of patrilineal clans lived in clan villages, which provided a framework for territorial organisation. They had their own systems of government, religion, education and culture, which were all an integral part of life."[15] Some of these systems of government have been thought to have been democratic with decentralized governments (for example, generational groupings made up of age groups). Some of the societies had central governments with a clear head of the government (whether these were kings, chiefs, Oloibonis, or Orkoiyot), with the power to negotiate with other communities and with external parties. But remarkably, there is no record of these communities actively pursuing the occupation and/or control of other communities, outside of the frequent skirmishes and wars for resources.

Economic activities were as varied as are the communities: "in more sedentary societies . . . pastoralism was combined with shifting cultivation",[16] while "unmarried youths were generally engaged in hunting, stock raiding and inter- or intra-tribal fighting, and were directed in these activities by older unmarried males, and younger married males."[17] "Both men and women were engaged in trade . . . men seemed to have monopolised the long-distance trade in both livestock and food-stuff" and using the "caravan" trade to carry out "barter trade between the Kikuyu and Masai, Kamba and Masai, and in the salt trade from Lake Magadi."[18] Trade, more than war, was actually more of the norm; for example, "the highland Gusii population practised labor-intensive cultivation, maintained high population densities, and produced sizeable grain surpluses for exchange against livestock from the lowland Luo, who produced less grains."[19]

In fact, quite to the contrary, some scholars have argued that the wars were not as prevalent or destructive as might be thought:

> while we can pinpoint a few destructive wars of this nature [wars that destroyed entire ethnic groups, such as the Purko Maasai's destruction of the Uasin Gishu Maasai], they were very few indeed. For the most part wars do not seem to have been concerned principally with killing people, but rather with the capture of women and livestock.[20]

Thus, although it is clear that there were often wars, conflicts and raids, it is also apparent that there was inter-group trade, contrary to some of the perceptions of African societies and the European incentive to "civilize" them.

Supporting this view, Wanyonyi writes that "studies carried out among the various pre-colonial people of Kenya seemed to affirm the existence of porous boundaries separating members of different communities".[21] Despite the seeming modern hostilities – such as those that have characterized electoral contests, Wanyonyi argues for a more heterogeneous people than scholarship characterizes, writing that

> the inhabitants of the interlacustrine region of East Africa commingled for a millennium within the region creating systems of production, exchange and redistribution which were predicted on local identities rather than specific Bantu or Nilotic language, culture and ethnic communities.[22]

Europeans arrive

The coming of the Europeans, the appropriation of land previously held by African societies, their settlement, imposition of different administrative systems and the full throttle of colonialism found militarily unprepared peoples, administratively utilizing different approaches (including, e.g., concepts of property ownership). Some of the treaties and agreements that some of the indigenous leaders signed covered aspects of access to trade and products, rather than the wholesale takeover of land; it was also widespread practice that the chiefs and their negotiators often had no idea what was in the treaties that they were signing. Indeed, as Lugard notes, "in many of these protectorates, no treaties had been made with outlying tribes, and regions as yet unexplored were included",[23] yet the land was taken over quite expeditiously.

Part of this almost-unwitting land giveaway was based on the differences in the concepts of ownership and the community practices relating to property holding and ownership. For example, land among the Kikuyu, a people who would be unrelenting in their immediate and later opposition to the colonialists' appropriation of the "White Highlands", "belonged to the clan and was transferred from generation to the other",[24] no deeds of ownership were required or developed; communal knowledge facilitated by a decentralized authority ensured peace and tranquility with organized dispute settlement mechanisms. Among the Nandi, a sub-group of the Kalenjin (others: Pokot, Tugen, Marakwet, Keiyo, Kipsigis, Sabaot, Sebu, Terik), "the basic political unit of the Nandi was based on autonomous territorial units known as *bororosiek* (*bororiet*-singular) each controlled by a council of elders. The latter were chosen for their wisdom and military skills."[25]

Because of the wall of hostility and resistance that the Europeans faced in their colonial quest, colonialism had to be imposed by force. Maloba calls "colonialism [was] a dictatorship. It was imposed by violence and maintained by violence. It . . . perfected a reign of terror by silencing its opponents through detentions, exile and even outright extermination."[26] Colonialism leveraged probably all the worst possible instruments of oppression, control and coercion: killing, imprisonment, appointment of administrators to stifle dissent, dictatorship, use of force of arms to implement decisions, social (and scientific) racism; "this racism given 'scientific' respectability was a distinct part of the culture of imperialism as Europeans advanced in Africa and was often used as a justification for this expansion."[27] It is little wonder then that virulent anti-colonialism existed.

The "strange white men" who were now entering the interior of Kenya included Indians. While they had been present at the coast, as seen, for example, in Alibhai Mulla Jeevanjee's argument – over the precedence of his arrival in Mombasa in 1890, Indian merchants and businessmen did not enter the interior of Kenya until the building of the Uganda railway.[28] After the building of the Uganda railway almost stalled around the Tsavo National Park due to refusals by Africans to provide both labor and the "Man-eaters of Tsavo", Indian "coolies" were recruited to help build the railway. Elkins estimated that the cost of the railway line was 6.5 million sterling pounds; it "imported over thirty thousand "coolies" from India, nearly a third of whom were killed or maimed by the punishing work, disease and frequent lion attacks."[29] Those who completed the work often led to their settling in different major cities, such as Nairobi, and going into business.

According to Elkins, the building of the railway displaced quite a number of people, and those who were not displaced, had to be pacified. "Thousands of Africans died at the hands of the British who came to pacify the local population in preparation for effective occupation, as formal colonial rule in Africa was called at the end of the nineteenth century."[30] This was after the determination by Eliot, the first British East African Protectorate commissioner, that Africans were lazy and insufficiently numerous to make the railway viable through farming. The initial confrontation with the British over the establishment of the British East Africa Protectorate, and later the Kenya Colony, did not last long: by 1905, most of the communities, including the Nandi, had been largely pacified.

This state of affairs would continue for most of the next 40 years, through the First World War. The Second World War proved to be enlightening for Kenyans, who fought, as part of the Kings African Rifles (KAR) on the side of the British in places as far off as Ceylon (Burma). Their services in the war opened them not only to the logic of armed resistance but also to the undesirability of colonization, considering the British were fighting to free themselves of foreign occupation. Thus, by the end of the war, armed with knowledge about organizing, about military tactics and using some of the same against the British, the Independence movement was ready to begin confronting the British, through organizations such as the Kikuyu Central Association (KCA) and, ultimately, the Mau Mau movement.

Protest, independence and the early republic

Despite the earlier "pacification" of the British East Africa Protectorate and subsequently Kenya, nascent nationalism, protest movements and socio-political organizing started a few years after the declaration of the Kenya Colony. The Young Kikuyu Association (YKA), led by Harry Thuku, was founded in 1921 but was quickly banned. A short year later, it was renamed the East Africa Association (EAA). In 1924, the Kikuyu Central Association was formed; it commissioned a publication, *Mũigwithania* (Reconciler) and was banned in 1940 at the height of the Second World War. Seeking to start an organization that was more multi-ethnic, the Kenya African Study Union was founded in 1944, becoming the Kenya African Union two years later. It was here that Jomo Kenyatta, educated in Britain, became more aggressive in seeking representation in the Legislative Council, Legco.

By 1952, the same year that the more militant Mau Mau began armed protest, the Legco had 28 members: 14 European, 1 Arab and 6 Asian elected members; 6 Africans and 1 Arab were further selected by the governor. Thus, Kenya's struggle for independence was carried out both peacefully and in the form of guerrilla war, whose major protagonists were the Mau Mau. Some of the Mau Mau fighters had taken part in wars in Asia, and in the British campaign in Somaliland, under the auspices of the KAR.

According to the government's version of the Mau Mau[31] uprising, revolt "was an atavistic eruption of 'African savagery' rather than a legitimate response to real grievances."[32] Clough adds that the British government's official report, issued in 1960, Historical Survey of the Origins and Growth of Mau Mau, suggested that Mau Mau was a political and social pathology. However, the appearance of published accounts by some of the Mau Mau fighters challenged this idea, for example, the publication of the volume *Mau Mau Detainee*, an account of J. M. Kariũki's experiences.[33]

Kenyatta, Odinga and Kimathi's prophecy

One of the most underrated aspects of the question of the impact of socio-cultural beliefs and traditions on the construction of a peoples' identity is the Kikuyu peoples' notion of leadership. The idea of who can be a leader is one of the most important ideas of the Kikuyu tradition and continues to have an impact on the (s)election of leaders in modern-day Kenya. In Clough's *Mau Mau Memoirs*, Dedan Kĩmathi wa Waciũri, the de facto Mau Mau leader executed by the British in 1957, was reported to have said,

> [T]he Whiteman has converted us into his private property, uncircumcised as he is. He is a clever man and we must prove to him that we are circumcised to get rid of all fear. We will fight the Whiteman until the last man. There will be no rest until we expel all Europeans to their countries of origin. All this will come about through God's help and the oath of unity that we took.[34]

The actual armed conflict against the Mau Mau was not lengthy: the state of emergency was declared in October 1952 by the then governor, Sir Evelyn Baring. Hostilities began shortly, thereafter, and Mau Mau fighters went into the Mount Kenya forest. Despite being poorly armed and facing an army that had not too long previously fought in Burma and Germany, the fighting did not end until 1957. In the initial fighting, "the army staff . . . diagnosed a failure to disrupt the Mau Mau gangs, ineffective tactics, lack of discipline and efficiency in many military units, poor liaison with other security forces, and incorrect intelligence methods."[35]

Yet, it must be remembered that this was an insurgency by a ragtag force of under-equipped and poorly trained Kikuyu tribesmen. Per Bennett, "three years later, the military campaign against the Mau Mau was won, the gangs (as the authorities described them) were reduced to negligible proportions and the civil authorities were largely able to govern without military help."[36] Despite the military victory, as history has come to teach victors, the cost of waging and the inability of winning military campaigns against guerrilla warfare are well chronicled; the political concessions that the Mau Mau insurrection caused saw Kenya become independent in just a short 12 years after the start of the Mau Mau insurrection.

It is perhaps useful to reflect on the Mau Mau struggle, which featured some rather unusual activities; one of the most conspicuous was "oath taking", in Kikuyu, referred to as "*muuma*". Recruits into the Mau Mau had to take an oath, which bound them to their comrades, on the pain of death. The goal of the oath was to prevent the oath takers from betraying the trust of the Mau Mau, even under questioning. The British recognized the import of such traditional practices, including the importance of music such as *Mwomboko*, that it was outlawed by the colonial government in 1950.[37]

One of the abiding questions, even as the Mau Mau continued with the armed struggle for independence, is the role of Jomo Kenyatta, Kenya's first African prime minister and, subsequently, president. According to the British colonial authorities, Kenyatta was "the manager of Mau Mau",[38] but other accounts (e.g., by Montagu Slater) argue that "they never managed to prove that Kenyatta was indeed an organizer, or even a member of Mau Mau."[39] In fact, arguments have been advanced that given the perceived radicalism and armed resistance of the

Mau Mau, Kenyatta was a more palatable negotiating partner, as the British faced the least-worst option. What was well "known" was that Kenyatta participated in the oath-taking ceremonies, although he "intentionally chose to know very little of what went on in the Mau Mau Central Committee meetings."[40]

Kenyatta's distance from the Mau Mau did not save him from being either scapegoated, or assessed to have been a member of the Mau Mau. As it were, on 21 October 1952, he was arrested for allegedly leading the Mau Mau, and sentenced to seven years' jail and hard labor on 8 April 1953, together with other leading nationalists, including Bildad Kaggia, Kûng'û Karumba, Fred Kubai, Paul Ngei and Achieng' Oneko. After his release in 1959, he became a member of the Legco. Kenya's independence, granted in 1963, followed several draft constitutions with the Boston Tea Party–esque questions about (unequal and preferential European) representation, particularly given the numbers of Europeans and Indians.

There were several conferences held at Lancaster House in the UK, most of which were opposed by the Europeans, who, according to Okoth, "called for white supremacy and for segregation in all fields, and opposed the idea of constitutional conference."[41] The Lancaster Conference ultimately ended the quest for white supremacy in both the Legco and in the Council of Ministers of pre-independence Kenya. Ultimately, Kenya would become independent with Jomo Kenyatta as the first prime minister in 1963.

It is useful to consider the political parties and the conditions under which Kenya gained independence. Previously, the conversation showed that political parties and, to a large extent, political activity were banned by the colonial government, particularly for Africans. One of the accomplishments of the Lancaster House conference was to lift a ban on political parties, which led to the immediate organizing of new political parties; according to Okoth, "by the end of 1960, two parties had come into existence – the Kenya African National Union (KANU) and the Kenya African Democratic Union (KADU)."[42]

KANU, the older of the two parties, was founded on 14 May 1960, with Dr. Gĩkonyo Kiano as its leader. (Some accounts, e.g., Okoth's, hold that the party was established in 1963.) KANU had emerged from the Kenya Independence Movement, which boasted among its ranks such national leaders as Oginga Odinga and Tom Mboya.[43] According to Okoth, the newly formed KANU political party "came to represent the two largest ethnic groups, the Agĩkũyũ and the Luo, as well as the Akamba and Abagusii."[44] Although the party's preference for its leader was Kenyatta, he was still imprisoned in Kapenguria, stemming from the 1952 arrest for supporting the Mau Mau. It is important to note that KANU's membership was primarily based on the larger of Kenya's tribes; after independence, this would become important in the management of politics in the country.

KADU, on the other hand, "came into being to protect the interests of smaller tribes, the coastal tribes, the Kalenjin of the Rift Valley and the Abaluyia of Western Province."[45] KADU's major figures were Ronald Ngala, Masinde Muliro, and Kenya's future second president, Daniel arap Moi.[46] The latter distrusted the idea of a central government, fearing domination by the larger tribes, but KANU, on the other hand, preferred a strong central government in order to unite the country. In the subsequent elections held in 1963, KANU won an overwhelming mandate[47] (perhaps because of the numbers of eligible voters from among the biggest ethnic groups or perhaps in order to speed up the process of attaining independence). As it was, in 1964, KADU voluntarily dissolved itself and joined KANU, and its major figures were offered positions in government. This assimilation would last but two years, before Oginga Odinga, the then vice president, broke away to form the Kenya Peoples' Union (KPU),[48] which was the officially recognized opposition party.

Two important notes: in the post-election violence that erupted in 2007, some of the major figures in the drama included Raila Odinga, the son of Oginga Odinga, the first vice president, and later the official opposition leader and KPU leader, and Uhuru Kenyatta, the son of the first independent Kenya's leader. The seeds of the 2007 conflict may thus have been sown more than 40 years before they erupted. At the same time, the other progressive members of KPU, including Oginga Odinga and Bildad Kaggia, were beginning to align themselves with the minority communities in the republic. Through its formation, KPU had definitely attracted the unwanted attention of the Kenyatta government and suffered its full-scale wrath.

One more issue is worth revisiting. Immediately after the formation of KPU, all members of parliament who allied themselves with KPU were required to immediately resign their seats in parliament and seek a fresh mandate. This was one of the ways in which the government would weaken the opposition: by forcing them to seek a fresh mandate. Jomo Kenyatta desired to show that KANU and his government had near-unanimous support, even among the Luo, the bastion of opposition support. As such, Kenyatta campaigned for KANU candidates. On his visit to Kisumu in 1969, in what is now described as the "Kisumu Massacre", "[p]residential guards gunned down over 100 people in Kisumu."[49]

As it was, the riots in Kisumu gave the Kenyatta government the pretext to ban KPU and thus destroy the last vestige of opposition in Kenya, making it a de facto one-party state. Folklore suggests that prior to the start of the massacre, Jomo Kenyatta, in response to the riots, stated "*nĩ-irue*" (i.e., let them be circumcised), implying that the political protests were driven by boy-like immaturity since the Luo did not, as standard practice, circumcise their males.[50] Whether or not this is true, the notion of what it means to be a man especially among Kenyan societies is widely associated with young people coming into adulthood. In subsequent politically violent episodes, these chants and sometimes actions, particularly against communities that do not, as standard practice, initiate their males, have been carried out with alacrity.

Setting the stage: the future of one-party state autocracy

The Kenyatta administration was accused of, ever since 1965, either carrying out or being complicit in a campaign of elimination of its enemies and people it did not agree with. Between 1965 and 1978, when Jomo Kenyatta died, three extremely high-profile assassinations, generally assumed to be political, occurred.

These included Pio Gama Pinto, Tom Mboya and J. M. Kariũki. Pio Gama Pinto, an Indian of Goan descent, was "an avowed communist with a clear Pan-African vision and strong linkages to the Mozambican liberation movement, which was becoming more radicalized."[51] On 25 February 1965, he was assassinated by Kisilu Mutua, who continued to profess innocence even as he was sentenced to death for the assassination. It is notable that his death sentence was never enforced.

Four years later, on 5 July 1969, it was the turn of the rapidly rising star Tom Mboya, a charismatic leader who had been active in the quest for independence in Kenya, in decolonization efforts, as a minister and an elected member of parliament, and in the airlift of African students and young professionals, which also brought to the US one Barack Obama Sr., father of the 44th president of the US. His death unleashed days of riots, particularly from his Luo ethnic community, but especially because he was "a figure that had played a central role in Kenyan affairs from the early 1950s."[52] According to Donde, "the entire nation rose up in anger and riots, with angry mobs running amok in the streets and threatening the very fabric of the young nation."[53]

Ultimately, Nahashon Isaac (Njenga) Njoroge was arrested and tried for the murder. Whether or not he was guilty (speculation has always been rife that he was not acting on his own accord), this, coupled with the subsequent incidents during Kenyatta's visit to Kisumu in October of the same year, did not improve relations between the Kikuyu and Luo communities. And as Murunga and Nasong'o argue, "the independence constitution provided the ideal framework for autocratic leadership",[54] including having little tolerance for dissent.

The run of unexplained murders did not quite stop there: Josiah Mwangi Kariũki, popularly known as J. M. Kariũki, the member of parliament for Nyandarua South was killed on 2 March 1975, leading to another bout of

> mass outbreak of popular anger. J. M. had been a private secretary to the president, Mzee Jomo Kenyatta, and was quite popular as a member of parliament. In some corners, J. M. Kariũki was seen as a possible contender to succeed the president; certainly, he was very well regarded in the country and in the West. As soon as Kariũki's death became public, angry students demonstrated, but were dispersed by the GSU.[55]

To date, the murder of J. M. Kariũki remains unsolved. In 12 short years, the country had gone from a blossoming multi-party democracy to one where mysterious assassinations were becoming more of the norm. More important, the levels of tolerance of differing political opinion was growing much lower and would continue to do so in the next administration. However, alternatives to reclaim political space would also begin to find increasing popularity.

The ethnic dimension

The debut of the issue of ethnicity can be seen in the very first interactions of the future Kenya with the Europeans. At the first contact, it was clear that the future

Kenya was a collection of ethnic communities, some aspiring to kingdoms, while others enjoyed looser forms of social and political organization. There was no such concept of a nation; individuals belonged, and owed allegiance, to their basic organizational unit but never on a "national" scale. The divisions were often based on family, clan and community. For example, this writer was introduced to the idea that he was a member of the "family" – *mbarĩ ya Mũcharĩ*, where *Mũcharĩ* is the writer's grandfather on the father's side (the Kikuyu society is overwhelmingly patrilineal). Past the mbarĩ, he was introduced to the *mũhĩrĩga*, literally, the clan. It was carefully explained to him that he belonged to the *angũi* clan, based on one of the nine proverbial daughters of *Gĩkũyũ* and *Mũmbi.* Although it is often the case that one never pays attention to the country that they are in, until they leave, the importance of being a member of the community, rather than the identity as a national of the particular country was emphasized in this – and possibly many other instances.

A lack of cohesion, the absence of a shared identity as a nation, coupled with the inherent weaknesses to be found in the existing "nations" – economically, militarily, and the lack of durable alliances, the kind that were to be found in Europe – and the sheer size of the nations (the population enclosed within the current boundaries of Kenya) numbered approximately 1 million in 1900; Kikuyus, who are today the most populous group in Kenya, can be estimated, based on population percentages, to have been close to 300,000 then.[56] Nevertheless, given *Guns, Germs and Steel*, and the conditions that the Europeans found, it was easy to conquer African peoples. It was also useful that Africans were divided into different ethnic groups; this, as the British found out, made "divide and conquer" quite easy, with members of other communities appointed to impose the will of the colonial government.

Thus, although hostilities already existed before colonialism, they became a useful tool to continue to divide the nation, by pitting one group against another. The armed struggle for independence through the Mau Mau movement, although benefitting the material and intellectual support of a cross-section of Kenyans, saw the Mau Mau especially involved in the guerrilla activities. This can be explained in several ways: first, that the Mau Mau, who were largely drawn from the Kikuyu, were fighting to reclaim their land, which had been converted to the White Highlands, and thus, the Kikuyus bore the brunt of the colonization of Kenya; second, that the ethnic groups were still so divided that the rest of the country did not necessarily see the Mau Mau struggle as part of their struggle; and, third, that some groups generally opted to cooperate with the colonialists; strategically, they saw little benefit in confronting the technologically superior British.

At independence, Kenya's communities were perhaps as divided as they had been prior to the coming of the British. Thus, those who stood to gain most from a newly independent Kenya were the elites (who were drawn from all across the country, even though their approaches to an independent Kenya differed) and their basis of support. Strengthened by a majority of numbers, the Kikuyu community appeared poised to benefit most from a newly independent republic.

The adoption of European approaches to property ownership, and the notion that Kenya was for all Kenyans, which appeared to ignore the traditional notions of community ownership, thus saw the stage set for grievances that have dominated the country since its independence, including the question of land ownership. Additionally, the question of "who gets what, when and how" continued to manifest itself – from appropriating land, to positions in government, the worst of British excesses had become the new realities of the republic.

Notes

1 W. McGregor Ross. *Kenya from within: A Short Political History*. (New York, NY: Routledge, 2006): 20.
2 P. L. McDermott. *British East Africa, or I B E A: A History of the Formation and Work of the Imperial British East Africa Company*. (London: Chapman and Hall, 1895): vi.
3 McDermott. *British East Africa*. vii.
4 Lord Frederick J.D. Lugard. *The Dual Mandate in British Tropical Africa*. (London, UK: Frank Cass & Co. Ltd., 1922. Digital Print: 2005): 14.
5 McDermott. *British East Africa*. 18.
6 The British Empire. "Kenya: Brief History." (Web). Accessed on 11/19/2016 from: www.britishempire.co.uk/maproom/kenya.htm
7 HM Stationery Office. "Colonial Reports – Annual. Colony & Protectorate of Kenya. Report for 1920–21, No. 1122." London, UK: HM Majesty's Office, 1922. (Web): 13–14.
8 HM Stationery Office. "Colonial Reports – Annual." 13–14.
9 Lugard. *The Dual Mandate in British Tropical Africa*. 3.
10 Lugard. *The Dual Mandate in British Tropical Africa*. 11.
11 Ross. *Kenya from within*. 21.
12 Ross. *Kenya from within*. 21.
13 See, for example, Marlene van Niekerk, "Understanding Trends in 'African Thinking': A Critical Discussion." In Pieter Hendrik Coetzee & A. P. J. Roux, Eds. *The African Philosophy Reader*. (New York, NY: Routledge, 1998): 100 and Derek Peterson. "Writing in Revolution: Independent Schooling & Mau Mau in Nyeri." In Eisha Stephen Atieno Odhiambo & John Lonsdale. *Mau Mau & Nationhood: Arms, Authority & Narration*. (Nairobi: East African Educational Publishers, 2003): 48.
14 Elizabeth Isichei. *A History of African Societies to 1870*. (New York: Cambridge University Press, 1997): 171; Eisha Stephen Atieno Odhiambo. "Matunda Ya Uhuru, Fruits of Independence: Seven Theses on Nationalism in Kenya." In E. S. Atieno Odhiambo & John Lonsdale, Eds. *Mau Mau & Nationhood: Arms, Authority & Narration*. (Nairobi: East African Educational Publishers, 2003): 43; Myles Osborne. *Ethnicity and Empire in Kenya: Loyalty and Martial Race among the Kamba, c. 1800 to the Present*. (New York, NY: Cambridge University Press, 2014): 42.
15 Shadrack Wanjala Nasong'o & Theodora O. Ayot. "Women in Kenya's Politics of Transition and Democratisation." In Godwin R. Murunga & Shadrack W. Nasong'o, Eds. *Kenya: The Struggle for Democracy*. (New York, NY: Zed Books, 2007): 172.
16 Gavin N. Kitching. *Class and Economic Change in Kenya: The Making of an African Petite-Bourgeoisie*. (New Haven, CT: Yale University Press, 1980): 14.
17 Kitching. *Class and Economic Change in Kenya*. 14.
18 Kitching. *Class and Economic Change in Kenya*. 19.
19 N. Thomas Hakansson. "Grain, Cattle, and Power: Social Processes of Intensive Cultivation and Exchange in Precolonial Western Kenya." *Journal of Anthropological Research*, 50, No. 3 (Autumn, 1994): 249.
20 Anne King & Roger M. A. Van Zwanenberg. *An Economic History of Kenya and Uganda, 1800–1970*. (Hampshire, UK: Macmillan Press, 1975): 6.

21 Pius Kaikai Wanyonyi. "Historicizing Negative Ethnicity in Kenya." In Mbugua wa Mungai & George M. Gona, Eds. *(Re)membering Kenya: Identity, Culture and Freedom*. (Nairobi, Kenya: Twaweza Communications, 2010): 33–34.
22 Wanyonyi. "Historicizing Negative Ethnicity in Kenya." 35.
23 Lugard. *The Dual Mandate in British Tropical Africa*. 14.
24 Julius Makong'o, Ephalina Maina, Wycliffe Oboka & The Kenya Institute of Education. *History and Government Form One*. (Nairobi, Kenya: East African Educational Publishers, 2003): 58.
25 Makong'o, Maina, Oboka & The Kenya Institute of Education. *History and Government Form One*. 64.
26 Wunyabari O. Maloba. "Decolonization: A Theoretical Perspective." In Bethwell A. Ogot & William Robert Ochieng, Eds. *Decolonization & Independence in Kenya, 1940*. (Athens, OH: Ohio University Press, 1995): 9.
27 Maloba. "Decolonization." 9.
28 Sana Aiyar. *Indians in Kenya*. (Boston, MA: Harvard University, 2015): 1.
29 Caroline Elkins. *Imperial Reckoning: The Untold Story of Britain's Gulag in Kenya*. (New York: Henry Holt and Co., 2005): 2.
30 Elkins. *Imperial Reckoning*. 2.
31 The Mau Mau group was also known formally as the Kenya Land and Freedom Army (KLFA).
32 Marshall S. Clough. *Mau Mau Memoirs: History, Memory, and Politics*. (Boulder, CO: Lynne Rienner Publishers, 1998): 2.
33 Clough. *Mau Mau Memoirs*. 1.
34 Clough. *Mau Mau Memoirs*. 127.
35 Huw Bennett. *Fighting the Mau Mau: The British Army and Counter-Insurgency in the Kenya Emergency*. (New York: Cambridge University Press, 2013): 11.
36 Bennett. *Fighting the Mau Mau*. 11.
37 Mich Nyawalo. "Redefining the Struggle: Remembering the Mau Mau through Hip Hop Music." In Msia Kibona Clark & Mickie Mwanzia Koster, Eds. *Hip Hop and Social Change in Africa: Ni Wakati*. (Lanham, MD: Lexington Books, 2014): 77.
38 S.M. Shamsul Alam. *Rethinking the Mau Mau in Colonial Kenya*. (New York, NY: Palgrave Macmillan, 2007): 114.
39 Alam. *Rethinking the Mau Mau in Colonial Kenya*. 115.
40 Alam. *Rethinking the Mau Mau in Colonial Kenya*. 114.
41 Assa Okoth. *A History of Africa: African Nationalism and the De-Colonisation Process*. (Nairobi, Kenya: East African Educational Publishers, 2006): 87.
42 Okoth. *A History of Africa*. 87.
43 Jim C. Harper. *Western-Educated Elites in Kenya, 1900–1963: The African American Factor*. (New York, NY: Routledge, 2006): 64.
44 Okoth. *A History of Africa*. 88.
45 Okoth. *A History of Africa*. 88.
46 Okoth. *A History of Africa*. 124.
47 David Seddon. *A Political and Economic Dictionary of Africa*. (New York, NY: Routledge, 2005): 287.
48 Adams G.R. Oloo. "The Contemporary Opposition in Kenya: Between Internal Traits and State Manipulation." In Godwin R. Murunga & Shadrack W. Nasong'o, Eds. *Kenya: The Struggle for Democracy*. (New York, NY: Zed Books, 2007): 96.
49 Bethwell Allan Ogot. "Essence of Ethnicity: An African Perspective." In Hiroyuki Hino, John Lonsdale, Gustav Ranis & Frances Stewart, Eds. *Ethnic Diversity and Economic Instability in Africa: Interdisciplinary Perspectives*. (New York, NY: Cambridge University Press, 2012): 115. See also: J. Oloka Onyango. *Battling over Human Rights: Twenty Essays on Law, Politics and Governance*. (Bamenda, Cameroon: Langaa RPCIG, 2015): 188 and Macharia Munene. *Historical Reflections on Kenya: Intellectual Adventurism, Politics and International Relations*. (Nairobi, Kenya: University of Nairobi Press, 2012): 121.

50 For context, all Kikuyu males, as a matter of tradition that continues to date, have to "go to the river" – a colloquial reference to circumcision of male members of the community. Prior to the invention of modern medicine, the initiates would go to the river, and dip in the cold water early in the morning. Among the Kikuyu, it was imperative to become circumcised; all who are not and have not been circumcised are referred to as *kĩhĩĩ* (sing; *ihĩĩ*, plural); traditionally, there was significant disregard for uncircumcised males, and they would never have been considered for any leadership.

51 David William Cohen & Eisha Stephen. Atieno Odhiambo. *The Risks of Knowledge: Investigations into the Death of the Hon. Minister John Robert Ouko in Kenya, 1990*. (Athens, OH: Ohio University Press, 2004): 4.

52 Edwin Gimode. *Thomas Joseph Mboya: A Biography*. (Nairobi, Kenya: East African Educational Publishers, 1996): 49.

53 Fredrick Donde. *Obama Senior: A Dream Fulfilled*. (Nairobi, Kenya: Kenway Publications, 2015): 60.

54 Maurice N. Amutabi. "Intellectuals and the Democratisation Process in Kenya." In Godwin R. Murunga & Shadrack W. Nasong'o, Eds. *Kenya: The Struggle for Democracy*. (New York, NY: Zed Books, 2007): 197.

55 Charles Hornsby. *Kenya: A History since Independence*. (New York, NY: I. B. Tauris & Co., 2012): 283. See also, David Goldsworthy. *Tom Mboya: The Man Kenya Wanted to Forget*. (Nairobi, Kenya: Heinemann Educational Books Ltd., 1982) and Godfrey Gitahi Kariuki. *The Illusion of Power: Reflections on Fifty Years in Kenya Politics*. (Nairobi, Kenya: Kenway Publications, 2001): 70.

56 Kikuyu tradition, e.g., forbids counting people, arguing that doing so will cause death.

References

Aiyar, Sana. *Indians in Kenya*. Boston, MA: Harvard University Press, 2015.

Alam, S. M. Shamsul. *Rethinking the Mau in Colonial Kenya*. New York, NY: Palgrave Macmillan, 2007.

Amutabi, Maurice N. "Intellectuals and the Democratisation Process in Kenya." In Godwin R. Murunga & Shadrack W. Nasong'o, Eds. *Kenya: The Struggle for Democracy*. New York, NY: Zed Books, 2007.

Bennett, Huw. *Fighting the Mau Mau: The British Army and Counter-Insurgency in the Kenya Emergency*. New York: Cambridge University Press, 2013.

The British Empire. "Kenya: Brief History." (Web). Accessed on 11/19/2016 from: www.britishempire.co.uk/maproom/kenya.htm

Clough, Marshall S. *Mau Mau Memoirs: History, Memory, and Politics*. Boulder, CO: Lynne Rienner Publishers, 1998.

Cohen, David William & E. S. Atieno Odhiambo. *The Risks of Knowledge: Investigations into the Death of the Hon: Minister John Robert Ouko in Kenya, 1990*. Athens, OH: Ohio University Press, 2004.

Cooper, Carole. *Kenya: The National Epic*. Nairobi, Kenya: Kenway Publications, 1993.

Donde, Fredrick. *Obama Senior: A Dream Fulfilled*. Nairobi, Kenya: Kenway Publications, 2015.

Elkins, Caroline. *Imperial Reckoning: The Untold Story of Britain's Gulag in Kenya*. New York: Henry Holt and Co., 2005.

Gimode, Edwin. *Thomas Joseph Mboya: A Biography*. Nairobi, Kenya: East African Educational Publishers, 1996.

Goldsworthy, David. *Tom Mboya: The Man Kenya Wanted to Forget*. Nairobi, Kenya: Heinemann Educational Books Ltd., 1982.

Hakansson, N. Thomas. "Grain, Cattle, and Power: Social Processes of Intensive Cultivation and Exchange in Precolonial Western Kenya." *Journal of Anthropological Research*, 50, No. 3 (Autumn, 1994): 249–276. Accessed on 11/19/2016 from: www.jstor.org/stable/3630179

Harper, Jim C. *Western-Educated Elites in Kenya, 1900–1963: The African American Factor*. New York, NY: Routledge, 2006.

Her Majesty's Stationery Office. "Colonial Reports – Annual, Colony & Protectorate of Kenya, Report for 1920–21, No. 1122." London, UK: HM Majesty's Office, 1922. (Web). Accessed from: http://libsysdigi.library.illinois.edu/ilharvest/Africana/Books2011-05/5530244/5530244_1920_1921/5530244_1920_1921_opt.pdf

Hornsby, Charles. *Kenya: A History since Independence*. New York, NY: I. B. Tauris & Co., 2012.

Isichei, Elizabeth. *A History of African Societies to 1870*. New York: Cambridge University Press, 1997.

Isichei, Elizabeth. *Voices of the Poor in Africa: Moral Economy and the Popular Imagination*. New York, NY: The University of Rochester Press, 2004.

Kariũki, Geoffrey G. *The Illusion of Power: Reflections on Fifty Years in Kenya Politics*. Nairobi, Kenya: Kenway Publications, 2001.

King, Anne & R. M. A. Van Zwanenberg. *An Economic History of Kenya and Uganda, 1800–1970*. Hampshire, UK: Macmillan Press, 1975.

Kitching, Gavin N. *Class and Economic Change in Kenya: The Making of an African Petite-Bourgeoisie*. New Haven, CT: Yale University Press, 2011.

Lugard, Lord Frederick J. D. *The Dual Mandate in British Tropical Africa*. London, UK: Frank Cass & Co. Ltd., 1922. Digital Print: 2005.

Makong'o, Julius, Ephalina Maina, Wycliffe Oboka & The Kenya Institute of Education. *History and Government Form One*. Nairobi, Kenya: East African Educational Publishers, 2003.

Maloba, Wunyabari O. "Decolonization: A Theoretical Perspective." In Bethwell A. Ogot & William Robert Ochieng', Eds. *Decolonization & Independence in Kenya, 1940*. Athens, OH: Ohio University Press, 1995.

McDermott, P. L. *British East Africa, or I B E A: A History of the Formation and Work of the Imperial British East Africa Company*. London: Chapman and Hall, 1895.

Munene, Macharia. *Historical Reflections on Kenya: Intellectual Adventurism, Politics and International Relations*. Nairobi, Kenya: University of Nairobi Press, 2012.

Nasong'o, Shadrack Wanjala & Theodora O. Ayot. "Women in Kenya's Politics of Transition and Democratisation." In Godwin R. Murunga & Shadrack W. Nasong'o, Eds. *Kenya: The Struggle for Democracy*. New York, NY: Zed Books, 2007.

Nyawalo, Mich. "Redefining the Struggle: Remembering the Mau Mau through Hip Hop Music." In Msia Kibona Clark & Mickie Mwanzia Koster, Eds. *Hip Hop and Social Change in Africa: Ni Wakati*. Lanham, MD: Lexington Books, 2014.

Odhiambo, E. S. Atieno. "Matunda Ya Uhuru, Fruits of Independence: Seven Theses on Nationalism in Kenya." In E. S. Atieno Odhiambo & John Lonsdale. *Mau Mau & Nationhood: Arms, Authority & Narration*. Nairobi: East African Educational Publishers, 2003.

Ogot, Bethwell Allan. "Essence of Ethnicity: An African Perspective." In Hiroyuki Hino, John Lonsdale, Gustav Ranis & Frances Stewart, Eds. *Ethnic Diversity and Economic Instability in Africa: Interdisciplinary Perspectives*. New York, NY: Cambridge University Press, 2012.

Okoth, Assa. *A History of Africa: African Nationalism and the De-Colonisation Process*. Nairobi, Kenya: East African Educational Publishers, 2006.

Oloo, Adams G. R. "The Contemporary Opposition in Kenya: Between Internal Traits and State Manipulation." In Godwin R. Murunga & Shadrack W. Nasong'o, Eds. *Kenya: The Struggle for Democracy*. New York, NY: Zed Books, 2007.

Onyango, J. Oloka. *Battling over Human Rights: Twenty Essays on Law, Politics and Governance*. Bamenda, Cameroon: Langaa RPCIG, 2015.

Osborne, Myles. *Ethnicity and Empire in Kenya: Loyalty and Martial Race among the Kamba, c. 1800 to the Present*. New York, NY: Cambridge University Press, 2014.

Otzen, Ellen. "Kenyan MP's Murder Unsolved 40 Years on." 11 March 2015. (Web). Accessed on 11/20/2016 from: www.bbc.com/news/world-africa-31817667

Peterson, Derek. "Writing in Revolution: Independent Schooling & Mau Mau in Nyeri." In E. S. Atieno Odhiambo & John Lonsdale, Eds. *Mau Mau & Nationhood: Arms, Authority & Narration*. Nairobi: East African Educational Publishers, 2003.

Ross, W. McGregor. *Kenya from within: A Short Political History*. New York, NY: Routledge, 2006 (Digital).

Seddon, David. *A Political and Economic Dictionary of Africa*. New York, NY: Routledge, 2005.

van Niekerk, Marlene. "Understanding Trends in 'African Thinking': A Critical Discussion." In Pieter Hendrik Coetzee & A. P. J. Roux, Eds. *The African Philosophy Reader*. New York, NY: Routledge, 1998.

Wanyonyi, Pius Kaikai. "Historicizing Negative Ethnicity in Kenya." In Mbugua wa Mungai & George M. Gona, Eds. *(Re)membering Kenya: Identity, Culture and Freedom*. Nairobi, Kenya: Twaweza Communications, 2010.

2 Post-independence, succession, autocracy and global geopolitics

The goal of this chapter is to review the transition from one presidency to another, that is, that of Jomo Kenyatta to that of Moi, and life under Daniel arap Moi. The transition was not smooth, neither was life under the Moi government. In fact, the one military coup that came closest to succeeding occurred early during Moi's rule, and it resulted in a government crackdown on dissent, on what it considered subversive activities and any form of dissent. Politically, the government introduced the one-party state with the Kenya African National Union (KANU) as the only legal party. The country became a *de facto* one-party state in 1982.

This in no way suggests that alternate schools of political thought did not exist; in fact, the 1980s gave rise to some of Kenya's most robust underground opposition movement. Moi continued to consolidate support from different ethnic groups, including creating the KAMATUSA (Kalenjin, Maasai, Turkana, Samburu) regional bloc to rival the Gikuyu, Embu, Meru Association (sometimes with the A denoting the Akamba) group. Yet, the seeds of the end of Moi's rule were sown by events taking place in Berlin and Moscow, rather than in Nairobi. Within 10 years of the *de facto* one-party state, the country would re-introduce multi-party politics, and with the change, what Moi had always warned against: that multi-party politics would inevitably herald 'tribal-based politics', where certain parties could clearly be identified through their tribes.

According to some analysts, Moi's regime quintessentially reflected the 1960–63 pre-independence realities – or, perhaps, fears – in Kenya. Then, Moi and members of the Kenya African Democratic Union (KADU), who were representatives from the smaller communities, had feared domination by the bigger tribes, such as the Kikuyu and the Luo. The KAMATUSA grouping would be a counterweight to the previously dominant Kikuyu community and, soon-to-be nemesis, the Luo community. Other groups would come under the government's alleged mistreatment, through "pacification" that turned out to be massacres, even as the government continued to attempt to stifle dissent and improve conditions for its citizens. As this chapter shows, these government attempts, while marginally successful, created even more resentment towards the government, while helping to develop a culture of resistance.

New kid on the block: Daniel Toroitich arap Moi

Mzee Jomo Kenyatta's succession, by the individual who would become the second president of the Republic of Kenya, was one of abiding interest to the nation; according to Ogot, "the question of the succession to Kenyatta had been raised in different forums by different Kenyans since 1964."[1] One of the reasons thereof was that Kenyatta had ascended to the presidency at the (estimated) ripe age of 71, and there was an obvious benefit to positioning oneself to succeed him. During the earlier years of the republic, a robust national debate generally also concerned itself with the role of the freedom fighters. By 1969, according to Ogot, the major contenders to succeed Kenyatta included Oginga Odinga, Tom Mboya and Ronald Ngala. With Odinga founding the Kenya Peoples' Union, thereby joining the opposition, Mboya's assassination in 1969 and Ronald Ngala's death in a road accident in 1972, the major contenders to succeed Kenyatta were eliminated.

According to Clough, some of the reasons for the apprehension surrounded the question of who Kenyatta's successor would be, and what the procedures for succession would entail, although they were outlined in the constitution.[2] Clough also argues that "by 1975, however, many Kikuyu from Mũrang'a, Nyeri, and Nyandarua were angry at the influence over the president of politicians from Kenyatta's home district of Kiambu"[3] and because of suspected complicity of the government in the death of J. M. Kariũki. These Kiambu politicians would later be referred to as the "Kikuyu clique", "the Family" and in derogatory terms as "the Kiambu Mafia." The other significant reason was whether Kenya would survive the death of the founding father or whether the country would disintegrate as many other African countries had.[4] Although attempts were made to change the constitution before the death of Kenyatta, the constitution specified the succession procedures as follows:

(1) If the office of the President becomes vacant by reason of the death or resignation of the President, or by reason of his ceasing to hold office by virtue of Section 10 or Section 12 of this constitution (qv) an election of a President shall be held within the period of ninety days immediately following the occurrence of that vacancy, and shall be held in a manner prescribed by Section 5 (5) of this Constitution (qv).
(2) While the office of the President is vacant as afore said, the functions of that office shall be exercised-

   (a) by the Vice-President; or
   (b) if there is no Vice President, or if the Vice-President considers that he is for any reason unable to discharge the functions of the office of the President, by such Minister as may be appointed by the Cabinet.[5]

Beginning late in 1976, a robust effort to amend the constitution, led by Nakuru North, MP; Kĩhĩka Kimani; and GEMA chairman, Njenga Karũme, got underway. The proposed changes intended to ensure that the Speaker of the National Assembly, rather than the vice president, would assume power until the election;

Widner holds that the goal was that GEMA (Kikuyu group) could secure the Speaker's position or, failing that, would have Dr. Njoroge Mũngai contest the presidency.[6] The ultimate goal of this effort was to deny the then vice president, Daniel Toroitich arap Moi, from ascending to power.

Daniel arap Moi had been appointed the vice president after the resignation of Joseph Zuzarte Murumbi in 1967; Murumbi served for less than a year and had been appointed to replace Jaramogi Oginga Odinga, who had resigned from office in order to found the opposition Kenya Peoples' Union in 1966. At the time, Moi was seen as an outsider, a holdover from the KADU group. The effort dominated public discourse, and those public officials who supported Moi's ascension to power, in accordance with the constitution (including Shariff Nassir and Stanley Oloitiptip), appeared to have a majority of the members of parliament (98 signatures of the 170 total members of the legislature, both elected and appointed). The attorney general, Charles Njonjo, a Kikuyu, issued a statement declaring that "it is a criminal offence for any person to encompass, imagine, devise, or intend the death or deposition of the President."[7]

On Kenyatta's death, Moi did indeed serve as acting president for the constitutionally stipulated 90 days, during which elections were held. Running on a KANU ticket, Moi was unchallenged, and the election cemented his leadership as the second president of the republic. Perhaps to assuage the fears of the Kikuyu elite, Moi "publicly declared that he would follow in Kenyatta's footsteps";[8] the concept of "*fuata nyayo*" (follow the footsteps – of Mzee Jomo Kenyatta) became a rallying cry.[9] Despite their public position as proponents of the "Change the Constitution Movement", members of the Family, including Mbiyũ Koinange, Dr. Njoroge Mũngai, Kĩhĩka Kimani, Njenga Karũme, Paul Ngei, James Gĩchũrũ and Jackson Angaine quickly got behind the new government,[10] although Cooper notes that President Moi "spoke of wolves in sheepskins, saying that many of those who had lavished him with praise were actually deadly enemies. The president said that he knew that nightly meetings were going on."[11] As it were President Moi came into office facing "a politically mobilized and nervous Kikuyu who also dominated the officer corps of the armed forces and police."[12]

Part of the support for Moi appeared to stem from the implications of the machinations of the Kiambu elite – the Family and the idea that another Kikuyu would succeed Kenyatta, thus bringing to reality the much-feared Kikuyu domination. As such, Moi appeared to be "the only real alternative to continued elite Kikuyu hegemony after Kenyatta's death."[13] The early years of the Moi presidency was a period of consolidation, whereupon the diverse ethnicity served both as a wedge and as a source of political patronage. Both critics and supporters agree that Moi was quite the accomplished politician, who earned the nickname "Professor of Politics", and was able to "protect Kalenjin interests by remaining close to Kenyatta."[14] But perhaps in a final nod to the Kikuyu, the new president, Daniel arap Moi, appointed Mwai Kibaki, a Kikuyu from Nyeri, as his vice president. His next vice president would also be a Kikuyu, although by then his rule was well established and most opposition was contained.

The early years of Moi's presidency were a period of both innovation and continuity. The new president had to "woo" the communities that did not support him full throttle but feared domination by not only the Kikuyu but also the Kikuyu and allied communities. Thus, by appearing to follow the late president's policies and not making initial drastic changes, Moi took time to consolidate his rule but leveraged other avenues, including the church. Moi "saw the churches as the obvious institutions to help legitimize his rule. Going beyond Kenyatta's call for the churches to act as the conscience of society, Moi explicitly invited them to play an active role in managing the country",[15] and as an appendage to his "Nyayo" pledge (to follow in the footsteps of Jomo Kenyatta), the Christian values of "peace, love and unity" were added. Additionally, the loyalty pledge was required to be recited in schools every Monday and sometimes Fridays. As such, according to Ahluwalia, there was an ongoing succession crisis that ultimately manifested itself in the 1 August 1982 attempted (but abortive) coup d'état, by junior officers of the 82 Air Force, led, rather ironically, by officers from the Luo community.[16]

Mutinies, creative democracy and political opposition

Kenya's flirtation with mutinies by the armed forces began almost as soon as the year following the granting of independence. During the Kenyatta reign, two such mutinies occurred in Kenya in 1964 and in 1971; indeed, they occurred in all the now newly independent East African countries (Kenya, Uganda and Tanzania) early in 1964, where the soldiers "demanded higher pay and the removal of expatriate British officers from the newly established national armies."[17] The 1964 army mutiny in Kenya was generally considered to have been over poor pay and was quickly quashed (the country was about to go to war in Somalia, from 1964–1967). A second attempted mutiny and plot to overthrow the government was discovered in 1970. According to Khapoya, this, too, was quickly quashed, and its ringleaders tried and convicted.[18]

Prior to the 2007 post-election violence, the most significant, disruptive event to occur in independent Kenya was the coup d'état staged in the early-morning hours of 1 August 1982. There is broad consensus that even before the coup d'état, Kenya had been increasingly trending authoritarian. For example, in May 1982, Kenyatta's nemesis, Oginga Odinga, was expelled from the *de facto* ruling party, KANU. Together with a former member of parliament, George Anyona Oginga, decided to launch the Kenya African Socialist Alliance (KASA),[19] which, in a new twist of politics, was described as "a GEMA-Luo combination that had the potential to rally enough support to force the issue of multipartyism to the floor of parliament."[20] One of the KASA's potential downsides was that it continued to be allied with socialism, which made its sources of support more tenuous than they would otherwise have been. It was also a continuation of the association between Oginga Odinga with socialism, a proposition that denied him potential support from the West and only incurred tepid support from the communist nations of the east. In response to Odinga and Anyona's moves, Moi re-introduced the practice of detention without trial; Anyona was detained, and Moi "set in motion the process of making Kenya a *de jure* one-party state. The law was pushed through parliament in 45 minutes on 9 June 1982."[21] These changes were met with protests by professors and students, with several of them being detained alongside Anyona.

Beginning midnight Sunday 1 August 1982, led by Hezekiah Ochuka Rabala, low-ranked officers of the Kenya Air Force took over the nation's radio station, Voice of Kenya, announcing an overthrow of the government, because "rampant corruption, tribalism, nepotism have made life almost intolerable in our society."[22] The rebels also seized the Jomo Kenyatta International Airport and the Embakasi, Eastleigh and Nanyuki air bases; the latter was used to "bomb" the capital, Nairobi (the bombs were dropped in the forest).[23] Although the coup plotters attempted to capture the president, who was at his farm in Kabarak, he was "evacuated from his home into a maize plantation."[24] By evening, the coup had been quashed, the masterminds fled to Tanzania, from whence they would be later extradited and Ochuka and Okumu executed. Hornsby adds that "the official death toll was 159, but unofficial estimates ranged from 600 to 1800."[25]

Among those who were arrested was Raila Odinga, while his father, Jaramogi Oginga Odinga was placed under house arrest. Most of the reactions to the coup were mixed, although Branch writes that "at the Kenyatta University College on the city's outskirts, news of the coup was met with jubilation. Students danced outside the campus housing of detained faculty members, but no attempts were made to join the uprising"[26] while the rest of the military forces, including the paramilitary General Service Unit did not join in as expected. Later, through the trials and detentions (of up to 3,000 people) it would be established – including through Raila's own biography – that the Odinga family was complicit in the coup attempts.[27] For Moi, it appeared that the ascension to the highest office had inherited him the immunities and challenges of the presidency. Kenyatta's contenders had come full circle: from opposition to Kenyatta and now to Moi.

Consolidation: one-party state and suppression of dissent

Although the aftermath of the 1982 coup d'état represented some of Kenya's darkest moments, with mass detentions of those opposed to the government and the hanging of the coup mastermind, Hezekiah Ochuka, in July 1987, the repressive regime straddled both Kenyatta's and, now, Moi's new regime, with a vengeance. Before he assumed the highest office, as Vice President, Moi announced "a screening of all Somalis after receiving reports that the Somali government was issuing passports to Kenyan Somalis to go to Somalia for military training";[28] Foulds adds that in 1980, the Garissa massacre killed hundreds of people. According to the Hansard (Kenya National Assembly record of 8 April 2010), the number of those killed in the operation was placed at more than 3,000. This account also suggests that there was a massacre in Isiolo in 1967 and a Malkamari Massacre in 1987, all directed at the Cushitic communities and nearly all occurring during a period where Moi was in power.[29]

Although other security operations in different parts of the country were carried out, including in the northwestern part of the country, where the primary economic activities are pastoralist in nature and the proliferation, use and availability of guns are especially widespread, almost disproportionately, wholesale suppression of communities appeared to target the northeast, where secessionist sentiment has been rampant because of marginalization by successive governments. During Moi's reign as president, but perhaps before that, Somalis had partially sided with Somalia's Great Somalia project and the attempt to annex the Northern Frontier District (NFD) during the 1964–1967 "Shifta War", "government repression of ethnic Somalis . . . continued."[30] At the same time, the government attempt to disarm communities in the region led to the infamous Wagalla massacre, which led to the deaths of up to 380, mostly men of the Degodia clan. Recent scholarship has suggested that although disarming the Degodia clan was one of the principal goals of the operation that led to the massacre, a political goal of the operation was to "muzzle the populous Degodia clan so that they would not shape NEP politics"[31] and as punishment for involvement in the Somali internal affairs.

The rise of Somalis who hailed from Garissa, including General Mahmood Mohamed, who was instrumental in suppressing the coup d'état, was seen as a counterbalance to the Degodia's greater population, and security concerns about potential secession drove some of the debates. Mahmoud attributes the massacre to political competition between two communities, the Ajuran and Degodia, for the Wajir West Parliamentary seat, where a candidate from the latter defeated two candidates from the former and thus occasioning the loss of the only parliamentary seat held by the community.[32] Furthermore, even after the Wagalla massacre and the uproar that followed its conclusion, the screening of Somalis continued, ostensibly to determine whether they were Kenyans or Somalis.[33] Thus, while the northeastern Cushitic and some northwestern Nilotic (especially pastoralist) communities were especially targeted for suppression in ways that were perhaps unique to their economic and historical circumstances, the more restive areas such as the Central Province and Nyanza Province were more economically, rather than politically, marginalized.

The purge, the underground and *Mlolongo*

Thus, by the late 1980s, less than a decade after ascending to power, the project to consolidate Moi's rule – and, with it, the one-party state – was complete. The Kikuyu elite had been thwarted in their attempt to stop his ascent to the presidency, an abortive coup had set forth the conditions necessary to turn the country into a one-party state, and thanks to Moi's devotion to religion through the Africa Inland Church, the church – and the broader religious community – was toeing the line. Elsewhere, the nation's children were being properly indoctrinated through a free school milk program, quite popular with pupils and the public alike, *Maziwa ya Nyayo* and loyalty pledges to the president and the republic, while the military opposition had been crushed. Those who had determined to change government by violent means had failed; the Kenya Air Force had been replaced with the 82 Air Force, with most of the senior officers purged, and the air force restructured ostensibly to remove those who would take up arms against their commander-in-chief.

In a nod to other tyrants and autocracies elsewhere, the academy was the next target. Although as previously highlighted, university students initially cheered the coup attempt, there had always an uneasy relationship between academics and the government. As early as May 1982, the crackdown on members of the learned professions had begun, with the arrest and incarceration of several leading academics and the severe crackdown on universities students' associations.[34] It was relatively easy to intimidate academics: after all, most of them were employed by the government in government-owned institutions, where the president was also the chancellor. Thus, the crackdown on the next source of resistance, the academy and future academics, and their subversive ideas, was at full throttle and through the Special Branch, detention without trial for "enemies of the state" happened with regularity. More important, as part of the consolidation of the state, Moi "proceeded to govern an ethnically divided Kenya with increasing authoritarianism. Urban Kikuyus of Nairobi charged him with cronyism as he appointed fellow Kalenjin tribesmen to lucrative government positions."[35]

The republic appeared to be secure, but the undercurrents of dissent procured such nascent underground protest movements such as Mwakenya. Mwakenya, Branch writes, stood for the "Union of Nationalists to Liberate Kenya . . . founded in 1985 as an umbrella group of isolated Nairobi-based dissidents who made up the last remnants of the 1982 coup plot.[36] The group's goal remained to "overthrow Moi's government as a first step towards breaking the 'stranglehold of Euro-American imperialism on our economy, politics and culture,'"[37] further exposing the socialist leanings espoused by the leading opposition figures. Simultaneously, there was growing clamor against the oppressive rule, the calls to "*tingisa kidole*" – the salute to show membership of KANU – was affirmed by shaking the right-hand index finger.

The Moi government, given the coup that had taken it by surprise, saw shadows everywhere; for example, Koigi wa Wamwere was accused of being a member of the proscribed Mwakenya group, merely for defending its accused.[38] The opposition, particularly Mwakenya, was not quite well organized; its existence was discovered, according to Wainaina, through the wife of one of its members, Maina Kĩongo. "Mrs. Kĩongo got wind of the existence of the movement and of its aims. Burdened by this knowledge, she then divulged it in church one Sunday before the entire congregation";[39] ultimately, the pastor encouraged Mrs. Kĩongo to alert the government, and by 1986 the movement had collapsed. Perhaps oathing, as had been done by the Mau Mau, might have helped Mwakenya solve that issue.

One of Kenya's rather unusually innovative attempts at electoral transparency was the idea of "*Mlolongo*" voting. *Mlolongo* is a Swahili word for "queue". Since independence, the process of voting was through secret ballot; however, in nearly every election, there were widespread complaints of rigging, stuffing of ballot boxes and other nefarious activities especially by the government, in order to obtain the preferential result. Since most of the tallying of the ballots would be done at a central location, and transportation of ballot boxes was provided by the government, sometimes across poor road infrastructure, and guarded by the police, the results often significantly differed from the peoples' preferences; to alleviate this, the government came up with the idea of *Mlolongo* – queue – voting.

Whereas the intention of the new system was to eliminate voting fraud, since in theory it was possible to see and count the number of votes for each candidate for each polling station, thus eliminating ballot-box stuffing or results alteration at the polling stations, there were quite a number of unintended consequences. These ranged from voter intimidation, when individuals voted for the "wrong" candidate, that is, one not preferred by the establishment,[40] to public shaming based on voting patterns, subtle pressure to vote for preferred candidates to "visits" by "hired thugs" in the subsequent days, resulting in assaults and beatings. The queue system was not necessarily unique to the Kenyan elections of 1988: Ajulu notes that the system had been used 24 years previously, under the British colonial administration for similar purposes.[41]

The use of "novel" institutions followed an established pattern, one in which Moi used the provincial administration to ensure compliance with the broader government vision, where "he used Harambee strategically to reward close supporters and weaken or divide enemies, reducing local power barons' independent ability to distribute patronage and gain support."[42] In addition, to consolidate his power and eliminate opposition, "he banned the Luo Union and all other "ethnic" associations; his weakness made them too great a threat to him."[43]

"Vibaraka", economics and the effect on domestic politics

Although Moi's government had managed to consolidate the political aspects of the republic, it could not hope to control everything. Perhaps one of the most significant external events that changed the trajectory of many African countries took place far away, in Moscow and other communist nations in Eastern Europe: the fall of the Berlin Wall in 1989 and the collapse of the Soviet Union in 1991. For most of their early years of independence, African countries sought, and leveraged, alliances with one or the other of the alliances pitting the US and its allies, on one hand, and the Soviet Union and its allies, on the other. Although African countries were almost without exception members of the Group of 77 Non-Aligned Movement nations, sometimes because of their prior colonization, or arising from conscious choices, they aligned themselves with one or the other bloc, occasionally switching and thus accruing more benefits, as was the case with Ethiopia/Somalia in the mid-1970s.

Under these conditions, it was easy to leverage the alliances, and as such, African countries could threaten to switch sides so as to relieve the pressure on them to enact social, political and/or economic reforms. Although the US had few direct alliances with African countries other than the sale of weapons, the friends of friends remained almost friends. Francophone African countries generally aligned themselves with France, a Western country, while Anglophone African countries, despite their independence, remained practically joined at the hip with the British. The collection of other countries formerly colonized by the Spaniards, Portuguese and Belgians were similarly allied. For Kenya, a former British colony allied with the British and the US, a stable, capitalist nation strategically located in the Horn of Africa, its continued affiliation with the West was critically important.

While Kenya was consolidating the one-party rule with token Western calls for more democratic societies, elsewhere, socialism had begun to weaken beginning in the early 1980s. It was coupled with economic reforms in China, the other major socialist economy, which led not only to a reconsideration of the economic and political paths of some African countries but also to the increasing ability of donors and lenders to attach conditions to any loans and development aid.[44] The collapse of the Soviet Union robbed African countries of the leverage borne of potentially pitting one superpower against another and, with it, any possibility of weathering the onslaught of demands to undertake social, political and economic reforms. At the same time, Africa's importance to Western countries declined, given the absence of a contending global power; African countries thus had less, if any, leverage.[45]

Barkan adds that the US's lack of commercial interest in Africa meant that donor countries could assert pressure based on their domestic conditions, to not spend their resources on countries unwilling to implement reforms. African countries – Kenya included – had to make economic and political adjustments as a precondition for aid.[46] The signs of strains on future funding, decreased future assistance and demands for political and economic changes were already there beginning the 1980s: American aid to Kenya after 1984 was already in decline, with the military loans and grants taking a bigger hit. For example, in 1985, total aid was US$100 million, whereas in 1988 it was slightly over US$60 million. At the height of the Kenya–Western donors' crisis from 1990 to 1992, it barely cracked US$40 million. Reflecting the geopolitical changes, US military aid to Kenya in 1991 and 1992 was approximately US$2 million.[47]

A less commonly cited external factor was the crumbling of the apartheid regime in South Africa and the release of Nelson Mandela from prison in February 1990 and the subsequent legalization of the African National Congress (ANC). Cumming writes that these events led to a resurgence of opposition politics in countries such as Kenya and Togo and a reconsideration of the wisdom of continued support for despots who might soon be swept out of power,[48] as was the case with the apartheid regime in the first free elections in South Africa. At the same time, the US and Western powers, despite suspending aid and loans to Kenya on several occasions – notably in 1991, 1997 and 2006 – continued to harbor a desire to keep Kenya especially in the American orbit even with the carrot-and-stick approaches, as Kenya was an important partner, a bulwark, and often provided bases for operations for humanitarian purposes, to counter rising powers such as China, against rising failed states (Somalia, Yemen) and in the fight against terrorism.[49]

Economics of failure and domestic impacts: structural adjustment programs

Although internally the government appeared to have control over social and the political situation, externally, the Washington Consensus would produce consequences that weakened the government's ability to provide social services, with severe negative outcomes. The genesis of structural adjustment programs (SAPs) dates as far back as the 1950s, but given the global geopolitical conditions prevailing in the world highlighted previously, political considerations, rather than economic ones, dominated the financiers' interests. Heidhues and Obare write of SAPs as the closely coordinated response between the International Monetary Fund (IMF; macroeconomic development and setting the policy agenda) and the World Bank (structural adjustment lending) to the African economic crisis of the 1970s; the SAPs intensified in the 1980s, were applied to Latin American countries and would continue to be the primary focus of the international financial institutions (IFIs) and their backers, the Western donor countries, through the 1990s.[50]

Some of the key features of SAPs were macroeconomic stabilization, private sector, free market, trade liberalization, reduction and control of budget deficits, free market, privatization especially of state-owned enterprises (SOEs), companies and services, the removal of subsidies to such companies and the introduction of user-fees controlling budget deficits, privatizing public-sector companies and services, dissolving parastatals, eliminating subsidies and the introduction of user fees for services.[51] Although they were enacted with a zeal akin to religious conviction, especially since now the economic realm was presumed to supersede the political after the fall of the Soviet Union, every country that sought loans or aid was prescribed the same pill. Rarely, if ever, did the pill heal; some studies suggest that aspects of SAPs brought about changes especially in macroeconomic indicators. Most scholarship finds that SAPs had an unintended consequence: poverty exacerbated as governments introduced user fees to basic services such as education, health and social services including school milk and school feeding programs' resources, community development services and agricultural extension services. Torn between paying for schooling or medical care, most families in the already-relatively poor countries removed their children from school and declined to seek medical care; Human Development Indices declined rapidly.

The Kenya government found itself torn between increasingly ebullient demands from the West and the actual domestic conditions. Spooner and Smith highlight this, writing that "the planned sequence of adjustment policy in Kenya does not appear to have been based on theoretical reasoning. The Kenyan government failed to implement some of the planned adjustment policies, often on the basis of good economic reasoning"[52] and with a good basis thereof: economic growth had shrunk from 6.6 percent per annum to 4.2 percent per annum but with a population growth of 3.8 percent. Its debt ballooned and required payments increased to US$881 million in 1980, compared with US$73 million in 1973; net agricultural production declined by 3.3 percent to 0.5 percent between 1978 and 1980; there was a greater need for social services as population grew, leading to more government spending on parastatals, unfavorable investment conditions and external conditions such as the dissolution of EAC, declining prices for principal exports and an increase in global oil prices.[53]

The Moi government, like many other African and Latin American countries operating under these strict, externally imposed conditions chafed: most Africans labeled the conditionalities neo-colonialism and argued that state sovereignty was being undermined. Mailafia highlights this argument, noting that Africa was not only a research lab for economic reforms, and the coupling between loss of funding from IFIs often followed the loss of funding from donor countries, blurring the lines between countries and organizations. Furthermore, Western donors have been accused of devising and imposing reform programs on countries, which have been imposed with "a powerful combination of arrogance, ignorance and absolute, unchecked power"[54] and, furthermore, increasing dependence of African countries on the Bretton Woods institutions. Often, Kenya's president called Western powers "Vibaraka" (neo-colonialists) and referred to pro-democracy agitators as agents of the "Vibaraka" but grudgingly implemented some of the conditionalities.

Criticism of IFIs and the governments that backed them was perhaps well deserved. Dollar and Svensson, analyzing the outcomes of SAPs in the 1980s, found "no evidence that any of the variables under the World Bank's control affect the probability of success of an adjustment loan",[55] whereas "domestic political-economy factors influence strongly the success or failure of reform programs supported by adjustment loans."[56] Endemic of Africa and Less Developed Countries (LDCs) as a laboratory for economic reform, the World Bank emphasized borrowing countries to undertake "policy conditions" prior to funding but subsequently began insisting on prior actions before being allocated funding.[57] At the same time, the initial analysis of the decade-long project was coming online; nearly uniformly, they mirrored Dollar and Svensson's findings: there were few instances in which SAPs had been successful; indeed, poverty increased. Perhaps the World Bank and Western countries underestimated the antecedent conditions in African countries between independence and the 1980s, the lack of private resources to invest into social services, the levels of poverty and the significant need for African governments' intervention in socio-economic developmental activities to foster social progress.

Initial post-independence conditions in Kenya were reported as difficult: "low income, low human development indicators, and a rather uneven distribution of income"[58] with a significant distribution in who owned what: 40 percent of the population controlled about 10 percent of wealth while the top 10 percent owned 46 percent of the wealth by the 1970s, and spending on social services averaged about 8 percent.[59] The reasons for poor social and economic outcomes for Kenya did not necessarily have their basis on the political conditions in the country. They included the combined effects of global decline in prices of commodities, lack of diversification of the economy, environmental conditions such as *El Nino* and *La Nina* in the early 1980s, followed by a major drought, decreasing political space to challenge government policy, and the gradual implementation of the Washington Consensus conditions and the introduction of user fees for social services. Ultimately the real gross domestic product (GDP) per capita grew by one of the slowest margins of 0.6 percent against a population growth of 3.5 and decreased by 0.8 in the early years of the 1990s, even as population growth remained at 3 percent.[60]

The relative peace that Kenya experienced, compared to its neighbors which were either wracked by conflict (e.g., Uganda), and socialism (Tanzania), ensured that Kenya's investment in, and therefore progress in social indicators was steady, although this trend began to reverse in the mid-1980s particularly in the north-east.[61] Where economic stagnation and reversals in gains occurred, Kenya's president blamed Western donors rather than the increasing lack of competition and a poor investment climate because of low Human Development Indicators (HDI), poor infrastructure and growing corruption. Evidence piled on that suggested that implementation of SAP was reversing social indicators' gains; as Abouharb and Cingranelli note, the World Bank was "stung by the rising tide of criticism of SAPs",[62] and its president "declared that, henceforth, poverty reduction would constitute the aim of the institution."[63]

Domestic populations in African countries such as Kenya generally blame their government for most of the social ills – as perhaps do most populations in other countries. In the case of Kenya, in addition to the World Bank's and the IMF's conditionalities, user fees and constricted political space threatened the government's control of the population. Any dissent, allegations of corruption and calls for good governance was often dismissed as neo-colonialism, and Western powers were more focused on containing communism rather than improving the lives of African peoples. But, coupled with global geopolitical occurrences, Kenya's government was losing the narrative, which led to even more oppression before space opened up for multi-party democracy, in part due to the consequences of events elsewhere.

Ethnic dimensions

The ethnic dimension of Kenyan politics began to manifest itself more blatantly and clearly during the presidency of Kenyatta, which gave way to the entrenchment of the Moi presidency. Although in the initial years of his presidency, Moi attempted to "*fuata nyayo*", subsequent challenges to his young presidency caused him to soon propose surrounding himself with people he could trust. In the selection of new government officials, as other communities would later argue, Kikuyus had populated all levels of government at ratios that did not reflect the ethnic diversity of the country and were more reflective of ethnic preferences. Even where political marriage reflecting the diversity had previously occurred, the removal of Jaramogi Oginga Odinga as vice president in 1966 reflected, in part, his socialist leanings, but the 1969 "Kisumu massacre" demonstrated the president's and "the Family's" thinking about the control, purpose, and exclusion of certain communities from government. Later, in the sunset years of President Kenyatta, the Family attempted to keep Daniel arap Moi from ascending to the presidency. Then, it was claimed, Jomo Kenyatta had implored, nee "*gũtiga kĩrumi*", that leadership should never cross west of Chania River, implying that Kenya's presidency was not to be allowed "western Kenya", broadly writ. Alternatively, it may be the case that the attempt to keep the leadership in the Kikuyu elite/Kiambu Mafia had more to do with the perks of leadership than the question of ethnicity.

Interestingly, following the first few years of Moi's presidency, much of the challenge to his rule did not come from the group/s that had attempted to deny him the presidency, primarily the Kikuyu. Although it can be treacherous slope to allege that the reasons for the attempted coup in 1982 and the growth of *Mwakenya* were ethnic, those largely associated with the movement were not from the Kikuyu community; rather, the diversification of the ethnic sources of political contestation saw the growth of opposition in the western Nyanza and Kisii regions and the Luo community's mantle in challenging the new government, just as they had challenged Kenyatta's government. Towards the beginning of the agitation for multi-party politics, a more cosmopolitan group of challengers emerged; these were especially drawn from the Academy and various ethnic, social, political and interest groups, as well as individuals who had, at one time, supported the president, including Moi's first vice president and several of his former ministers.

Yet, the return of ethnicity, both as a reward and to punish any non-cooperating ethnic group featured prominently in Moi's administration, and in the conduct of multi-party democratic elections, as the next chapter shows. The latter part of the pre-multi-party politics era saw significant pushback because nepotism and ethnic preferences in appointing civil servants and was cited as one of the causes of the coup d'état in 1982 and the rise of Mwakenya. Thus, although less pronounced in public, and although the country appeared peaceful, there were still those undercurrents that could be leveraged and exploited at nearly a moment's notice, to upend the peace and challenge the government. At the same time, the 1980s saw the strengthening of the security state; the Special Branch turned the disappearance of opposition figures an art, while torture in the infamous Nyayo House basement became all too well known but rarely talked about.

Thus, the years of consolidation saw several significant developments: Moi began by attempting to reassure a restive Kikuyu Elite who attempted to dethrone him, followed by progressive consolidation of the one-party rule, an abortive military coup d'état that led to the adoption of KANU as the only legal political party, crackdown on opposition and the rise of underground movements that were always at risk of infiltration by the security agencies. A sham "*Mlolongo*" election in 1988 demonstrated the depths to which the political corruption had sunk. Elsewhere, the winds of change blowing across Eastern Europe and the Soviet Union, the eventual collapse of communism and triumph of capitalism eliminated the need to cozy up to dictators as a bulwark against communism, and a combination of IFIs of Bretton Woods institutions and the donor countries' pressure led to the re-introduction of multi-party politics, but with that, the return of somewhat credible elections and participation. The policies that Kenyatta had put in place, for example, regarding property ownership, and the idea of a Kenya for all Kenyans, together with the competition attributed to ethnic-based parties, would be the causes of the next installment of ethnic conflict.

Notes

1 Bethwell A. Ogot. "The Politics of Populism." In Bethwell A. Ogot & William Robert Ochieng, Eds. *Decolonization & Independence in Kenya, 1940–1993*. (Athens, OH: Ohio University Press, 1995): 187.
2 Marshall Clough. "Kenya after Kenyatta: An Introduction." *Africa Today*, 26, No. 3, Kenya after Kenyatta (3rd Qtr., 1979): 5.
3 Clough. "Kenya after Kenyatta." 5.
4 Richard Hodder-Williams. "Kenya after Kenyatta." *The World Today*, 36, No. 12 (December, 1980): 476.
5 Jennifer A. Widner. *The Rise of a Party-State in Kenya: From 'Harambee!' to 'Nyayo!'*. (Berkeley, CA: The University of California Press, 1992): 113.
6 Widner. *The Rise of a Party-State in Kenya*. 114.
7 Widner. *The Rise of a Party-State in Kenya*. 116.
8 Clough. "Kenya after Kenyatta." 6.
9 David K. Leonard. *African Successes: Four Public Managers of Kenyan Rural Development*. (Berkeley, CA: University of California Press, 1991): 169.
10 Carole Cooper, Ed. *Kenya: The National Epic*. (Nairobi, Kenya: Kenway Publications, 1993): 243.
11 Cooper. *Kenya*. 247.
12 Leonard. *African Successes*. 169.
13 Daniel Branch. *Kenya: Between Hope and Despair, 1963–2011*. (New Haven, CT: Yale University Press, 2011): 127.
14 Branch. *Kenya*. 129.
15 Galia Sabar. *Church, State and Society in Kenya: From Mediation to Opposition 1963–1993*. (New York, NY: Frank Cass & Co. Ltd., 2005): 179.
16 D. Pal S. Ahluwalia. *Post-Colonialism and the Politics of Kenya*. (New York: Nova Science Publishers, 1996): 22.
17 Timothy Parsons. "The Lanet Incident, 2–25 January 1964: Military Unrest and National Amnesia in Kenya." *The International Journal of African Historical Studies*, 40, No. 1, Continuities in Governance in Late Colonial and Early Postcolonial East Africa (2007): 51.
18 Vincent B. Khapoya. "The Politics of Succession in Africa: Kenya after Kenyatta." *Africa Today*, 26, No. 3, Kenya after Kenyatta (3rd Qtr., 1979): 9.
19 Charles Hornsby. *Kenya: A History since Independence*. (New York, NY: I. B. Tauris & Co., 2012): 374.
20 Sabar. *Church, State and Society in Kenya*. 179.
21 Sabar. *Church, State and Society in Kenya*. 179.
22 Hornsby. *Kenya*. 374.
23 Hornsby. *Kenya*. 374.
24 Hornsby. *Kenya*. 376.
25 Hornsby. *Kenya*. 377.
26 Branch. *Kenya*. 156.
27 Branch. *Kenya*. 156–157.
28 Kim Foulds. "The Somali Question: Protracted Conflict, National Narratives, and Curricular Politics in Kenya." In Denise Bentrovato, Karina V. Korostelina & Martina Schulze, Eds. *History Can Bite: History Education in Divided and Postwar Societies*. Goettingen: V&R unipress GmbH, 2016): 47.
29 National Assembly. *Kenya National Assembly Official Record (Hansard) Apr 8, 2010*. (Nairobi: Government Printer, 2010): 38.

30 Ben Rawlence & Human Rights Watch. *'Bring the Gun or You'll Die': Torture, Rape, and Other Serious Human Rights Violations by Kenyan Security Forces in the Mandera Triangle*. (New York, NY: Human Rights Watch, 2009): 13.
31 Keren Weitzberg. *We Do Not Have Borders: Greater Somalia and the Predicaments of Belonging in Kenya*. (Athens, OH: Ohio University Press, 2017): 145.
32 Hussein A. Mahmoud. "Conflict and Constraints to Peace among Pastoralists in Northern Kenya." In Mwesiga Laurent Baregu, Ed. *Understanding Obstacles to Peace: Actors, Interests, and Strategies in Africa's Great Lakes Region*. (Kampala, Uganda: Fountain Publishers, 2011): 156.
33 Rasna Warah. *War Crimes: How Warlords, Politicians, Foreign Governments and Aid Agencies Conspired to Create a Failed State in Somalia*. (Bloomington, IN: AuthorHouse UK Ltd., 2014): 134.
34 See Samson Kaunga Ndayi. "Reassessing Jomo Kenyatta's Crackdown on Theater for Education and Development." In Mickie Mwanzia Koster, Michael Mwenda Kithinji & Jerono P. Rotich, Eds. *Kenya after 50: Reconfiguring Education, Gender, and Policy*. (New York, NY: Palgrave Macmillan, 2016) and Matthew Firestone, Stuart Butler, Paula Hardy and Adam Karlin. *Kenya*. (Lonely Planet, 2016, eBook).
35 Francis Wiafe-Amoako. *Africa 2016–2017*. (Lanham, MD: Rowman & Littlefield, 2016): 221.
36 Branch. *Kenya*. 162.
37 Branch. *Kenya*. 163.
38 Koigi Wa Wamwere. *I Refuse to Die: My Journey for Freedom*. (New York, NY: Seven Stories Press, 2002): 264.
39 Binyavanga Wainaina. *Kwani? 02*, Vol. 2. (Nairobi, Kenya: Kwani Trust, 2004): 306.
40 Wiafe-Amoako. *Africa*. 221.
41 Eok Ajulu. "Thinking through the Crisis of Democratisation in Kenya: A Response to Adar and Murunga." *African Sociological Review/Revue Africaine de Sociologie*, 4, No. 2 (2000): 147.
42 Stephen Orvis. "Conclusion: Bringing Institutions Back into the Study of Kenya and Africa." *Africa Today*, 53, No. 2, Creating the Kenya Post-Colony (Winter, 2006): 106.
43 Orvis. "Conclusion." 106.
44 Joel D. Barkan. "Divergence and Convergence in Kenya and Tanzania: Pressures for Reform." In Joel D. Barkan, Ed. *Beyond Capitalism vs. Socialism in Kenya and Tanzania*. (Boulder, CO: Lynn Rienner Publishers, 1994): 3.
45 Barkan. "Divergence and Convergence in Kenya and Tanzania." 3.
46 Barkan. "Divergence and Convergence in Kenya and Tanzania." 3.
47 Hornsby. *Kenya*. 468.
48 Gordon Cumming. *Aid to Africa: French and British Policies from the Cold War to the New Millennium*. (New York, NY: Routledge, 2017): 247.
49 Babere Kerata Chacha & Muniko Zdphaniah Marwa. "Kenya's Foreign Policy Challenges of Terrorism in the Post-Cold War." In Malinda S. Smith, Ed. *Securing Africa: Post-9/11 Discourses on Terrorism*. (New York, NY: Routledge, 2016): 168.
50 Franz Heidhues & Gideon Obare. "Lessons from Structural Adjustment Programmes and Their Effects in Africa." *Quarterly Journal of International Agriculture*, 50, No. 1 (2011): 57.
51 Heidhues & Obare. "Lessons from Structural Adjustment Programmes." 58.
52 Neil J. Spooner & Lawrence D. Smith. *Structural Adjustment Policy Sequencing in Sub-Saharan Africa*. (Rome, Italy: Food and Agricultural Organization, 1991): 73.
53 Spooner & Smith. *Structural Adjustment Policy Sequencing in Sub-Saharan Africa*. 73–74.
54 Obed O. Mailafia. *Europe and Economic Reform in Africa: Structural Adjustment and Economic Diplomacy*. (New York, NY: Routledge, 1997): 22.
55 David Dollar & Jakob Svensson. *What Explains the Success or Failure of Structural Adjustment Programs?* Policy Research Working Paper, Issue 1938. (Washington, DC: The World Bank, 1998): 4.

56 Dollar & Svensson. *What Explains the Success or Failure of Structural Adjustment Programs?* 3–4.
57 M. Rodwan Abouharb & David Cingranelli. *Human Rights and Structural Adjustment.* (Oxford, UK: Cambridge University Press, 2008): 63.
58 United Nations Development Programme. *Human Development Report 1990.* (New York, NY: Oxford University Press, 1990): 55.
59 UNDP. *Human Development Report 1990.* 55.
60 Kempe Ronald Hope, Sr., *The Political Economy of Development in Kenya.* (New York, NY: Continuum International Pulishing Group, 2012): 6.
61 Klugman Jeni, Neyapti Bilin & Stewart Frances. *Development Centre Studies Conflict and Growth in Africa, Vol. 2: Kenya, Tanzania and Uganda.* (Paris, FR: OECD, 1999): 102.
62 Abouharb & Cingranelli. *Human Rights and Structural Adjustment.* 63.
63 Abouharb & Cingranelli. *Human Rights and Structural Adjustment.* 63.

References

Abouharb, M. Rodwan & David Cingranelli. *Human Rights and Structural Adjustment.* Oxford, UK: Cambridge University Press, 2008.

Ahluwalia, D. Pal S. *Post-Colonialism and the Politics of Kenya.* New York: Nova Science Publishers, 1996.

Ajulu, Rok. "Thinking through the Crisis of Democratisation in Kenya: A Response to Adar and Murunga." *African Sociological Review/Revue Africaine de Sociologie*, 4, No. 2 (2000): 133–157. (Web). Accessed on 11/22/2016 05:57 UTC from: www.jstor.org/stable/24487394

Barkan, Joel D. "Divergence and Convergence in Kenya and Tanzania: Pressures for Reform." In Joel D. Barkan, Ed. *Beyond Capitalism vs. Socialism in Kenya and Tanzania.* Boulder, CO: Lynn Rienner Publishers, 1994.

Branch, Daniel. *Kenya: Between Hope and Despair, 1963–2011.* New Haven, CT: Yale University Press, 2011.

Chacha, Babere Kerata & Muniko Zdphaniah Marwa. "Kenya's Foreign Policy Challenges of Terrorism in the Post-Cold War." In Malinda S. Smith, Ed. *Securing Africa: Post-9/11 Discourses on Terrorism.* New York, NY: Routledge, 2016.

Clough, Marshall S. "Kenya after Kenyatta: An Introduction." *Africa Today*, 26, No. 3, Kenya after Kenyatta (3rd Qtr., 1979): 5–6. Accessed on 11/212016 from: www.jstor.org/stable/4185872

Cooper, Carole, Ed. *Kenya: The National Epic.* Nairobi, Kenya: Kenway Publications, 1993.

Cumming, Gordon. *Aid to Africa: French and British Policies from the Cold War to the New Millennium.* New York, NY: Routledge, 2017.

Dollar, David & Jakob Svensson. *What Explains the Success or Failure of Structural Adjustment Programs?* Policy Research Working Paper, Issue 1938. Washington, DC: The World Bank, 1998.

Firestone, Matthew, Stuart Butler, Paula Hardy & Adam Karlin. *Kenya.* Melbourne, Australia: Lonely Planet, 2016 (eBook).

Foulds, Kim. "The Somali Question: Protracted Conflict, National Narratives, and Curricular Politics in Kenya." In Denise Bentrovato, Karina V. Korostelina & Martina Schulze, Eds. *History Can Bite: History Education in Divided and Postwar Societies.* Goettingen: V&R Unipress GmbH, 2016.

Heidhues, Franz & Gideon Obare. "Lessons from Structural Adjustment Programmes and Their Effects in Africa." *Quarterly Journal of International Agriculture*, 50, No. 1 (2011): 55–64.

Hodder-Williams, Richard. "Kenya after Kenyatta." *The World Today*, 36, No. 12 (December, 1980): 476–483. Accessed on 11/21/2016 from: www.jstor.org/stable/40395163

Hope, Kempe Ronald, Sr. *The Political Economy of Development in Kenya*. New York, NY: Continuum International Publishing Group, 2012.

Hornsby, Charles. *Kenya: A History since Independence*. New York, NY: I. B. Tauris & Co., 2012.

Jeni, Klugman, Neyapti Bilin & Stewart Frances. *Development Centre Studies Conflict and Growth in Africa, Vol. 2: Kenya, Tanzania and Uganda*. Paris, FR: OECD, 1999.

Khapoya, Vincent B. "The Politics of Succession in Africa: Kenya after Kenyatta." *Africa Today*, 26, No. 3, Kenya after Kenyatta (3rd Qtr., 1979): 7–20. Accessed on 11/21/2016 from: www.jstor.org/stable/4185873

Leonard, David K. *African Successes: Four Public Managers of Kenyan Rural Development*. Berkeley, CA: University of California Press, 1991.

Mahmoud, Hussein A. "Conflict and Constraints to Peace among Pastoralists in Northern Kenya." In Mwesiga Laurent Baregu, Ed. *Understanding Obstacles to Peace: Actors, Interests, and Strategies in Africa's Great Lakes Region*. Kampala, Uganda: Fountain Publishers, 2011.

Mailafia, Obed O. *Europe and Economic Reform in Africa: Structural Adjustment and Economic Diplomacy*. New York, NY: Routledge, 1997.

National Assembly. *Kenya National Assembly Official Record (Hansard)*. 8 April 2010. Nairobi: Government Printer, 2010.

Ndayi, Samson Kaunga. "Reassessing Jomo Kenyatta's Crackdown on Theater for Education and Development." In Mickie Mwanzia Koster, Michael Mwenda Kithinji & Jerono P. Rotich, Eds. *Kenya after 50: Reconfiguring Education, Gender, and Policy*. New York, NY: Palgrave Macmillan, 2016.

Ogot, Bethwell A. "The Politics of Populism." In Bethwell A. Ogot & William Robert Ochieng, Eds. *Decolonization & Independence in Kenya, 1940–93*. Athens, OH: Ohio University Press, 1995.

Orvis, Stephen. "Conclusion: Bringing Institutions Back into the Study of Kenya and Africa." *Africa Today*, 53, No. 2, Creating the Kenya Post-Colony (Winter, 2006): 95–110. (Web). Accessed on 11/22/2016 05:57 UTC from: www.jstor.org/stable/4187774

Parsons, Timothy. "The Lanet Incident, 2–25 January 1964: Military Unrest and National Amnesia in Kenya." *The International Journal of African Historical Studies*, 40, No. 1, Continuities in Governance in Late Colonial and Early Postcolonial East Africa (2007): 51–70. Accessed on 11/21/2016 from: www.jstor.org/stable/40034790

Rawlence, Ben & Human Rights Watch. *'Bring the Gun or You'll Die': Torture, Rape, and Other Serious Human Rights Violations by Kenyan Security Forces in the Mandera Triangle*. New York, NY: Human Rights Watch, 2009.

Sabar, Galia. *Church, State and Society in Kenya: From Mediation to Opposition 1963–1993*. New York, NY: Frank Cass & Co. Ltd., 2005.

Spooner, Neil J. & Lawrence D. Smith. *Structural Adjustment Policy Sequencing in Sub-Saharan Africa*. FAO Economic and Social Development Paper 104. Rome, Italy: Food and Agricultural Organization, 1991.

United Nations Development Programme. *Human Development Report 1990*. New York, NY: Oxford University Press, 1990.

Wainaina, Binyavanga. *Kwani? 02*, Vol. 2. Nairobi, Kenya: Kwani Trust, 2004.

Warah, Rasna. *War Crimes: How Warlords, Politicians, Foreign Governments and Aid Agencies Conspired to Create a Failed State in Somalia*. Bloomington, IN: AuthorHouse UK Ltd., 2014.

Wa Wamwere, Koigi. *I Refuse to Die: My Journey for Freedom*. New York, NY: Seven Stories Press, 2002.
Weitzberg, Keren. *We Do Not Have Borders: Greater Somalia and the Predicaments of Belonging in Kenya*. Athens, OH: Ohio University Press, 2017.
Wiafe-Amoako, Francis. *Africa 2016–2017*. Lanham, MD: Rowman & Littlefield, 2016.
Widner, Jennifer A. *The Rise of a Party-State in Kenya: From 'Harambee!' to 'Nyayo!'*. Berkeley, CA: The University of California Press, 1992.

3 Democracy, our way and multi-party politics

By the early 1990s, it was clear that global geopolitics and events far away from Kenya's capital, Nairobi, were driving the new realities to which Africa would find itself in the grip of, unable to influence, significantly influenced by or on the brink of disaster. All over the continent, these winds of change had different outcomes: from the disintegration of the Somali state to the rapid introduction of multi-party politics in different countries, despite stiff opposition by the ruling parties, which almost uniformly had moved from multi-party politics to one-party rule within a decade of independence. Kenya was no exception; despite the consolidation of one-party rule that had occurred within the previous decade, overbearing pressure from inside and outside would lead to rapid adoption of multi-party politics, although the incumbent would continue to rule for another 10 years, conceding and effecting transfer of power in 2002.

Kenya's changes were not without challenges: indeed, those ethnic divisions that have been highlighted in previous chapters were now visible in greater relief. KANU, the only "legal" party, faced a divided opposition and twice won elections with a minority of votes and, in the first election, resorted to one of the most significant episodes of corruption and raiding of the economy in the Goldenberg gold export scheme, in order to raise money with which it would "buy" the election of 1992. Other strategies, discussed in this chapter, would come into operation: these included ballot-box stuffing, disenfranchising voters, defection by candidates (more like incentivization to drop out of the races), changing political sides in parliament thus prompting by-elections, and ethnic violence in order to both buy votes and disenfranchise potential opposition. The rest of this chapter examines the global geopolitics and internal conditions that prompted changes that led to the re-introduction of multi-party politics and the contentious elections that followed these changes.

Global winds of change, unintended local consequences

Scholars generally agree that the third wave of democratization began somewhere around the fall of the Berlin Wall, on 9 November 1989, and extended all the way to the collapse of the Soviet Union in 1991.[1] The first wave is thought to have started during the 1820s and the second wave between 1974 and 1990. In between, some 47 African, in addition to the former Eastern European countries, managed to hold multi-party elections. It was indeed a fortuitous time for democracy, although the reasons for the changes were not a sudden discovery of the inherent value of democracy.

Rather, it was generally a combination, for most countries, of internal pressure and activism, for example, in the previously highlighted case of the underground Mwakenya and seismic shifts in global geopolitics. There was, so to say, a new sheriff in town. The US was now the sole global superpower, and the conditions for "doing business" had dramatically changed. A combination of poor economic outcomes in the previous decade, leading many countries to lean on the international finance institutions (IFIs), especially the World Bank and International Monetary Fund, both dominated by Western liberal democratic powers, required several micro- and macroeconomic reforms, as well as reforms in governance. Countries that were ruled as single-party polities had pressure brought to bear to reform their institutions.

Kenya's situation was no different. Some attribute the start of the pro-democracy activism to the massive discontent following the "*Mlolongo*" elections of 1988, where blatant rigging demonstrated the government's lack of commitment to the purported notion of transparency (losing candidates often found themselves back in office, while popular candidates somehow "lost" the elections, and the president's prerogative to nominate 12 members of parliament also saw him return "preferred" candidates whom the electorate rejected). Although most of the opposition had been gutted, a re-energized underground opposition, with the support of alternate press and the Academy, restarted the rumblings.

Additionally, the church, which had been co-opted with the idea of "peace, love and unity", also became more vocal, as the number and frequency of crackdowns on meetings, detention without trial and incidences of torture increased. The government's position was not helped by the appearance of support for the protests and clamor for opening up of the democratic space by one of the most combative diplomats that the country has ever had the (dis)pleasure of hosting. In May 1990, according to Muigai, Smith Hempstone "fired the first salvo when in a speech to Kenyan businessmen he stated that the U.S. would give preference in its grants of foreign aid to those countries which nourished democratic institutions, defended human rights, and practiced multiparty politics."[2]

Kenya benefitted indirectly from the Cold War rivalry between the US and its allies; US allies included Kenya's past colonizer, Britain. Generally, Kenya was "co-opted into the Western camp",[3] and as long as this was the case, the pro-democracy forces did not find a sympathetic ear in London or Washington, D.C. Perhaps to indicate that it was a sovereign republic, Kenya often flirted with other alliances, for example, in 1964, when "Jaramogi Oginga Odinga led a high-powered Kenyan 'good-will' delegation to Beijing to discuss enhanced ties between the two countries."[4] But if Kenya was signalling one way, it was also doing so forcefully in the other direction. Two years after Jaramogi's visit to Beijing, Kenya "expelled the third secretary in the Chinese embassy, Yao Chun, on suspicions of plotting subversion."[5] The back and forth over where Kenya's alliances would lie continued, through elites pushing for different agenda and recruiting allies in the East and West to support their ventures. For example, Jaramogi Oginga Odinga "now got onto the socialist circuit – Guinea, East Germany, Chinese People's Republic and the Soviet Union",[6] while on the other hand, Tom Mboya continued with his widely supported airlift to America. All this while, Kenya strongly asserted its Non-Aligned Movement affiliation and G-77 membership throughout the Cold War but allowed Western troops to use its territory for training and other purposes.

Democracy was clearly secondary to other Western strategic interests. But alas, wasn't the country already tending democratic? There were regularly held elections, beginning as far back as 1963, including 1978, the very general elections that put Moi in office as the second president. Did the general elections of 1988, for president, members of parliament and councillors (ward representatives) not introduce the *Mlolongo* – queue – voting system? Whereas this was the case, the only legal party was KANU, and as such, Kenya was not classified as a democracy; indeed, during Moi's entire presidency, Kenya's Polity IV (as measured through the polity 2 variable) averaged −5 and only recorded a score of above 5 (considered the threshold of democracy) once, in 2002, Moi's last year in office. In 1988, during the touted *Mlolongo* elections, the polity 2 value was −7.

The march towards Saba Saba

The tropical storm that would build to become the hurricane that led to the repeal of Section 2 a) of the Kenyan constitution (that had made Kenya a *de jure* one-party state) thus had its start in places as near as the *Mlolongo* polling stations and as far away as Prague and Warsaw and Berlin and Moscow and Got Alila. In the latter, a sleepy village outside of Kisumu, the stronghold of the Luo, the "new" minister for foreign affairs, the well-liked and respected Dr. Robert Ouko, "disappeared", and his charred remains were found four days later. The government suggested that he had achieved what might have been otherwise an impossible feat: he committed suicide by shooting himself, then set himself on fire and somehow managed to break his legs, which seemed nigh impossible in both sequencing and logic.

Perhaps recalling the blatant murder of Tom Mboya, riots erupted in both Nairobi and Kisumu. The investigators from Scotland Yard were called in, but four investigations later, no one has ever been convicted of complicity in the death of the minister.[7] According to Makinda,

> the Scotland Yard team concluded that Ouko had been murdered for two reasons. First, he had been preparing a detailed report for the President in connection with corruption, in which the former Energy and Industry Minister, Nicholas Biwott, was the principal. Second, Ouko and Biwott had disagreed strongly in Washington during their visit there which ended on 2 February 1990.[8]

Ouko's death led to "spontaneous demonstrations . . . in Nairobi, Nakuru, Eldoret and Kisumu."[9]

In quick succession, the elections of 1988 that also resulted in the "demotion" Mwai Kibaki, the fall of the Berlin Wall and its implications, the murder of a popular, even Washington-beloved diplomat generally thought to have been capable of better leadership, the growing assertiveness of the church and civil society, an unusually combative US ambassador to Kenya and a Washington establishment that was growing less tolerant of dictatorships, coupled with the third wave of democratizations elsewhere, would ultimately lead to Saba Saba (Swahili for 7–7, or 7 July), when leading Kenyan "opposition" politicians (together with a very young, politically inactive author of this volume) were clubbed and teargassed when they attempted to hold a political rally at Kamukunji grounds. Muigai recounts that "on that fateful Saturday morning thousands upon thousands of Kenyans turned up at Kamukunji. Many waved green branches symbolizing that they were nonviolent and flashed the two finger salute, which had become the symbol for the proponents of multiparty politics";[10] the government attempt to quell these protests resulted in the deaths of 13, with many more injured.

By August 1990, the "government superficially compromised in August 1990 by appointing a KANU Review Committee to consider constitutional reforms",[11] recommending "cosmetic changes that would allow more openness in KANU, sidestepping the grievances that had animated the protests."[12] The pressure would become relentless; from Ambassador Hempstone's warnings (earning him the title "Rogue Ambassador") to pressure groups calling for a freeze in Kenya's foreign aid from Washington to the public excoriation and singling out by Canada (PM Brian Mulroney, Commonwealth Heads of States Summit, Zimbabwe) as a human rights offender,[13] accompanied by unrelenting street protests, a coherence in the message under the rallying cry that "Moi Must Go."[14]

By the end of 1991, Kenya was facing the suspension of US$350 million by the Paris Club of donors, pegging its resumption on "the early implementation of political reforms, including greater pluralism, the importance of the rule of law and respect for human rights, notably basic freedom of expression and assembly and . . . firm action to deal with corruption."[15] Norway joined the fray, requiring good governance and a shift to multi-party politics; Moi's response was to break diplomatic relations, losing US$50 million in pledged development aid in the process. None of these actions alleviated the pressure for reforms, not even Moi's oft-repeated claim that a one-party state was the wish of the majority. By the mid- to end of 1991, the pressure had grown to such a crescendo that at a National Delegates Conference, the ruling party, KANU, moved for a repeal of section 2 a) of the Constitution of Kenya that made the country a *de jure* one-party state was repealed, and by 10 December 1991, the era of multi-party politics had returned to Kenya.

Multi-party and the return of ethnic politics

Remarkably, the early months of the clamor for a return to multi-party politics saw a united front, one that superseded the ethnic angle. Jaramogi Oginga Odinga led the way with the application for the registration of the National Democratic

Party (NDP) in 1991, even before the country returned to multi-party politics. The group of initial opposition movement leaders was drawn from all across the country and ethnicities, although primarily from the more populous ethnic communities such as the broader GEMA (Gikuyu, Embu and Meru Association, and sometimes the Akamba), the Luo and the Luhya. Subsequently, some of the leading figures in the budding opposition would include "former Cabinet ministers Kenneth Matiba and Charles Rubia, and then political activist Raila Odinga";[16] these were some of the first politicians to be detained. Subsequently, the list of opposition leaders who were ultimately detained, imprisoned or placed under house arrest expanded to include "Charles Rubia, Matiba, Jaramogi Odinga, Gitobu imanyara, Mohammed Ibrahim, Masinde Muliro, Martin Shikuku, and James Orengo."[17] Others like Mwai Kibaki, only four years previously Moi's vice president, joined the opposition movement later on.

But just as quickly as the efforts to achieve multiparty democracy and unseat the incumbent government gained support, the temporary unity frayed. The government did help, by frustrating registration, limiting the ability to organize and outlawing meetings and invoking the Public Order Act, a relic of colonial administration's strategies for denying freedom of speech to its African subjects. The first election held under the aegis of a country with a plurality of parties took place on 29 December 1992. By the time the elections came around, the inevitable disagreements that have characterized Kenyan politics for half a century repeated. One of the major political parties, the Forum for Restoration of Democracy (FORD), which had been registered with two of the doyens of politics – Kenneth Matiba and Jaramogi Oginga Odinga, as its leaders, had already split into FORD-Asili, led by Kenneth Matiba, and FORD-Kenya, which was led by Odinga.

One might see a repeat of the early to mid-1960s here: Jomo Kenyatta, from the populous Kikuyu community, facing off against Jaramogi Oginga Odinga, from the third-most populous community, differed; this time around it was Matiba against Odinga, with Kibaki, another Kikuyu, in the mix. It is helpful to think of the demographics of the country in the early 1990s. Towards the election, Kenya's population was slightly north of 25 million:

> [T]he largest group are the Kikuyu (21 per cent), mainly living in the central part of the country. Then come the Luhya (14 per cent) in western Kenya, the Luo (13 per cent) near Lake Victoria, the Kalenjin (11 per cent) in the central Rift Valley, the Kamba (11 per cent) living east and south-east of Nairobi, the Kisii (6 per cent) in the south-west and the Meru (5 per cent).[18]

The results of the election were a self-defeating exercise for the now-fractured opposition, which was helped along by some of the pre-election machinations of the government. According to Nasong'o, the vote counts were as follows: Moi/KANU, 1.927 million; Matiba/FORD-Asili, 1.35 million; Kibaki/DP, 1.04 million; and Oginga Odinga/FORD-Kenya, .903 million.[19] In terms of percentage votes (that exceeded 1 percent), the three opposition candidates together garnered approximately 3.3 million votes to Moi's 1.93 million votes, or about 63 percent of the votes, thus handing Moi another term in office, despite the constraints that the ruling government attempted to put in place prior to the elections.[20] Similarly, had the two Kikuyu candidates simply supported one, their combined votes would have been approximately 600,000 votes short of those of Moi. Clearly, Moi had outwitted the opposition, a self-inflicted wound, although some of the additional requirements imposed to constrain the new parties and people included the requirement for the winning candidate to secure at least 25 percent of the votes in at least five provinces, rather than determining the winner based on a simple majority.

KANU zone, Kikuyus unwelcome

KANU's plans to win the elections, even though greatly aided by the disarray in the opposition ranks, benefitted from some of its own improvisation: eviction of the Kikuyus and other ethnic groups from the then Rift Valley Province. A little background here might be in order: upon independence, as a unitary country, Kenyatta took the step of disregarding the traditional ideas of what community owned what or who was settled where. In an address aimed at especially the former British colonialists who were leaving in droves, worried about the future of the white man in a majority African country, Kenyatta gave his "*uhuru na kazi*" speech and encouraged Kenyans to settle everywhere in Kenya. In contrast, KADU, fearing domination by the major ethnic groups, had preferred a Majimbo (regional) system, one that would give much greater autonomy to the provinces (regions) and be able to manage (or curtail) such issues as settlement.

As it was, Kenyans settled everywhere, but of special import,

> Kalenjin resentment of Kikuyu settlement in the Rift Valley grew during the 1960s as European farms were bought up and settlement schemes became scarce. Many self-identified local or indigenous residents decried how their interests were being neglected in favor of Kenyatta's Kikuyu community.[21]

Kanyinga adds that because of the political marginalization of the Kalenjin peoples, since they had no senior political figures in government until Moi's appointment as vice president to Kenyatta's government in 1967, they were unable to defend their rights. "Inevitably, therefore, settlement schemes in the Rift Valley remained sites of intense competition between the Kikuyu and the Kalenjins."[22] The significance of this settlement of the Kikuyus, from their supposed "ancestral districts" of Kiambu, Mũrang'a and Nyeri, ultimately saw "two districts that were home to the largest numbers of the Kikuyu in the diaspora, the Nakuru and Laikipia districts, [which] had about one-third of the 154 settlement schemes",[23] out of 418 settlement schemes. Another "diaspora" district for the Kikuyu, Nyandarua (generally considered to encompass land that belonged to the Maasai before colonialism) counted 90 land settlement schemes.

The land grievances, together with issues of perceived lack of support and betrayal in agitating for a return to multi-party politics, rekindled debate on "who was from where." "Particularly infamous", writes Lynch,

> were the "majimbo rallies" held in the Rift Valley in September 1991, at which speakers castigated advocates for multipartyism and called for a majimboism that would require outsiders to behave like "guests" and thus either display loyalty to President Moi and KANU or "return" to their "homelands."[24]

Kanyinga concurs, writing that

> the Kalenjin politicians allied with Moi and KANU picked the land question to mobilise ethnic sport in the Rift Valley. They argued that those in the political opposition demanding multiparty democracy, and the Kikuyu, in particular, had secured land in the Rift Valley meant for the Kalenjin and the Masai who had historical territorial claims to the area.[25]

The dry run of practices that would be repeated five years later in 1997 and 10 years later, in 2007 on a far grander scale, the displacement of "outsiders" prior to the election, with the goal of ensuring that the preferred candidates were voted into government began. In addition, since individuals are required to generally vote in the same location where they registered, and the re-registration periods often were shortened, having "outsiders" register in one area and then relocated would ensure that they did not vote, thus inflating the importance of the KANU votes. Similarly, the disenfranchisement would extend to the opposition (presidential) candidates, since the Kikuyus (and other "outsiders") would have no chance to cast their vote. Khadiagala writes that "by June 1992, ethnic attacks had killed an estimated 800 people and displaced 60,000 in Rift Valley and the neighboring Western Province. This pro-government – and sometimes government-perpetrated – violence, along with splits within the opposition, assured the KANU's victory in the elections of December 1992, as it won 100 of the 188 contested seats"[26] and as the winning party, KANU had the prerogative to appoint another 12 members, giving KANU 112 of 200 seats. Other machinations included nullifying electoral victories while alleging voting malpractices and encouraging defections by the opposition on promises of, or being provided with incentives and the continuation of ethnic violence in the Rift Valley.[27] Although this subject is addressed much later in the book, it is important to highlight that the estimated deaths from the 1991–93 election period was 800 with 60,000 persons replaced, while the death toll of the post-election violence in 2008 was 1133, approximately 333 more than in the 1991–1993 period but with more than 600,000 persons displaced internally. Yet, there was little national, regional or international re-/action to these tribal clashes, in part because the government still controlled media and free movement.

It would be inaccurate to characterize the violence simply as a pre-election activity, or necessarily targeted at the Kikuyu ethnic group alone. There had been significant fears, some articulated by Moi, that Kenya was more stable under one-party rule and that multi-party politics would stoke ethnic divisions; this did happen before and after the first democratic elections held under a multi-party system, in 1992. Chege notes that this occurred as "bands of armed Kalenjins attacked Luo, Luhya, Kisii, and Kikuyu farmers within or just beyond the border of the Rift Valley between December 1991 and March 1992";[28] later, the Maasai began "burning, looting and killing" Kikuyu farmers in ancestral Maasai lands.[29] Were they to happen today, these then so-called tribal clashes may have risen to the level of crimes against humanity in the context of the modern-day Rome Statute of the International Criminal Court (ICC).

Suffice it to say, the results of the elections on the other side and the wholesale rejection of KANU were almost flawless; one might rightly consider this to be the "humiliation of KANU." The government, under KANU, did not win any seats in the Central Province. So uniform was the KANU's rejection that in the Kinangop Constituency (where the author had first-person experience), a rather eccentric religious zealot by the name of Mary Wanjiru, who also put out that she could cure HIV, was elected, much to the chagrin and five-year duration of mortal, perhaps eternal, embarrassment of the constituents. In a neighboring constituency, Kipipiri, the death of the FORD-Asili member of parliament Laban Muchemi necessitated a by-election. The desire to flip the seat and have at least one KANU seat in Central Kenya, a Kikuyu stronghold, and, perhaps in an effort to remove the sting of wholesale rejection, saw almost comical economic stick-and-carrot activities by the president, Moi. At the time, it was alleged that President Moi postponed his birthday in order to campaign for the KANU candidate. The desperate vote-hunting tactics included make-believe electric power grid spread – trenches were dug, wire dumped and electric poles delivered. Yet, Githiomi Mwangi, of the Mwai Kibaki-led Democratic Party won, and that was the end of the "quest for fire" at least until Kibaki's presidency.[30]

Likoni violence

If the 1992 general election was contentious, the elections of 1997 took everything from 1992 to a different level, both pre- and post-election. As part of the 1991/2 reforms, presidential term limits of a maximum two five-year terms had been imposed; if he did not change the constitution, as had happened in other countries in Africa, this would be the last time that Daniel arap Moi would be contesting elections as a presidential candidate. On the side of the opposition, further fracturing had continued to occur. According to Maxon and Ofcansky, "the December 1997 elections featured 15 presidential candidates and more than twice as many parties as the general elections of 1992."[31] In additional to the usual suspects (KANU, DP, FORD-Asili and FORD-Kenya), other major newcomers included FORD-People (Kĩmani wa Nyoike), the National Development Party (led by Charity Ngilu), the Kenya Social Congress (George Anyona), the Kenya National Congress (Katama Mkangi), Kenya National Democratic Alliance (Koigi wa Wamwere) and the Liberal Party of Kenya (Wangarĩ Maathai).[32]

Multi-party politics in Kenya had ushered in a new era after the 1992 elections. The opposition sought to maintain relevance in the face of an unrelenting Moi and the KANU government. KANU, recognizing the lack of support in opposition-dominated areas, sought to reinvent itself and to diversify itself, even as KANU itself faced internal divisions. Kanyinga notes that "the party was also wracked by intra-elite rivalries. These rivalries began with the 1993 party national elections in which ethnic balancing in the distribution of national party positions took precedence over all other factors."[33] Communities that had supported KANU agitated for leadership "positions" in the party and government. Nevertheless, the belief of the need to reward the Kikuyu people was not universally shared; for example, "John Keen, the party's Secretary General at the time, pointed out that this [Meru underrepresentation in KANU] was not a serious problem because the Kikuyu are the 'cousins' of the Meru and would, therefore, represent Meru interests in the party",[34] but it apparently incensed the Meru. It appeared that the era of multi-party politics was also going to be the era of a careful balancing of ethnic interests.

More important, the doors to open acknowledgment of the role of ethnicity in multi-party politics appeared to be at full throttle, but so were the efforts to re-consolidate support for both KANU and the opposition (the latter was less successful). Ethnic and bloc negotiation between broader ethnic coalitions began; for example, "the broad Kikuyu bloc subsumes the Embu and Meru (and is thus sometimes referred to collectively as GEMA – the acronym for the Gĩkũyũ [Kikuyu], Embu, and Meru Association,"[35] while "the broader Kalenjin coalition is commonly referred to in the Kenyan press by the acronym KAMATUSA (*Ka*lenjin, *Ma*asai, *Tu*rkana, *Sa*mburu"[36] started talks.[37]

Even before the talks started, Moi continued to maintain contacts with both his business partners, some of whom were Kikuyus, and several "point-men" in the community, including, for example, the KANU secretary general, J. J. Kamotho; Steeves writes further that "in 1993, Moi undertook a strategy designed to 'reach out' to the Kikuyu and attempt to bring them back within KANU."[38]

To bring the Kikuyu back into the fold, despite the Mwangi Githiomi debacle alluded to previously, "in 1995, the 'reach-out' strategy deepened with the launch of the GEMA-KAMATUSA talks"[39] led by Njenga Karume, a wealthy entrepreneur, on the Kikuyu side, while on the KAMATUSA side, Nicholas Biwott, a close confidante of President Moi, was the leader. The second front of the GEMA-KAMATUSA talks saw Joseph Kamotho, G. G. Kariũki and Kuria Kanyingĩ provide a second "entry-point" for engagement with the Kikuyu. Furthermore, according to Steeves, "under the table, the talks sought a political accommodation between the Kikuyu and KANU (read KAMATUSA)."[40] On the side of the Kikuyu, the goal of attending the talks was to arrive at

> de-escalating the Rift Valley land purification clashes pitting Kalenjin against Kikuyu; greater representation in cabinet if electoral inroads could be made in Central Province by KANU in 1997; and an opportunity to be positioned centrally for a run at the presidency when Moi completes his maximum two terms,[41]

and to offset the continuing significant losses that they had incurred due to the evictions during the clashes.

This in no way suggests that the Kikuyu were all in; "some party members [of Mwai Kibaki's Democratic Party] DP questioned the relevance of the dialogue in the light of widespread suggestions that the Kalenjin were involved in provoking the Rift Valley Clashes".[42] Even as the GEMA–KAMATUSA talks continued, the government continued to harass the rest of the opposition. For example, as recorded in the Hansard (Kenya National Assembly's official record), Raila Odinga, one of the opposition party members of parliament, inquired:

> licenses for meetings to be addressed by the GEMA and KAMATUSA leaders have been issued for this coming weekend, whereas FORD (K), which applied for a permit to hold a rally in Mbita Constituency, a month ago, has been denied permit for a rally on the 6th of August, 1995. What criteria does the Minister use in issuing licenses to non-registered organisations like GEMA and KAMATUSA and denying a registered political party permits to hold a rally?[43]

Even as the reach-out efforts were ongoing, within KANU, it appeared to be splitting the party into KANU "A" and KANU "B"; the "A" faction led by the pro-rapprochement group, while the "B" faction was led by an alliance of the Kisii, Maasai, Luhya ethnic groups. The B faction was afraid that the Kikuyu would re-dominate KANU if rapprochement was achieved, even after the wholesale abandonment of KANU by the Kikuyu. At the same time, the math made sense for KANU to co-opt as many Kikuyu as possible, so that it could split the Democratic Party, FORD-Asili and FORD-People, led by Kikuyus, and thus give KANU a better chance of winning the next elections in less than two years hence. If the Kikuyu did rejoin KANU, the talks would also have achieved the goal of "neutralising the presence of the opposition in the Rift Valley."[44] The tent did appear to be insufficient to accommodate all the members.

The general climate, approaching the 1997 elections, had been one of contentious engagement between the opposition, which demanded for more constitutional reforms, including specifically reducing the role of the Provincial Administration which had been accused of frustrating political rallies, arbitrary arrests and harassment. At the same time, despite the ethnic fractionalization, the parties knew that they had to attract some votes from outside their region and their blocs. This in no way stopped the rekindling of ethnic conflict and eviction of "outsiders" from some regions of the country. For the 1997 elections, it was the turn of the coastal region to exclude "*watu wa bara*" – literally, Swahili for "people from up-country".

Likoni clashes: a complex coastal history

The coastal region of Kenya has always had a difficult, if not outright contentious history, with the rest of the country. Before the coming of the Europeans, the coastal strip, about 10 miles of it, was ruled by the sultan of Zanzibar, after splitting off from the sultan of Oman rule. Coastal Kenya did some trade with the interior, with Europeans and with the islands of Kilwa, Zanzibar, Pemba and Lamu (Lamu, Manda and Pate), with its control alternating between the Portuguese Empire, the Sultanate of Oman, the Portuguese (again), the Sultanate of Oman (again), and was ceded to the British Empire for two years, before reverting to the Sultanate of Oman and finally becoming part of the British East Africa Protectorate.[45] Through the past century, one of the complaints of the coastal area was due to neglect.

Kresse, for example, writes that "the structural neglect of the Kenyan coast (economic, educational, etc.) is one feature of such 'disorder' (an inverse 'order') – understandably leading to the common complaint among Muslims of being second-class citizens in their own home region."[46] Given the neglect that the region has endured, despite its contribution to the Kenyan economy – until 1997, tourism, particularly at the coast, was the second-highest contributor to Kenya's gross domestic product (GDP) and a significant income earner for the country; the argument was that the coast was much neglected given its contribution to the economy. Indeed, by 2007, the Mombasa Republican Council (MRC), a "proscribed" party, had begun using the slogan "*Pwani Si Kenya*" (the coast is not part of Kenya).[47] In part, this slogan articulated the historical control by Oman/Zanzibar sultanates, the different religious persuasion, ethnic composition and the traditional socio-economic neglect that the coast has been subjected to by successive Kenyan governments.

In the context of the greater national narrative, the re-ethnicization of different regions beginning 1992, it was no surprise that the Likoni–Kwale area of the Coast Province of Kenya erupted in ethnic cleansing from August 1997 through November 1997. "Precise figures are unavailable and estimates of fatalities vary from 70 to as many as 1,000. Many more were injured and their homes or businesses destroyed. The threat of further violence displaced 100,000–200,000 people."[48] The cause of the clashes, particularly at the coast, was especially land. "On the coast, land tenure was also perceived as favoring ethnic groups not indigenous to the area, such as the Luo, Kikuyu, Kisii, and Kamba, commonly called 'upcountry' ethnicities."[4950] Ironically, the clashes led to many countries issuing travel advisories against Kenya, affecting the tourism business to the extent that major hotels had to fire workers, exacerbating the economic marginalization issue;[51] the sector has not recovered to date.

The elections of 1997 were held on 29 December, with an extended day of voting in some areas of the country. As he had done previously, through suppression of the vote, intimidation and splitting of the opposition vote, and benefitting from an opposition that refused to consolidate, Moi gained "40.12 percent of the vote (2,445,801 votes) and at least 25 percent of the vote in five provinces";[52] the other candidates trailed Moi thus: Kibaki, 31.09 percent of the vote; Odinga, 10.92 percent; Wamalwa, 8.29 percent; Ngilu, 7.71 percent, with KANU securing 107 seats, against 103 for the opposition.[53] Once again, the opposition had practically given Moi the presidency given their refusal to coordinate their campaigns and/or step down for one of them.

After the election, the same pattern of ethnic violence continued. "Members of opposition-supporting ethnicities were once again targeted in the Rift Valley as punishment for supporting the 'wrong' side."[54] The post-election violence was less understandable, particularly given the fact that the intended outcomes had already been accomplished – that of "intimidation and violence to expel non-indigenous residents by . . . promising the return of land to the control of its pre-colonial inhabitants and that the regions would gain greater autonomy vis-à-vis the central government."[55]

Democracy and elections' ethnic dimension: lessons learnt

As President Moi had predicted, or because as the head of state he had command of apparatus that could have fomented or constrained it, the advent of multi-party politics led to the heightening of tensions between different communities. It must be remembered that in the first instance, Moi was one of the founding members of the Kenya African Democratic Union, KADU, in 1960. KADU's political platform, "Majimboism", advocated for the devolution of power to the regions; these regions were to be ethnically based and would retain autonomy from the central government. Now that one of KADU's founders was president, was there some relationship between his presidency and the platform he had advocated a mere 18 years previously, especially considering the settlement by "outsiders" in these "majimbo", roughly defined by provincial boundaries?

According to Oucho, the post-election violence between 1991 and 1995 occurred in three phases: "call for majimboism accompanied by inflammatory statements by politicians in Rift Valley Province, pre-election violence in the form of ethnic clashes of October 1991 through December 1992 and the post-election conflict which lingered on up to 1995."[56] The first ethnically motivated attack occurred on 29 October 1991 at Meteitei farm, in Nandi District, asking the Luo and other non-Kalenjins to leave the area.[57] Post election, the violence appeared to intensify, going on until 1995. As such, the ethnic division had more than electoral outcomes: it both punished "outsiders" while rewarding ethnic groups considered to belong to certain geographical areas, including by resettlement on the abandoned farms but also hiving off forest land for resettlement and land acquisition. The Likoni–Kwale clashes seven years later followed the same patterns: evicting "outsiders" from the coastal areas.

Overall, according to Halakhe,

> violence during electoral periods in Kenya has killed at least 4,433 people and displaced over 1.8 million since the introduction of the multi-party system in 1991. Electoral violence developed as a result of a combination of factors, including politicization of ethnicity, corruption, nonadherence to the rule of law, a centralized and highly personalized form of governance, inequitable development and a "winner-takes-all" form of politics perceived as benefiting one ethnic constituency to the detriment of all others. Only the 2002 and 2013 elections have not been seriously marred by violence.[58]

The open outbreak of ethnic hostilities served certain functions, some of them outlined by Brown. They include, *inter alia*, punishment of opposition to one-party rule and KANU, disenfranchisement of hundreds of thousands of opposition supporters by making sure they could not vote, ensuring opposition candidates did not secure 25 percent votes in at least five provinces as stipulated by the constitution, post-election punishment of communities that did not support KANU (and providing land that was often resettled by the "native communities"), and, thus, fifth, as a reward for pro-KANU supporters by appropriating the fertile land abandoned by victims of the ethnic conflict.[59]

With government complicity, ethnic divisions became one of the most important tools for political fractionalization and disenfranchisement of certain ethnic groups. But more important, the short-term gains accrued from evicting outsiders had long-term consequences; for example, the tourism sector collapsed and has never recovered. The prior agricultural production activities decreased as a result of upsetting farming and production process. More pertinent was the missed opportunity: by focusing on short-term electoral gains and using every tool at its disposal, especially ethnic division, the chance to mold a modern, democratic polity, with politics based on ideology, rather than ethnicity, the country cemented the proposition that Kenya's electoral contests were based on ethnic divisions rather than on policies. Ethnicity and ethnic strife demonstrated themselves to be "credible, legitimate" political tools and strategies, despite the destructiveness of its use to communities, the country and its reputation as a haven for peace. More important, it set the template for 2008, when the ethnic conflict would lead to the displacement of a third of the 1.8 million internally displaced persons and nearly a third of the 4,000 deaths from ethnic violence recorded in Kenya.

Notes

1 See: Larry J. Diamond. "Is the Third Wave over?"*Journal of Democracy*, 7, No. 3 (1996): 20; Samuel P. Huntington. *The Third Wave: Democratization in the Late Twentieth Century*. (Norman, OK: University of Oklahoma Press, 1993): 3 and Scott Mainwaring. *Rethinking Party Systems in the Third Wave of Democratization: The Case of Brazil*. (Stanford, CA: Stanford University Press, 1999): 21.
2 Githu Muigai. "Kenya's Opposition and the Crisis of Governance." *Issue: A Journal of Opinion*, 21, No. 1–2 (1993): 26.
3 Ken Walibora Waliaula. "Reflections on Intellectual Life and Knowing as a Problem in Alamin Mazrui's Shadows of the Moon." In Kimani Njogu & Garnette Oluoch-Olunya, Eds. *Cultural Production and Social Change in Kenya: Building Bridges*. (Nairobi, Kenya: Twaweza Communications, 2007): 218.
4 Michael Chege. "Economic Relations between Kenya and China, 1963–2007." In Jennifer G. Cooke, Ed. *U.S. and Chinese Engagement in Africa: Prospects for Improving U.S.-China-Africa Cooperation*. (Washington, DC: Center for Strategic and International Studies, 2008): 16.
5 Chege. "Economic Relations between Kenya and China, 1963–2007." 16.
6 Keith Kyle. *The Politics of the Independence of Kenya*. (New York, NY: Palgrave Macmillan, 1999): 109.
7 David William Cohen & E. S. Atieno Odhiambo. "Reading the Minister's Remains: Investigations into the Death of the Honourable Minister John Robert Ouko in Kenya,

February 1990." In Della Pollock, Ed. *Exceptional Spaces: Essays in Performance and History*. (Chapel Hill, NC: The University of North Carolina Press, 1998): 77; David William Cohen. "Robert Ouko's Pain: The Negotiation of a 'State of Mind'." In Michael S. Roth & Charles G. Salas, Eds. *Disturbing Remains: Memory, History, and Crisis in the Twentieth Century*. (Los Angeles, CA: The Getty Research Institute, 2001): 17; David William Cohen. "The Uncertainty of Africa in an Age of Certainty." In David William Cohen & Michael D. Kennedy, Eds. *Responsibility in Crisis: Knowledge Politics and Global Publics*. (Ann Arbor, MI: University of Michigan University Library, 2005): 248 and Samuel M. Makinda. "Kenya: Out of the Straitjacket, Slowly." *The World Today*, 48, No. 10 (October, 1992): 191.

8 Makinda. "Kenya." 191.

9 Godwin Rapando Murunga. "Urban Violence in Kenya's Transition to Pluralist Politics, 1982–1992." *Africa Development/Afrique et Développement*, 24, No. 1–2, The Political Economy of Conflicts in Africa/Economie politique des conflits en Afrique (1999): 187.

10 Muigai. Kenya's Opposition and the Crisis of Governance." 27.

11 Gilbert M. Khadiagala. "Kenya: Gradual Pluralization Fails to Buffer Shocks." In Alan J. Kuperman, Ed. *Constitutions and Conflict Management in Africa: Preventing Civil War through Institutional Design*. (Philadelphia, PA: University of Pennsylvania Press, 2015): 56.

12 Khadiagala. "Kenya." 56.

13 Khadiagala. "Kenya." 57.

14 Michael Chege. "Economic Relations between Kenya and China, 1963–2007." 48.

15 Khadiagala, "Kenya." 58

16 Fred Oluoch. "Agitation That Shaped Today's Politics." *Daily Nation*. Posted 10 July 2013. (Web).

17 Maureen Murimi. "Kenyans Mark Saba Saba Day." *Citizen Digital*. 7 July 2015. (Web).

18 Dick Foeken & Ton Dietz. "Of Ethnicity, Manipulation and Observation: The 1992 and 1997 Elections in Kenya." In John Abbink & Gerti Hesseling, Eds. *Election Observation and Democratization in Africa*. (London, UK: Macmillan Press, 2000): 123.

19 Shadrack Wanjala Nasong'o. "Negotiating New Rules of the Game: Social Movements, Civil Society and the Kenyan Transition." In Godwin R. Murunga & Shadrack W. Nasong'o, Eds. *Kenya: The Struggle for Democracy*. (New York, NY: Zed Books, 2007): 39.

20 Guy S. Goodwin-Gill. *Free and Fair Elections*. (Geneva, Switzerland: Inter-Parliamentary Union, 2006): 145.

21 Gabrielle Lynch. "*Majimboism* and Kenya's Moral Economy of Ethnic Territoriality." In Bruce J. Berman, André Laliberté & Stephen J. Larin, Eds. *The Moral Economies of Ethnic and Nationalist Claims*. (Vancouver, BC: University of British Columbia Press, 2016): 56.

22 Karuti Kanyinga. "The Legacy of the White Highlands: Land Rights, Ethnicity and the Post-2007 Election Violence in Kenya." In Peter Kagwanja & Roger Southall, Eds. *Kenya's Uncertain Democracy: The Electoral Crisis of 2008*. (New York, NY: Routledge, 2010): 77.

23 Kanyinga. "The Legacy of the White Highlands." 77–78.

24 Lynch. "*Majimboism* and Kenya's Moral Economy of Ethnic Territoriality." 57.

25 Kanyinga. "The Legacy of the White Highlands." 78.

26 Khadiagala. "Kenya." 59.

27 Khadiagala. "Kenya." 59.

28 Chege. "Economic Relations between Kenya and China, 1963–2007." 69.

29 Chege. "Economic Relations between Kenya and China, 1963–2007." 69.

30 Stephen Njogo. "Kenya: Kipipiri Power Project on Course." *The Standard*. 7 December 2002. (Web): n.p.

31 Robert Maxon & Thomas P. Ofcansky. *Historical Dictionary of Kenya*. (Lanham, MD: Rowman & Littlefield, 2014): 116.
32 Maxon and Ofcansky. *Historical Dictionary of Kenya*. 116.
33 Karuti Kanyinga. "Contestation over Political Space: The State and the Demobilisation of Opposition Politics in Kenya." In Adebayo O. Olukoshi, Ed. *The Politics of Opposition in Contemporary Africa*. (Stockholm, Sweden: Nordiska Afrikainstitutet, 1998): 68.
34 Kanyinga. "Contestation over Political Space." 68.
35 Daniel N. Posner. *Institutions and Ethnic Politics in Africa*. (New York, NY: Cambridge University Press, 2005): 261.
36 Posner. *Institutions and Ethnic Politics in Africa*. 261.
37 Posner adds that "the Kalenjin are a linguistic umbrella category linking members of the Nandi, Kipsigis, Tugen, Pokot, Elgeyo, Keiyo, Marakwet, Seibi, Dorobo, Terik, and Sabaot tribes, and sometimes also the Maasai, Turkana and Samburu." Posner. *Institutions and Ethnic Politics in Africa*. 261.
38 Jeffrey S. Steeves. "Re-Democratization in Kenya: 'Unbounded Politics' and the Political Trajectory toward National Elections." In D. Pal S. Ahluwalia & Paul F. Nursey-Bray, Eds. *The Post-Colonial Condition: Contemporary Politics in Africa*. (Commack, NY: Nova Science Publishers, Inc., 1997): 47.
39 Steeves. "Re-Democratization in Kenya." 47.
40 Steeves. "Re-Democratization in Kenya." 48.
41 Steeves. "Re-Democratization in Kenya." 48.
43 Government of Kenya. *Kenya National Assembly Official Record (Hansard)*. 4 July 1995. 7th Parliament, 4th Session, Vol. 7, No. 36. (Nairobi, Kenya: Government Printer, 1995): 1695.
44 Kanyinga. "Contestation over Political Space." 68.
45 Cynthia Brantley. *The Giriama and Colonial Resistance in Kenya, 1800–1920*. (Berkeley, CA: University of California Press, 1981): 16.
46 Kai Kresse. "Muslim Politics in Postcolonial Kenya: Negotiating Knowledge on the Double-Periphery." In Filippo Osella & Benjamin Soares, Ed. *Islam, Politics, Anthropology*. (Malden, MA: Wiley-Blackwell, 2010): 87.
47 Ngala Chome. "'The Grassroots Are Very Complicated': Marginalization and the Emergence of Alternative Authority in the Kenyan Coast 2013 Elections." In Marie-Aude Fouere, Susan Mwangi, Mildred Ndeda & Christian Thibon, Eds. *Kenya's Past as Prologue: Voters, Violence and the 2013 General Election*. (Nairobi, Kenya: Twaweza Communications, 2014): 254.
48 Stephen Brown. "Quiet Diplomacy and Recurring 'Ethnic Clashes' in Kenya." In Chandra Lekha Sriram & Karin Wermester, Eds. *From Promise to Practice: Strengthening UN Capacities for the Prevention of Violent Conflict*. (Boulder, CO: Lynne Rienner Publishers, 2003): 72.
49 Brown. "Quiet Diplomacy and Recurring 'Ethnic Clashes' in Kenya." 72.
50 Brown's alternate estimate of the total fatalities in the coastal region is more conservative; "some 70–199 people were killed and a further 100,000 to 200,000 were displaced." (Stephen Brown. "Lessons Learned and Forgotten: The International Community and Electoral Conflict Management in Kenya." In David Gillies, Ed. *Elections in Dangerous Places: Democracy and the Paradoxes of Peacebuilding*. (Montreal, CA: McGill-Queen's University Press, 2011): 131.
51 Government of Kenya. *Kenya National Assembly Official Record (Hansard)*. 18 November 1998. Parliamentary Debates. (Nairobi, Kenya: Government Press, 1998): 2365.
52 Maxon and Ofcansky. *Historical Dictionary of Kenya*. 117.
53 Maxon and Ofcansky. *Historical Dictionary of Kenya*. 117–118.
54 Brown. "Lessons Learned and Forgotten." 131.
55 Human Rights Watch. *Playing with Fire*. (New York, NY: Human Rights Watch, 2002): 25.

56 John O. Oucho. *Undercurrents of Ethnic Conflicts in Kenya*. (Leiden, The Netherlands: Koninklijke Brill NV, 2002): 89.
57 Oucho. *Undercurrents of Ethnic Conflicts in Kenya*. 91.
58 Abdullahi Boru Halakhe. "'R2P in Practice': Ethnic Violence, Elections and Atrocity Prevention in Kenya." Global Centre for the Responsibility to Protect, 2013. (Web): 5.
59 Stephen Brown. "Quiet Diplomacy and Recurring 'Ethnic Clashes' in Kenya." 74.

References

Brantley, Cynthia. *The Giriama and Colonial Resistance in Kenya, 1800–1920*. Berkeley, CA: University of California Press, 1981.

Brown, Stephen. "Lessons Learned and Forgotten: The International Community and Electoral Conflict Management in Kenya." In David Gillies, Ed. *Elections in Dangerous Places: Democracy and the Paradoxes of Peacebuilding*. Montreal, CA: McGill-Queen's University Press, 2011. Ch. 9, pp. 127–146.

Brown, Stephen. "Quiet Diplomacy and Recurring 'Ethnic Clashes' in Kenya." In Chandra Lekha Sriram & Karin Wermester, Eds. *From Promise to Practice: Strengthening UN Capacities for the Prevention of Violent Conflict*. Boulder, CO: Lynne Rienner Publishers, 2003. Ch. 4, pp. 69–100.

Chege, Michael. "Economic Relations between Kenya and China, 1963–2007." In Jennifer G. Cooke, Ed. *U.S. and Chinese Engagement in Africa: Prospects for Improving U.S.-China-Africa Cooperation*. Washington, DC: Center for Strategic and International Studies, 2008.

Chege, Michael. "The Return of Multiparty Politics." In Joel D. Barkan, Ed. *Beyond Capitalism vs. Socialism in Kenya and Tanzania*. Boulder, CO: Lynne Rienner Publishers, 1994. Ch. 2, pp. 47–74.

Chome, Ngala. "'The Grassroots Are Very Complicated': Marginalization and the Emergence of Alternative Authority in the Kenyan Coast 2013 Elections." In Marie-Aude Fouere, Susan Mwangi, Mildred Ndeda & Christian Thibon, Eds. *Kenya's Past as Prologue: Voters, Violence and the 2013 General Election*. Nairobi, Kenya: Twaweza Communications, 2014. pp. 247–265.

Cohen, David William. "Robert Ouko's Pain: The Negotiation of a 'State of Mind'." In Michael S. Roth & Charles G. Salas, Eds. *Disturbing Remains: Memory, History, and Crisis in the Twentieth Century*. Los Angeles, CA: The Getty Research Institute, 2001.

Cohen, David William. "The Uncertainty of Africa in an Age of Certainty." In David William Cohen & Michael D. Kennedy, Eds. *Responsibility in Crisis: Knowledge Politics and Global Publics*. Ann Arbor, MI: University of Michigan University Library, 2005.

Cohen, David William & Eisha Stephen Atieno Odhiambo. "Reading the Minister's Remains: Investigations into the Death of the Honourable Minister John Robert Ouko in Kenya, February 1990." In Della Pollock, Ed. *Exceptional Spaces: Essays in Performance and History*. Chapel Hill, NC: The University of North Carolina Press, 1998.

Foeken, Dick & Ton Dietz. "Of Ethnicity, Manipulation and Observation: The 1992 and 1997 Elections in Kenya." In John Abbink & Gerti Hesseling, Eds. *Election Observation and Democratization in Africa*. London, UK: Macmillan Press, 2000.

Goodwin-Gill, Guy S. *Free and Fair Elections*. Geneva, Switzerland: Inter-Parliamentary Union, 2006.

Government of Kenya. *The Kenya Gazette*. 8 September 1995. Nairobi, Kenya: Government Press, 1995.

Government of Kenya. *Kenya National Assembly Official Record (Hansard)*. 4 July 1995. 7th Parliament, 4th Session, Vol. 7, No. 36. Nairobi, Kenya: Government Printer, 1995.

Government of Kenya. *Kenya National Assembly Official Record (Hansard)*. 18 November 1998. Parliamentary Debates. Nairobi, Kenya: Government Press, 1998.

Halakhe, Abdullahi Boru. "'R2P in Practice': Ethnic Violence, Elections and Atrocity Prevention in Kenya." Global Centre for the Responsibility to Protect, 2013. (Web). Accessed on 11/24/2016 from: www.globalr2p.org/media/files/kenya_occasionalpaper_web.pdf

Human Rights Watch. *Playing with Fire*. New York, NY: Human Rights Watch, 2002.

Huntington, Samuel P. "Democracy's Third Wave." *Journal of Democracy*, 2, No. 2 (Spring, 1991): 12–34. doi:10.153/jod.1991.0016

Huntington, Samuel P. *The Third Wave: Democratization in the Late Twentieth Century*. Norman, OK: University of Oklahoma Press, 1993.

Kanyinga, Karuti. "Contestation over Political Space: The State and the Demobilisation of Opposition Politics in Kenya." In Adebayo O. Olukoshi, Ed. *The Politics of Opposition in Contemporary Africa*. Stockholm, Sweden: Nordiska Afrikainstitutet, 1998. Ch. 2, pp. 39–90.

Kanyinga, Karuti. "The Legacy of the White Highlands: Land Rights, Ethnicity and the Post-2007 Election Violence in Kenya." In Peter Kagwanja & Roger Southall, Eds. *Kenya's Uncertain Democracy: The Electoral Crisis of 2008*. New York, NY: Routledge, 2010.

Khadiagala, Gilbert M. "Kenya: Gradual Pluralization Fails to Buffer Shocks." In Alan J. Kuperman, Ed. *Constitutions and Conflict Management in Africa: Preventing Civil War through Institutional Design*. Philadelphia, PA: University of Pennsylvania Press, 2015. pp. 51–70.

Kresse, Kai. "Muslim Politics in Postcolonial Kenya: Negotiating Knowledge on the Double-Periphery." In Filippo Osella & Benjamin Soares, Eds. *Islam, Politics, Anthropology*. Malden, MA: Wiley-Blackwell, 2010.

Kyle, Keith. *The Politics of the Independence of Kenya*. New York, NY: Palgrave Macmillan, 1999.

Lynch, Gabrielle. "*Majimboism* and Kenya's Moral Economy of Ethnic Territoriality." In Bruce J. Berman, André Laliberté & Stephen J. Larin, Eds. *The Moral Economies of Ethnic and Nationalist Claims*. Vancouver, BC: University of British Columbia Press, 2016. Ch. 2, pp. 59–69.

Maingi, Grace. "The Kenyan Constitutional Reform Process: A Case Study on the Work of FIDA Kenya in Securing Women's Rights." *Feminist Africa*, 15 (2011): 66. Accessed on 11/23/2016 from: http://agi.ac.za/sites/agi.ac.za/files/fa_15_case_study_grace_maingi.pdf

Mainwaring, Scott. *Rethinking Party Systems in the Third Wave of Democratization: The Case of Brazil*. Stanford, CA: Stanford University Press, 1999.

Makinda, Samuel M. "Kenya: Out of the Straitjacket, Slowly." *The World Today*, 48, No. 10 (October, 1992): 188–192. Accessed on 11/24/2016 from: www.jstor.org/stable/40396340

Maxon, Robert M. & Thomas P. Ofcansky. *Historical Dictionary of Kenya*. Lanham, MD: Rowman & Littlefield, 2014.

Muigai, Githu. "Kenya's Opposition and the Crisis of Governance." *Issue: A Journal of Opinion*, 21, No. 1–2 (1993): 26–34. Accessed on 11/22/2016 from: www.jstor.org/stable/1166282

Murimi, Maureen. "Kenyans Mark Saba Saba Day." *Citizen Digital*. 7 July 2015. Accessed on 11/24/2016 from: https://citizentv.co.ke/news/kenyans-mark-saba-saba-day-93061/

Nasong'o, Shadrack Wanjala. "Negotiating New Rules of the Game: Social Movements, Civil Society and the Kenyan Transition." In Godwin R. Murunga & Shadrack W. Nasong'o, Eds. *Kenya: The Struggle for Democracy*. New York, NY: Zed Books, 2007.

Njogo, Stephen. "Kenya: Kipipiri Power Project on Course." *The Standard*. 7 December 2002. (Web). Accessed on 11/24/2016 from: http://allafrica.com/stories/200212070091.html

Ogot, Bethwell A. "Transition from Single-Party to Multiparty Political System 1989–1993." In Bethwell A. Ogot & William Robert Ochieng, Eds. *Decolonization & Independence in Kenya, 1940–93*. Athens, OH: Ohio University Press, 1995.

Oluoch, Fred. "Agitation That Shaped Today's Politics." *Daily Nation*. Posted 10 July 2013. Accessed on 11/24/2016 from: http://mobile.nation.co.ke/lifestyle/Kenya-Multiparty-politics/-/1950774/2020838/-/format/xhtml/-/13vfvi4/-/index.html

Oucho, John O. *Undercurrents of Ethnic Conflicts in Kenya*. Leiden, The Netherlands: Koninklijke Brill NV, 2002.

Posner, Daniel N. *Institutions and Ethnic Politics in Africa*. New York, NY: Cambridge University Press, 2005.

Steeves, Jeffrey S. "Re-Democratization in Kenya: 'Unbounded Politics' and the Political Trajectory toward National Elections." In D. Pal S. Ahluwalia & Paul F. Nursey-Bray, Eds. *The Post-Colonial Condition: Contemporary Politics in Africa*. Commack, NY: Nova Science Publishers, Inc., 1997. Ch. 3, pp. 31–54.

Waliaula, Ken Walibora. "Reflections on Intellectual Life and Knowing as a Problem in Alamin Mazrui's Shadows of the Moon." In Kimani Njogu & Garnette Oluoch-Olunya, Eds. *Cultural Production and Social Change in Kenya: Building Bridges*. Nairobi, Kenya: Twaweza Communications, 2007.

4 Change to believe in

New beginnings

The politics of succession: 2002 and term limits

Elections in many African countries have been interesting, both in terms of the conduct, and the results. It is the exception, rather than the norm, for incumbent parties to lose elections. Elections have always been, at a minimum, one of the indicators of the citizens' ability to express their preferences. But as the prior discussions have shown, governments, particularly in the Kenyan context, have utilized a myriad of oppressive tools to manipulate the elections: from ballot-box stuffing to ethnic violence and displacement of "opposition-leaning" populations, as happened in Rift Valley from 1991 to 1995, after the 1998 elections and the Coast Province in 1997, to the use of the Provincial Administration to frustrate the ability to organize and hold political rallies, arrest and detention of opposition politicians, among several other strategies.

In the earliest iteration of the third wave of democratization, only four African countries out of the 47 that had multi-party elections saw a change in government. Granted, many countries were holding elections even before the multi-party politics; thus, by themselves, elections were not a remarkable achievement, although Crawford and Lynch hold that repeated elections "appear to have a positive impact on human freedom and democratic values."[1] Free and fair elections were a more useful threshold to determine the level of democratization. Indeed, in addition to low levels of democracy (as measured by Freedom House and the Center for Systemic Peace's Polity IV data set) have persisted across Africa, and Lynch and Crawford record democratic reversals in repeated years since 2006.[2]

Hanging on to power is not necessarily an "African thing", but it has been such part of the norm for the many African countries that at the conclusion of a term-limited presidency, there is general expectation that a few months to years before such an election the head of state would attempt to muck the environment to set up the possibility of a subsequent term. Term limits, for the most part, came about together with the agitation for multi-party democracy and the constitutional amendments and/or changes that occurred, during the third wave of democratization in the late 1980s to early 1990s. Quinn, for example, writes that "many African countries . . . established term limits for presidential tenure: something nearly unthinkable for most African polities during the Cold War."[3]

Despite the imposition of term limits by constitutional changes, there were, nevertheless, attempts to cling on to power; quite a few leaders of African countries asserted "the will of the people" in nearly almost immediately suggesting the scrapping of term limits. There was good reason to consider term limits as limiting and not good for the ruling parties. As Rupiya notes, quoting Daniel Vencovsky's *ITA: Presidential Term Limits in Africa*, "during the era of the one-party state between 1960 and 1990, no ruling party lost an election".[4] Of course, the probability of losing an election is forestalled by all kinds of governmental interference. Such interference sometimes takes on features of imaginary, impending coup d'états, temporary and sometimes prolonged episodes of delayed elections. The Democratic Republic of the Congo, alleging the fighting in the eastern part of the country, has been one of the ones to postpone elections severally.

Several scholars acknowledge this view and point to African politics and the frequency of incumbent presidents' attempts to change term limits.[5] Dundas writes that "there are some 18 AU member states at the time of writing without term limits for the Head of State – Algeria, Cameroon, Chad, Egypt, Equatorial Guinea, Gabon, Lesotho, Libya, Mauritius, SADR, Somalia, Swaziland, The Gambia, Togo, Tunisia, Uganda and Zimbabwe."[6] On the other hand, 30 states have term limits, and some have three-term limits, others, like Niger, one-term limit. In some cases, term limits were successful: Prempeh argues that "term limits have ended the tenure of fourteen presidents in Africa since 1990."[7] The CQ Researcher adds that "while more than half of African countries introduced presidential term limits between 1990 and 1994, 12 governments reversed themselves and abolished term limits in the 10 years ending in 2009."[8]

One of the most vexing manifestations of democracy is the notion of checks and balances, which, in the case of African countries (but also in most parliamentary and hybrid democracies), has never been quite as robust. For most African countries, Kenya included, the president has traditionally had the power to appoint legislators (either the president or the head of the ruling party) and to appoint members of the judiciary. In nearly all African countries, prior to the third wave of democratization and the constitutional changes, there were very few instances where the judiciary was independent or had tenure. Thus, as the appointing authority, the head of state had almost unchecked power, and the judiciary was beholden to him or her. In Quinn's words, "within the African context, the executive branch has faced limited legislative and judicial constraints on its power."[9] Indeed, Kenya's executive continued to face almost unlimited constraints until the promulgation of the new constitution in 2010.

Why have African leaders sought to cling to power? Different reasons have been hypothesized, ranging from prophetic visions of leading their people, divine leadership (e.g., in the case of Ahmed Yahya Jammeh) perceived popularity, allegations of lack of other suitable leaders to take over, coming to power by doubtful means (Paul Biya), the "need to serve the people", subtly interpreted as the need to continue enriching themselves, and fear of prosecution stemming from abuses of power and illegal activities carried out while in office, should they leave power. Indeed, many African presidents and their families have grown quite wealthy through corruption, misappropriation of public resources, cronyism, nepotism and all other manner of "isms". As the Nobel Peace Prize–winning Wangari Maathai almost prophetically wrote,

> politicians tend to change with the tide. For instance, they become 'democrats' when democracy is seen as the route to power. But when another route appears that is shorter, they are often willing to take it, even if it means joining a rival group or faction.[10]

The case of the new republic of South Sudan fits perfectly into this mold.

A separate phenomenon has begun to manifest itself, even in the face of processes meant to implement contestation of political office, one that bucks the trend of accepting the results of elections and conceding defeat. "As seen in both Kenya and Zimbabwe in 2008, clinging to power in the face of electoral defeat is a great temptation for African leaders."[11] Notably, the same happened in the Ivory Coast, leading to the intervention by the French, and the eventual prosecution of Laurent Gbagbo, who refused to concede the election to Alassane Ouattara, leading to crimes against humanity and the intervention of the International Criminal Court (ICC). Thus, although Isanga notes that "many African leaders have been viewed by some in the international community as a 'new breed' of African leaders because of their rule of law reforms"; he argues that "they cleverly navigated the new constitutional configurations to extend their hold on power."[12]

It is indeed striking, the level of differences in the practices in African countries of clinging to power, including through change-the-constitution strategies, versus those of more established democracies and the role of tradition in setting up executive leadership. Gardner, for example, notes that in the US,

> the first president, George Washington, faced no constitutional restriction as to the number of four-year terms he could serve. Still, he chose to step aside after two, judging that the orderly transition of power from one president to another was needed to consolidate the constitution.[13]

It was not until over 150 years later that the Twenty-Second Amendment to the US Constitution, imposing term limits to a maximum of two terms of four years each. As Gardner notes, while many African country leaders have attempted to outlast constitutions, ironically, "'the most powerful man in the world' cannot change the constitution" to extend his time in office.[14]

Sometimes, though, prior conditions in African countries can plunge countries into confusion; for example, in Burundi, there was a question of whether the president, Pierre Nkurunziza, was eligible to run for another term in 2015. Nkurunziza's situation was quite unusual, as was the Constitutional Court ruling:

> The Court concluded that, despite the two-term limit and because of the ambiguity of a transitional provision in the Constitution, Nkurunziza – who

had been indirectly elected by parliament in 2005 and directly elected in 2010 – could run for an additional term.[15]

In the neighboring Rwanda, Paul Kagame, who has been president since 2000 and who was constrained by the two-term limit, recently benefitted from a move to change the constitution to remove presidential term limits, which, according to the revisions, he could potentially run for office until 2034.[16]

There have been several stands in the sand, instances when presidents wanted to change the constitution but did not have the support to do so; African democracy might yet catch on. Some of the countries that managed to reject the move to change constitutions included "Nigerian Senate's rejection in May 2008 of a bill that would have enabled President Olusegun Obasanjo to stand for a third-term and that of Malawi where the Malawian parliament did not support President Muluzi's attempt to abolish term limits."[17] These outcomes in some way demonstrated to the heads of state their folly, and the limit of their powers, constrained by the domestic audiences.

What is rather curious, though, is the outcome of elections for the third term: Rupiya argues that "currently, when a president seeking a third term goes for an election, he normally wins hands down;"[18] one might wonder, then, whether, as they claim, the presidents actually do have quite the support or whether the machinations of the government see the actualization of the Stalin-esque view that it did not matter who voted; what mattered is who counted the votes. After all, in places such as Chechnya, the Russian prime minister won by a margin of 107 percent of the votes cast. Then again, as has been shown elsewhere, presidents often win elections by a minority: KANU and Moi won the 1992 and 1997 elections with 36 percent and 40 percent of the vote, respectively, for each of the aforesaid elections.

Moi's Kenya or Kenya's Moi: a third term?

In a country where young children grew up pledging their loyalty "to the President and the Republic of Kenya", implying that perhaps they did not have an opinion (or the choice to disagree), it was curious whether there would be a new government after Moi or whether there would be an "after Moi" in the first place. Given the longevity of the executive, the lack of fidelity to the rule of law, the constant violations to the constitution and the precedent of leaders who had attempted to change the term limits, or simply blatantly ignored them, in the context of Kenya, it was expected that Moi would attempt to either cling on to power, have the constitution amended to remove term limits or craft some other way of staying in power.

Moi's strategy was somewhat different: he aimed to rule through his "project", Uhuru Kenyatta. Materu writes that there was "a perception emerged that Moi's succession plans [were] crafted deliberately to enable him continue ruling Kenya indirectly after his formal retirement."[19] Moi made it well known that he preferred to support Uhuru Kenyatta, under the umbrella of KANU. But as would become quite evident in the next few months, Uhuru again managed to split the vote with Kibaki, but Kibaki won about twice the number of votes as were cast for Kenyatta. Thus, the much-touted plan did not work, as was expected, given the results. The elections were largely peaceful, although Rutten and Owuor write that "the post-election showed hardly any violent flare-ups before. However, ahead of the 2002 election some people lost their lives in election-related violence."[20] The violence was somewhat different: "foreigners" were not evicted en masse from their current land holdings.

The campaign, election and outcomes

One of the most observed, the most peaceful and, so far, the most credible elections in Kenya occurred in 2002. The elections were happening after 40 years of near authoritarian rule going back to Kenya's independence in 1963, and the subsequent shift towards a one-party state. The 2002 elections promised to usher in a new political reality for Kenya. For the first time in quite a long time, there were no significant pre-or post-election clashes. The National Rainbow Alliance (NARC) won 62 percent of the vote, the single largest majority by any government in the multi-party era.[21]

The elections were monumental, because it was the sunset of the Moi years, and there were questions of whether Moi would willingly give up power, or whether the pre- and post-election violence of 1997 would be repeated.

Furthermore, the 2002 presidential election was the first time that the country was choosing a new president; the incumbent was not taking part. However, he had "groomed" and appointed an heir, a preferred presidential candidate. Questions abound as to why Moi chose Uhuru Kenyatta (the fourth president). Was it perhaps rewarding the son of his former boss? Or was it to ensure power continued to be concentrated in a family that had such significance for independent Kenya, and leadership for the first 15 years of the republic, thus securing "regime secrets" might best remain with the Kenyattas and the Mois? The main contestants were Mwai Kibaki, of NARC, who garnered 3.65 million votes, and Uhuru Kenyatta, with 1.84 million votes, while the next highest candidate, Simeon Nyachae, garnered slightly more than 300,000 votes. James Orengo and David Ng'ethe, the other two candidates, managed less than 25,000 and 10,500 votes, respectively.

The campaigns and general elections of 2002 also showed, for the first time, that the possibility of putting aside ethnic hostilities existed, at least for the short term. The results of the election were surprising, achieving a rare feat; that of bundling out of power a party that had been in power for the entirety of Kenya's independence. The results also indicated that the notion of "self-interest" overrode the ethnic factor: the joint outcomes of removing Moi from power, after 24 years, and defeating his "anointed" successor were more important than each of the candidates running for office in a way that could split the vote along ethnic lines, especially given that Raila Odinga and Mwai Kibaki were two of the leading contenders.

Thus, although conventional wisdom would have suggested that it would have been easier for a presidential candidate like James Orengo, a Luo, running on the Social Democratic Party's platform, or Simeon Nyachae, a Kisii, running on the FORD-People platform, to attract the "ethnically inclined votes" of communities that did not support not one, but two candidates, both Kikuyus. Mwai Kibaki, who was ultimately elected president, ran under the banner of NARC while Uhuru Kenyatta, Moi's appointed successor, ran under the banner of the 1960 independence and then ruling party, KANU. The two Kikuyu presidential candidates garnered a total of 5.48 million votes.

The election also illustrated an important, often under-emphasized factor in Kenyan and African politics: that with the right kind of leadership, the proper motivation, the desire for change and the prospect for change, it was possible to select a different course of action and drive the country in a different direction. It also demonstrated that the previous instances of ethnic cleansing could be avoided, that it was driven by self-serving politicians and that the government could, when it wanted to, regulate such conflict and reinforce the importance of the rule of law.

The New KANU that got indigestion

The cross-ethnic cooperation that was evident in the latter months of 2002, and the recognition that the opposition might lose again to Moi's preferred successor led to the formation of NARC. The process was not as natural as perhaps it might appear; rather, it was a culmination of quite a lot of maneuvering, negotiations and bringing together of the regionally based parties. These maneuvers included the structure of the new party, which was expanded to welcome disgruntled partners from other parties. Determining who the appointed successor to Moi was going to be and how they were going to be defeated ultimately triumphed over personal and ethnic preferences.

Perhaps as a result of the Kenyatta succession battle, this became *the* issue, especially since Moi quite clearly indicated that he preferred Uhuru Kenyatta. Uhuru was often seen as a "newbie", one who should "wait his turn" just as others, such as Saitoti, had. Although long-term planning had been one of Moi's strengths, his rapprochement with Kenyatta, a newcomer in politics who had first contested political office in 1997, was unusual and somewhat baffling. Over the course of his 24-year presidency, Moi had acquired the title "Professor of Politics", and this was quite evident in the post-1998 election. The election gave KANU a slightly larger share of the vote than 1992 (41 percent, as opposed to 36 percent) but also strengthened a more united opposition; Moi returned to wooing opposition members of parliament who could either defect or, at a minimum, cooperate with the government. To do this, he turned to the National Democratic Party, now led by Raila Odinga, the son of Moi's one-time nemesis, Jaramogi Oginga Odinga. (Jaramogi had passed on 20 January 1994; the mantle of Luo community leadership had fallen to his son, Raila Odinga).

Khadiagala notes that Moi needed to do this, since the 41 percent vote in the 1997 elections

> would have made it difficult to govern without support from one of the opposition parties. But after the elections, further schisms in the opposition allowed Moi to co-opt new defectors into KANU, most notably Raila Odinga's National Democratic Party (NDP), with its populous Luo base.[22]

As a reward for his "cooperation with the KANU government, Raila was appointed minister for energy, which also consolidated his prospects for the future succession. This is what Hornsby calls "the Western strategy", and its implications would extend to the upcoming election. Raila had successfully contested the 1997 elections through NDP as a presidential candidate and had emerged third. On the broader level, this "cooperation" would begin what Wanyonyi calls "mergers", "partnerships" and "cooperation".[23]

The New KANU that wasn't, NAK and NARC

Determining the prudent course of action as being retirement, rather than seek a change in the constitution or to prolong his rule (some feared that Moi might do this through the military), Moi kept the question of his succession "interesting", although constitutionally, it was not clear how he would influence the election, outside of carrying out a last credible election. Whereas his predecessor, Jomo Kenyatta, had not acted decisively to forestall anyone succeeding him (especially Moi himself, despite "the Family's" preference for a Kikuyu successor), Moi did not necessarily support his vice president, George Saitoti, who had suffered the indignity of being dropped as vice president on 8 January 1998. Saitoti was reappointed on 3 April 1999, a little less than 15 months later. Saitoti, who did not quite enjoy the support of his boss as his successor, ultimately jumped ship in August 2002, perhaps hedging his bet as the next logical choice to be president. Hornsby recounts that "on 18 March [2002] NDP and KANU formally merged in a conference at Kasarani stadium (known as 'Kasarani II') where 6,000 delegates dissolved the NDP and elected a new KANU leadership."[24] Since Moi had been increasingly expressing his preference for a successor, this was one of the key factors in doing what KANU would otherwise not have done: it drove the opposition in the direction of unity.

The most significant problem with the proposed successor reflected Moi's preference for a younger heir. Hornsby adds that

> there were intense factional fights between the presidential contenders in the build-up to the merger, during which it became clear that the Rift Valley had abandoned Saitoti and Kamotho in favour of the new leadership of Kenyatta and Odinga. Moi was open that he wanted someone form this younger generation to succeed him.[25]

Yet, even if this was true, Raila was more than 20 years older than Uhuru. Perhaps Moi intended, after all, to repay his old boss by anointing his son to be his successor, although cynics suggest that Uhuru probably knew where the skeletons from his father's administration were buried.

Pre-election maneuvering and Kibaki Tosha

In the pre-election maneuvering, Saitoti rejected KANU and in quick succession joined the Rainbow Alliance (later the Liberal Democratic Party, LDP), then joined the National Alliance of Kenya and ultimately joined the "NARC Summit", the coalition's key organ. The formation of NARC itself was in part a response to the New KANU (the merger of KANU and the NDP). "The formation of the short-lived New KANU alliance had sent signals to the opposition parties that if they resorted to contesting the elections individually in the 2002 elections, they would lose".[26] Elischer agrees, writing that "in particular, Charity Ngilu was keen on forming an alliance with Kibaki and Wamalwa and managed to convince both to agree to the formation of the National Alliance of Kenya (NAK)".[27] Mwai Kibaki was subsequently selected as the presidential flag bearer for this particular alliance.

For Moi, Saitoti's departure from KANU was a gift, since it paved the way for Musalia Mudavadi to be appointed vice president for a period of a little less than two months, from November 2002 until the inauguration of the new Kibaki government in 2003. Mudavadi had the distinction of being the shortest-serving vice president in the history of Kenya. Moi, it appeared, used the next highest office in the land as political bait: by offering the vice presidency to Mudavadi, he planned to entice the Luhya community, the second-most populous in Kenya, to vote for his preferred successor, Uhuru Kenyatta, ultimately the fourth president. In the rapidly shifting, fluid situation, Moi continued to use the ethnic card to maintain the fragile coalition. The opposition (NARC Alliance) mirrored Moi's moves and utilized the ethnic card as a powerful signaling tool. For example, when Moi appointed Musalia Mudavadi the vice president, NARC elevated Moody Awori, another Luhya, to the NARC Summit – Awori would ultimately be appointed Kibaki's running mate and became the vice president after Kibaki's election.

Yet, there remained members of the New KANU who were skeptical of Uhuru but, even more important so incensed that Moi declared, "I have chosen Uhuru to take over leadership when I leave. This young man Uhuru has been consulting me on leadership matters. I have seen that *he is a person who can be guided.*"[28] The idea that Kenya needed someone "who can be guided" by Moi, after 24 years of leadership in the country, was met with veritable hostility. There would be quite the backlash, and his preferred candidate might not make it. Together with the votes of the Kikuyu (if they voted for Uhuru) and the Kalenjin, the ethnic arithmetic made sense: together, these three groups could vote in the next president of Kenya.

There were many slights to Moi's attempts to influence his successor; his preferred ticket, with the "appointed" successor Uhuru Kenyatta and his vice presidential running mate Musalia Mudavadi were roundly beaten. Moi's attempts also required careful maneuvering so as not to aggravate any of the potential successors; his Western strategy to impose Uhuru on the country bore evidence to this. Nevertheless, by the dawn of 2002, Kenya had a president who was not beholden to Moi's entreaties.

The coronation of Kibaki appeared to happen late in 2002, when the general election campaigns were in full swing. The stakes were high and the signs unmistakable, that Moi was determined to select Uhuru to run on the KANU ticket. Raila Odinga's "new" outfit, the Liberal Democratic Party (LDP – recall that the National Democratic Party had been dissolved in its "union" with KANU into New KANU) appeared to be out in the cold, and Raila was on the brink of becoming irrelevant. LDP held its first rally at Uhuru Park on 14 October 2002, parallel to Uhuru's selection as the KANU flag bearer, to which NAK was invited. It was at this rally where Raila uttered the words thought to have crowned Kibaki as (future) president: "Kibaki Tosha" (Kibaki is enough).[29] This endorsement was as strategic as it was practical: many of the possible alliances had already been formed (with KANU and its four regional vice presidencies), while NAK had drawn in the opposition factions of the other communities. As such, Raila considered that LDP could not win an election on its own or even agree to a presidential candidate, given the lessons of history. Also, given the prior ethnic considerations, it would be a more promising proposition to add the splinter Kikuyu vote that would go to Kibaki to that of the Luo, Luhya and Kamba votes and thus secure the election.[30]

Post-election: memoranda, broken promises and the coming storms

The euphoria surrounding the elections and what promised to be a new beginning, a new nation, the beginning of the Kibaki presidency, riding on a 62 percent mandate, was palpable. It was so palpable that in December 2002, Gallup reported that Kenyans were the most optimistic people in the world.[31] From all appearances, the Moi government had failed to drive its preferred successor to victory and had lost the country to the opposition, and for the first time KANU was out of power and in the opposition, with its candidate conceding the election. Just as it had failed to execute a successful election, it appeared to fail to plan for the inauguration ceremonies, including the security of the heads of state and governments who attended and other high-ranking officials. The incoming president, Mwai Kibaki, had broken his leg in a pre-election accident and was confined to a wheelchair, and what appeared to be inadequate preparations to confront this physical challenge compounded the appearance of chaos. The crowds, eager to let the outgoing president know their delight, booed and pelted the former president all the way to the dais as he left. The indignity was confounded by parts of Kibaki's speech, offering that "[t]he era of 'anything goes' is now gone forever. Government will no longer be run on the whims of individuals. The era of roadside decisions, declarations have gone. My government's decisions will be guided by teamwork and consultations."[32]

Over and above the chaos that marked the ceremony itself, the government's new reign started off with the implementation and realization of some of the promises that the (now) NARC government had made. In January 2003, Free Primary Education (FPE) was introduced, and quickly attracted the promise of funding from the British Department for International Development and the US Agency for International Development. In March 2003, a commission to re-investigate the murder of the former foreign affairs minister, Robert Ouko, in 1990, was established, questioning among others the former president. Ultimately, the commission failed to resolve the murder of the former minister.[33] The president also appointed individuals from different ethnic groups to his cabinet, especially the principals of the different parties that formed the NARC coalition. The prevailing view was that Kibaki was appointing the most qualified people to different posts, although there was a view that the politics of patronage were beginning to make a comeback.[34]

Despite this mixed record of accomplishments, Kibaki's government largely brought about significant changes and rapid economic growth. These included a 400 percent growth in the volume of trading at the Nairobi Stock Exchange, the successful privatization of several public enterprises with half a million new local investors, 1.3 million pupils going to school in 2003 under the FPE program, doubling of the number of children enrolled in schools, salary increases for police and teachers, a 5.5 percent annual growth rate for the economy during Kibaki's first administration and an almost 100 percent increase in the tax collection.[35] Still, there were economic difficulties: these benefits went to the top 25 percent of the wealthiest population, inflation rose and corruption showed no signs of abating.

Memoranda of understanding, strains and fissures

Although the new government fulfilled some of its campaign promises, significant differences in the coalition partners' positions emerged, beginning to crack open the coalition. The majority of the citizens identified a new constitution as one of the new government's mandates. During the campaigns, NARC had promised one "within the first 100 days of its administration."[36] Orwenjo argues that "the new president, having tasted the benefits of incumbency and the massive presidential powers that the draft constitution had sought to drastically trim and devolve, started dilly dallying on the issue."[37] Still, within 100 days, a Constitutional Conference was inaugurated in April 2003, with the mandate to collect the views of the public, ultimately draft a new constitution and determine the process of its ratification. On its part, and perhaps in an indication of things to come, LDP proposed an executive prime minister with a weak presidency (in the model of Israel), but Kibaki and his supporters advocated to retain a strong presidency. Ultimately, after the constitutional review process began, it would be presented to the electorate in a referendum in 2005, completing the split between the NARC partners, as Raila and his supporters voted down the proposed constitution.[38]

But the more things changed, the more they remained the same. The first instance of what LDP considered betrayal appeared to stem from the so-called

Memorandum of Understanding (MoU) signed between the NARC principals. To wit, the MoU had promised Raila Odinga the position of prime minister, based on a 50/50 power-sharing arrangement in terms of the appointment of cabinet ministers. After the elections, this was not done, and Kibaki asserted constitutional executive authority to appoint members of government.[39] Thus, the non-fulfillment of the conditions stipulated in the MoU continued the tradition and legacy of "use and dump", which Raila had alleged, when he had left the New KANU party. In August 2003, the then vice president, Michael Kijana Wamalwa, passed on. Because he was from the Luhya community, there was pressure to appoint another member of the community, in keeping with the "regional balance". On 25 September, a month later, Moody Awori, also a Luhya, was appointed the ninth vice president of Kenya. The ethnic balance had been retained.

In other areas, the Kibaki government was not quite as accommodating, or different from, the previous Moi and Kenyatta governments. Ayittey writes of the return of the "Mount Kenya mafia", just as there had been "the Family" (the Kikuyu elite) during the Kenyatta presidency. The Mount Kenya mafia, according to *The Economist*,

> as the Kikuyu cabal became known within weeks of Mr. Kibaki's inauguration, appears to have renounced reform in favour of shoring up its ailing patron's power. In particular, its members seem determined to shut out Raila Odinga, a firebrand leader of the Luo, whose pre-election defection to Mr. Kibaki delivered him victory.[40]

The new government's tactics appeared to mirror those of old; for example, Odhiambo Mbai, the major proponent for a parliamentary system of government with a powerful prime minister (interpreted to infer Raila Odinga) was assassinated in his residence, the perpetrators of which were never apprehended.

On the foreign policy front, despite the traditional friendship that Kenya maintained with both the US and the UK, Kibaki began to chart an independent foreign policy course, with a "tilt" towards China and Asia more broadly. Granted, the beginning of his presidency corresponded with the start of the war in Iraq. Kibaki's view was that Kenya would pursue its interests in collaboration with those countries that supported it but would collaborate with the US and its allies, read the UK and Israel, to fight terrorism.[41] Yet, Kenya bucked joining "the coalition of the willing", when the US invaded Iraq in 2003 without authorization by the United Nations. In retaliation, the US and the UK issued travel advisories to Kenya, causing another massive blow to the tourism sector on the Kenyan coast.[42]

Breaking point: constitutional review revolt, 2005

The constitutional review process was one of the most significant sources of disagreements in the new government, primarily because of the positions taken by the partners. The Kibaki government's stated preference was for the retention of a strong presidency and a ceremonial prime minister, while Raila and his LDP partners pushed for an executive prime minister with a largely ceremonial presidency. Once again, the fluidity of the alliances and the positions staked manifested itself across parties. There was no clear ethnic angle as to which communities supported what position, or the merits thereof, other than based on the leadership of the parties, although Elischer (2013) and Stidsen (2006) note that the only "Yes" votes for the constitution to be adopted were only in the Central Province of Kenya.

The completion of the draft process of the constitution review produced what was generally known as the "Bomas Draft". Within the act authorizing the constitutional review activities was a stipulation for Parliament to ratify the draft before it was put to the country in a referendum. According to the Hansard, Parliament was requested to debate the contentious clauses and to resolve these, per the act. The contentious clauses were Chapter 4 (Citizenship; on the question of Dual Citizenship), Chapter 6 (Bill of Rights, Articles 34: Right to Life, Article 50: Freedom of the Media and Article 51: Access to Information), Chapter 11 (the Legislature, Articles 120 to 122 on the Senate), Chapter 12 (the Executive, Article 152: President and Deputy President and Article 172: The Prime Minister and the Cabinet), Chapter 14 (Judicial and Legal Systems; Articles 198 and 199 on the Kadhi's Courts), Chapter 14 (Devolved Government)[43] and Chapter 18 (Additional Constitutional Commissions).[44]

Whereas the preceding issues were contentious, Elischer summarizes the points of departure as primarily the differences in the two drafts: the Bomas Draft (which is referred to earlier, in the Hansard discussions) and the "Wako" or "Kilifi" Draft, which was the version put to the electorate; the differences were primarily around the executive and devolution. Briefly, the Bomas Draft suggested a largely ceremonial president as head of state and the prime minister with executive power. On devolution, it advocated for a quasi-federal system with strong regional governments (Majimbo). The Wako/Kilifi Draft, on the other hand, had the president as the chief executive, who appointed and dismissed the prime minister and who could be impeached by 75 percent of the members of parliament. On devolution, it advocated for districts as basic units of devolution with an elected district assembly.[45]

The Wako/Kilifi Draft, while attempting to resolve the questions that were raised in the Bomas Draft[46] was considered a betrayal of the citizen-driven process and an attempt to continue the presidential system with its unchecked powers. In fairness, the Bomas Draft was seen, for example, as legitimating Kadhi's courts, thus giving Islam a preference while not according other religions and traditional societal processes the same consideration. Other initiatives, whose suggestions were included in the Wako Draft, included, for example, the "Ufungamano Initiative", which suggested neutral language, suggesting in the (new) Paragraph 111 of Religious Courts: "The jurisdiction of Religious Courts must be limited to matters of personal law to which the parties are subject."[47] Given the proposed changes in the draft coming out of the Bomas process, Kibaki's "betrayal" regarding the MoU signed before the 2002 election, there was palpable opposition to the draft. The LDP faction of NARC, together with some of KANU's members, opposed the ratification of the new constitution (the No people) and adopted an orange as their symbol. On the other side, those advocating for the adoption of the constitution (the Yes people) adopted a banana symbol.

Stidsen argues that the defeat of the Wako draft was not just about the constitution; it was about sending a message to Kibaki and his administration, as the president campaigned "hard" to win the referendum:

> Hence it is said that the referendum vote was as much against the draft as against this group, who were its proponents. The referendum defeat was said to constitute the 'third liberation' (the first being from colonialism, and the second being the overthrow of the ruling KANU party in 2002 after 40 years in power.[48]

Stidsen adds that the Kikuyu, Embu and Meru people (of the GEMA fame), (are) pejoratively referred to as the "Mount Kenya Mafia", on account of their being perceived as corrupt and conceited, since they see themselves as constituting 'the government'.[49] The referendum results were conclusive: in seven of the eight provinces, the vote was an overwhelming "No", rejecting the proposed constitution. In four of the seven provinces, more than 75 percent of the voters rejected the proposed constitution, with the overall (winning) tally against the new constitution at 58 percent, while the percentage of those voting for the constitution was 41.8 percent.[50]

After the defeat of the "Yes" camp, the "Orange" camp constituted itself into a political party, the Orange Democratic Movement (ODM), under whose banner Raila Odinga would contest the presidency in 2007.[51] The referendum had not only denied Kenya a new constitution; it had also effectively fractured the government, with NARC being reconstituted into NARC-Kenya (NARC-K), based on an alliance between FORD-Kenya, FORD-People, DP, KANU and other smaller parties.[52] And just as Moi's government had previously attempted to co-opt additional members of the communities represented by the opposition, ODM in this case, NARC-K attempted the same feat. Still, the schisms ran deep, and it was not clear that they would be bridged in ways that would continue to ensure the tranquility of 2002 in the impending 2007 general election.

Ethnic dimensions: the New KANU, NARC and *Umoja* at last

There were two important outcomes, which actually had outcomes going in two directions in terms of the outcomes (collaboration and conflict). Although the previous discussions have shown that in 2002 the leading figures in the opposition were ready and did indeed achieve unity, if only for the purposes of the election, there were still undercurrents leading up to the 2002 elections. The most significant of these revolved around attempting to keep the different communities happy, offering them incentives and disincentives. For example, Hornsby recalls the structure of the New KANU; it was to have four party vice-chairmen, as opposed to the regular one:

> KANU's constitution was changed (during the 2002 delegates conference) to keep its leadership options open, by creating four party vice-chairmen rather than one. As expected, Mudavadi took one post for Western, Ngala the second for the Coast and Musyoka the third for Eastern.[53]

This change, in addition to elevating Uhuru to one of the vice presidencies, the vice president, Saitoti, was dropped from the vice presidency in the party.

More important, the four vice-chairmen roughly represented four regions, in effect rewarding four different regions of concentration of ethnic groups. Moi was effectively acknowledging that Kenya was ethnically divided and that in an era of multi-party politics, the only way to win was by giving ethic groups a stake in the forthcoming elections. The most interesting aspect of these arrangements, though, was that the two major candidates for president came from one ethnic group, the Kikuyu; together they had garnered more than 5.5 million votes, which accounted for more than 90 percent of all votes cast in that election. Was Kenya better off, then, having fewer presidential candidates represented fewer ethnic groups? The firm opposition to a Kikuyu presidency appeared to wither in the face of a predecessor who was determined to continue having an influence on the country. Perhaps as one of the ways to contain electoral violence that occurred with the predictable frequency of elections. Was it possible that if Kenya had leadership arrangements that took into account its distribution of ethnic groups (much as Iraq has), there would be peace?

On the positive side, the 2002 elections were peaceful, and the violence that had marked the previous two elections under the multi-party system was not witnessed, despite the possible future dominance by one of the communities that had been especially affected by the violence. Elischer especially notes that the different principals in the NARC coalition (Kibaki, Raila, Ngilu, Musyoka and Wamalwa) campaigned together, thus modeling inter-ethnic cooperation, while urging their constituents to vote in large numbers but avoiding "the negative rhetoric that had characterized previous campaigns."[54] They were also considered some of the most credible elections, with an outcome that saw power transition. Thus, despite his Kikuyu roots, "the strong position for Kibaki in other parts of the country gives the image of a national leader."[55]

The fears that had characterized the atmosphere around previous multi-party elections, the history of violence and the greater continental challenge of having peaceful transitions appeared to have been overcome. The new government was implementing the election promises, including introducing FPE with a million new learners. Although the ethnic divisions – rather, ethnic promises – at the heart of NARC and its now infamous MOU would begin to re-divide government over unfulfilled promises, the transitional election had concluded peacefully. Perhaps the ethnic identity and its role in Kenyan politics were, after all, beginning to lose their importance.

Notes

1 Gabrielle Lynch & Gordon Crawford. "Democratization in Africa 1990–2010: An Assessment." In Gordon Crawford & Gabrielle Lynch, Eds. *Democratization in Africa: Challenges and Prospects*. (New York, NY: Routledge, 2012): 3.
2 Lynch and Crawford. "Democratization in Africa 1990–2010." 4.
3 John James Quinn. *Global Geopolitical Power and African Political and Economic Institutions: When Elephants Fight*. (Lanham, MD: Lexington Books, 2016): 161.
4 Martin Rupiya. "Conclusions." In Martin Rupiya, Gorden Moyo, & Henrik Laugesen, Eds. *The New African Civil-Military Relations*. (Pretoria, South Africa: The African Public Policy and Research Institute (APPRI), 2015): 208.
5 See for example, Dundas (2012), Isanga (2012), Aall (2016), and Quinn (2016), among others.
6 [Sahrawi Arab Democratic Republic]. Carl W. Dundas. *Close Elections and Political Succession in the African Union*. (Bloomington, IN: AuthorHouse UK Ltd., 2012): 70.
7 H. Kwasi Prempeh. "Presidents Untamed." In Larry Diamond & Marc F. Plattner, Eds. *Democratization in Africa: Progress and Retreat*, 2nd Ed. (Baltimore, MD: The Johns Hopkins University Press, 2010): 19.
8 CQ Researcher. *Issues in Comparative Politics: Selections from CQ Researcher*. (Thousand Oaks, CA: Sage Publications, 2012): 78 and Rita Biswas & Eric Ofori. "Democracy and Stock Market Development: The African Experience." In John W. Kensinger, Ed. *Overlaps of Private Sector with Public Sector around the Globe*. (Bingley, UK: Emerald Group Publishing, 2015): 79.
9 Quinn. *Global Geopolitical Power and African Political and Economic Institutions*. 163.
10 Wangari Muta Maathai. *The Challenge for Africa*. (New York, NY: Pantheon Books, 2009): 116.
11 John Yoder. "Elections as a Stress Test of Democratization in Societies: A Comparison of Liberal, Sierra Leone, and the Democratic Republic of the Congo." In Cassandra Rachel Veney & Dick W. Simpson, Eds. *African Democracy and Development: Challenges for Post-Conflict African Nations*. (Lanham, MD: Lexington Books, 2013): Ch. 6, pp. 109–144, 125.
12 Joseph M. Isanga. "Rethinking the Rule of Law as Antidote to African Development Challenges." In David K. Linnan, Ed. *Legitimacy, Legal Development and Change: Law and Modernization Reconsidered*. (New York, NY: Routledge, 2012): 65.
13 Gardner Thompson. *African Democracy: Its Origins and Development in Uganda, Kenya and Tanzania*. (Kampala, Uganda: Fountain Publishers, 2015): 39.
14 Thompson. *African Democracy*. 40.
15 Stef Vandeginste. "Burundi." In John Abbink, Sebastian Elischer, Andreas Mehler & Henning Melber, Eds. *Africa Yearbook, Vol. 12: Politics, Economy and Society South of the Sahara in 2015*. (Leiden, The Netherlands: Koninklijke Brill NV, 2016): 76.
16 Reuters. "Rwandan President Paul Kagame to Run for Third Term in 2017." Posted Friday 1 January 2016. (Web): n.p.
17 Tyodzua Atim. *African Politics and Society in the 21st Century*. (Bloomington, IN: AuthorHouse UK Ltd., 2013): 119.
19 Sosteness Francis Materu. *The Post-Election Violence in Kenya: Domestic and International Legal Responses*. (The Hague, The Netherlands: T.M.C. Asser Press, 2015): 29.
20 Marcel Rutten & Sam Owuor. "Weapons of Mass Destruction: Land, Ethnicity and the 2007 Elections in Kenya." In Peter Kagwanja & Roger Southall. *Kenya's Uncertain Democracy: The Electoral Crisis of 2008*. (New York, NY: Routledge, 2010): 56.
21 Mara Roberts. "Conflict Analysis of the 2007 Post-Election Violence in Kenya." In Akanmu Gafari Adebayo, Ed. *Managing Conflicts in Africa's Democratic Transitions*. (Lanham, MD: Lexington Books, 2012): 142.
22 Gilbert M. Khadiagala. "Kenya: Gradual Pluralization Fails to Buffer Shocks." In Alan J. Kuperman, Ed. *Constitutions and Conflict Management in Africa: Preventing Civil*

War through Institutional Design. (Philadelphia, PA: University of Pennsylvania Press, 2015): 63.

23 Pius Kakai Wanyonyi. "Historicizing Negative Ethnicity in Kenya." In Mbũgua wa Mũngai & George M. Gona, Eds. *(Re)membering Kenya: Identity, Culture and Freedom*. (Nairobi, Kenya: Twaweza Communications, 2010): 43.

24 Charles Hornsby. *Kenya: A History since Independence*. (New York, NY: I. B. Tauris & Co., 2012): 671.

25 Hornsby. *Kenya*. 671

26 Materu. *The Post-Election Violence in Kenya*. 30

27 Elischer. *Political parties in Africa*. 79

28 Materu. *The Post-Election Violence in Kenya*. 29.

29 See Gavin Brent Sullivan & Rose Ruto-Korir. "Is Collective Pride Possible after Intergroup Violence? A Case Study of Kenya Following the Post-Election Violence of 2007 and 2008." In Gavin Brent Sullivan, Ed. *Understanding Collective Pride and Group Identity: New Directions in Emotion Theory Research and Practice*. (New York, NY: Routledge, 2014); Felix Nguzo Kioli. "Ethnicity: The Jinx to Kenyan Politics and Economic Development." In Kimani Njogu, Ed. *Citizen Participation in Decision Making: Towards Inclusive Development in Kenya*. (Nairobi, Kenya: Twaweza Communications, 2013); Daniel Branch. *Kenya: Between Hope and Despair, 1963–2011*. (New Haven, CT: Yale University Press, 2011) and Sebastian Elischer. *Political Parties in Africa: Ethnicity and Party Formation*. (New York, NY: Cambridge University Press, 2013), among others.

30 Elischer. *Political Parties in Africa*. 81.

31 John Githongo. "Fear and Loathing in Nairobi: The Challenge of Reconciliation in Kenya." *Foreign Affairs*, 89, No. 4 (July/August, 2010): 3.

32 BBC News. "Kibaki and Moi Speech Excerpts." *BBC News*. (Web). Posted on Monday 30 December 2002.

33 Taylor & Francis Group. *The Europa World Year: Book 2004, Vol. 2: Countries: Kazakhstan – Zimbabwe*. (New York, NY: Taylor & Francis, 2004): 2435.

34 Kioli. "Ethnicity." 78.

35 Githongo. "Fear and Loathing in Nairobi." 3.

36 Daniel Ochieng Orwenjo. "Political Grandstanding and the Use of Proverbs in African Political Discourse." *Discourse & Society*, 20, No. 1 (January, 2009): 127.

37 Orwenjo. "Political Grandstanding and the Use of Proverbs in African Political Discourse." 127.

38 Taylor & Francis Group. *The Europa World Year*. 2435.

39 Elischer. *Political Parties in Africa*. 81. [In retrospective analysis, it is not clear that Kibaki had the authority to appoint a Prime Minister, a position that was not provided for in the Constitution; neither was there a move to subject this to the authority of parliament. As the MoU remained secret, its enforceability was at best questionable – a gentlemen's agreement]

40 *The Economist*. "Kenya's Government: Going Wrong?" 9 October 2003.

41 Macharia Munene. *Historical Reflections on Kenya: Intellectual Adventurism, Politics and International Relations*. (Nairobi, Kenya: University of Nairobi Press, 2012): 29. Cooperation to tackle terrorism was especially important to Kenya, given the US embassy bombing in 1998 and the loss of 212 Kenyan citizens in the attack, the Kikambala bombing and attempt to take down an Israeli airliner in 2002 and other sporadic attacks.

42 See Munene. *Historical Reflections on Kenya*. 29; see also: Jeremy Prestholdt. "Fighting Phantoms: The United States and Counterterrorism in Eastern Africa." In Everard Meade & William J. Aceves, Eds. *Lessons and Legacies of the War on Terror: From Moral Panic to Permanent War*. (New York, NY: Routledge, 2013): 137.

43 The Hansard noted that this entire chapter (14) was contentious, as the draft constitution advocated for regionalism.

44 The National Assembly. *Kenya National Assembly Official Record (Hansard) Jun 30, 2005*. (Nairobi, Kenya: Government Press, 2006): 2070.
45 Elischer. *Political Parties in Africa*. 86.
46 For example, according to Chesworth (2009), the proposed "Bomas draft" Articles 198 and 199 read as follows:

> 198 (1) There is established the Kadhi's Court.
> (2) The Kadhi's Court shall –
>
> (a) consist of the Chief Kadhi and such number of other Kadhis, all of whom shall profess the Islamic faith; and
> (b) be organized and administered as may be prescribed by an Act of Parliament.
>
> 199 The Kadhis' Court shall be a subordinate court with jurisdiction to determine questions of Islamic law relating to personal status, marriage, divorce and matters consequential to divorce, inheritance and succession in proceedings in which all the parties profess the Islamic faith.

47 John Chesworth. "The Church and Islam: *Vyama Vingi* (Multipartyism) and the Ufungamano Talks." In Ben Knighton, Ed. *Religion and Politics in Kenya: Essays in Honor of a Meddlesome Priest*. (New York, NY: Palgrave Macmillan, 2009): 174.
48 Sille Stidsen. *The Indigenous World 2006*. (Copenhagen, Denmark: The International Work Group for Indigenous Affairs, 2006): 440.
49 Stidsen. *The Indigenous World 2006*. 440.
50 Robert Maxon & Thomas P. Ofcansky. *Historical Dictionary of Kenya*. (Lanham, MD: Rowman & Littlefield, 2014): 61.
51 Chesworth. "The Church and Islam." 176.
52 Elischer. *Political Parties in Africa*. 87.
53 Hornsby. *Kenya*. 671.
54 Elischer. *Political Parties in Africa*. 82.
55 Anders Närman. "Elections in Kenya." *Review of African Political Economy*, 30, No. 96, War & the Forgotten Continent (June, 2003): 347.

References

Aall, Pamela. "Conflict Management Capacity in Africa: Understanding the Problem and Designing the Solution." In Pamela Aall & Chester A. Crocker, Eds. *Minding the Gap: African Conflict Management in a Time of Change*. Waterloo, ON: Center for International Governance Innovation, 2016.

Atim, Tyodzua. *African Politics and Society in the 21st Century*. Bloomington, IN: AuthorHouse UK Ltd., 2013.

Ayittey, George B. N. *Africa Unchained: The Blueprint for Africa's Future*. New York, NY: Palgrave Macmillan, 2005.

BBC News. "Kibaki and Moi Speech Excerpts." *BBC News*. Posted on Monday 30 December 2002. (Web). Accessed on 11/27/2016 from: http://news.bbc.co.uk/2/hi/not_in_website/syndication/monitoring/media_reports/2615369.stm

Biswas, Rita & Eric Ofori. "Democracy and Stock Market Development: The African Experience." In John W. Kensinger, Ed. *Overlapsof Private Sector with Public Sector around the Globe*. Bingley, UK: Emerald Group Publishing, 2015. Ch. 4, pp. 65–86.

Branch, Daniel. *Kenya: Between Hope and Despair, 1963–2011*. New Haven, CT: Yale University Press, 2011.

Chesworth, John. "The Church and Islam: *Vyama Vingi* (Multipartyism) and the Ufungamano Talks." In Ben Knighton, Ed. *Religion and Politics in Kenya: Essays in Honor of a Meddlesome Priest*. New York, NY: Palgrave Macmillan, 2009. Ch. 6, pp. 155–180.

CQ Researcher. *Issues in Comparative Politics: Selections from CQ Researcher*. Thousand Oaks, CA: Sage Publications, 2012.

Dundas, Carl W. *Close Elections and Political Succession in the African Union*. Bloomington, IN: AuthorHouse UK Ltd., 2012.

The Economist. "Kenya's Government: Going Wrong?" *The Economist*. 9 October 2003. (Web). Accessed on 11/27/2016 from: www.economist.com/node/2126505

Elischer, Sebastian. *Political Parties in Africa: Ethnicity and Party Formation*. New York, NY: Cambridge University Press, 2013.

Frankenberg, Günter. *Order from Transfer*. Northampton, MA: Edward Elger Publishing, 2013.

Githongo, John. "Fear and Loathing in Nairobi: The Challenge of Reconciliation in Kenya." *Foreign Affairs*, 89, No. 4 (July/August, 2010): 2–9. Accessed 11/27/2016 22:58 UTC from: www.jstor.org/stable/25680975

Isanga, Joseph M. "Rethinking the Rule of Law as Antidote to African Development Challenges." In David K. Linnan, Ed. *Legitimacy, Legal Development and Change: Law and Modernization Reconsidered*. New York, NY: Routledge, 2012. Ch. 3, pp. 59–84.

Kioli, Felix Nguzo. "Ethnicity: The Jinx to Kenyan Politics and Economic Development." In Kimani Njogu, Ed. *Citizen Participation in Decision Making: Towards Inclusive Development in Kenya*. Nairobi, Kenya: Twaweza Communications, 2013. Ch. 5, p. 78.

Linnan, David K., Ed. *Legitimacy, Legal Development and Change: Law and Modernization Reconsidered*. New York, NY: Routledge, 2012.

Lynch, Gabrielle & Gordon Crawford. "Democratization in Africa 1990–2010: An Assessment." In Gordon Crawford & Gabrielle Lynch, Eds. *Democratization in Africa: Challenges and Prospects*. New York, NY: Routledge, 2012.

Maathai, Wangari Muta. *The Challenge for Africa*. New York, NY: Pantheon Books, 2009.

Materu, Sosteness Francis. *The Post-Election Violence in Kenya: Domestic and International Legal Responses*. The Hague, The Netherlands: T.M.C. Asser Press, 2015.

Maxon, Robert M. & Thomas P. Ofcansky. *Historical Dictionary of Kenya*. Lanham, MD: Rowman & Littlefield, 2014.

Munene, Macharia. *Historical Reflections on Kenya: Intellectual Adventurism, Politics and International Relations*. Nairobi, Kenya: University of Nairobi Press, 2012.

Närman, Anders. "Elections in Kenya." *Review of African Political Economy*, 30, No. 96, War & the Forgotten Continent (June, 2003): 343–350. Accessed on 11/27/2016 from: www.jstor.org/stable/4006777

The National Assembly. *Kenya National Assembly Official Record (Hansard) Jun 30, 2005*. Nairobi, Kenya: Government Press, 2006. p. 2070.

Orwenjo, Daniel Ochieng. "Political Grandstanding and the Use of Proverbs in African Political Discourse." *Discourse & Society*, 20, No. 1 (January, 2009): 123–146. Accessed on 11/27/2016 from: www.jstor.org/stable/42889246

Prempeh, H. Kwasi. "Presidents Untamed." In Larry Diamond & Marc F. Plattner, Eds. *Democratization in Africa: Progress and Retreat*, 2nd Ed. Baltimore, MD: The Johns Hopkins University Press, 2010.

Prestholdt, Jeremy. "Fighting Phantoms: The United States and Counterterrorism in Eastern Africa." In Everard Meade & William J. Aceves, Eds. *Lessons and Legacies of the War on Terror: From Moral Panic to Permanent War*. New York, NY: Routledge, 2013. Ch. 6, pp. 127–156.

Quinn, John James. *Global Geopolitical Power and African Political and Economic Institutions: When Elephants Fight*. Lanham, MD: Lexington Books, 2016.

Reuters. "Rwandan President Paul Kagame to Run for Third Term in 2017." Posted Friday 1 January 2016. (Web). Accessed on 11/25/2016 from: www.theguardian.com/world/2016/jan/01/rwanda-paul-kagame-third-term-office-constitutional-changes

Roberts, Mara. "Conflict Analysis of the 2007 Post-Election Violence in Kenya." In Akanmu Gafari Adebayo, Ed. *Managing Conflicts in Africa's Democratic Transitions*. Lanham, MD: Lexington Books, 2012.

Rupiya, Martin. "Conclusions." In Martin Rupiya, Gorden Moyo & Henrik Laugesen, Eds. *The New African Civil-Military Relations*. Pretoria, South Africa: The African Public Policy and Research Institute (APPRI), 2015.

Rutten, Marcel & Sam Owuor. "Weapons of Mass Destruction: Land, Ethnicity and the 2007 Elections in Kenya." In Peter Kagwanja & Roger Southall. *Kenya's Uncertain Democracy: The Electoral Crisis of 2008*. New York, NY: Routledge, 2010. Ch. 3, pp. 46–65.

Stidsen, Sille. *The Indigenous World 2006*. Copenhagen, Denmark: The International Work Group for Indigenous Affairs, 2006.

Sullivan, Gavin Brent & Rose Ruto-Korir. "Is Collective Pride Possible after Intergroup Violence? A Case Study of Kenya Following the Post-Election Violence of 2007 and 2008." In Gavin Brent Sullivan, Ed. *Understanding Collective Pride and Group Identity: New Directions in Emotion Theory Research and Practice*. New York, NY: Routledge, 2014.

Taylor & Francis Group. *The Europa World Year: Book 2004, Vol. 2: Countries: Kazakhstan – Zimbabwe*. New York, NY: Taylor & Francis, 2004.

Thompson, Gardner. *African Democracy: Its Origins and Development in Uganda, Kenya and Tanzania*. Kampala, Uganda: Fountain Publishers, 2015.

Vandeginste, Stef. "Burundi." In John Abbink, Sebastian Elischer, Andreas Mehler & Henning Melber, Eds. *Africa Yearbook, Vol. 12: Politics, Economy and Society South of the Sahara in 2015*, Vol. 12. Leiden, The Netherlands: Koninklijke Brill NV, 2016. Part 5, pp. 274–283.

Wanyonyi, Pius Kakai. "Historicizing Negative Ethnicity in Kenya." In Mbũgua wa Mũngai & George M. Gona, Eds. *(Re)membering Kenya: Identity, Culture and Freedom*. Nairobi, Kenya: Twaweza Communications, 2010.

Yoder, John. "Elections as a Stress Test of Democratization in Societies: A Comparison of Liberal, Sierra Leone, and the Democratic Republic of the Congo." In Cassandra Rachel Veney & Dick W. Simpson, Eds. *African Democracy and Development: Challenges for Post-Conflict African Nations*. Lanham, MD: Lexington Books, 2013. Ch. 6. pp. 109–144.

5 Reconfiguring the politiscape

Return of history and the end of hope

Re-entrenching the historical schisms

The 2005 constitutional review did more than defeat the proposed constitution: it led to a splintering of the government along alliance (and to some extent, ethnic) fissures. It also led to the split of the Orange Democratic Movement, which had triumphed on the "No" side, into the Orange Democratic Movement (ODM) and the Orange Democratic Movement-Kenya (ODM-Kenya). It also led to the death of seven people during the campaign activities for the referendum.[1] During the constitutional review process, those opposed to the new "Wako" Draft constitution unified and solidified opposition against Mwai Kibaki; the "No" camp that had adopted the orange symbol soon transformed itself from a protest into a political movement, ODM, in preparation to contest the elections of 2007.

Given the extent of division of the country, the forthcoming elections would potentially be a further repudiation of the Kibaki presidency, and the campaign was framed as such. The election, then, would seek to cobble together an alliance, one that would favor Kibaki's 2002 NARC, which dethroned KANU and its Moi-imposed heir, Uhuru Kenyatta. The politics were more complex than this oversimplified version; for example, even after attempting and failing to install Kenyatta as his heir, Moi supported a change in the constitution based on the Wako Draft. At the same time, further complicating post-Moi KANU affairs, Kenyatta opposed the draft constitution, teaming up with Raila Odinga, Kalonzo Musyoka, Najib Balala, Anyang' Nyong'o, Ochilo Ayacko, Linah Kilimo and William ole Ntimama, who were members of Kibaki's cabinet (from the Luo, Kalenjin, Maasai and Kamba and "coastal Muslim" communities).[2]

Yet, by the time elections were approaching, the erstwhile Orange Democratic Movement split into two: ODM and ODM-Kenya; both were deemed sufficiently different from each other that they were allowed registration by the Registrar of Societies. The former was led by Raila Odinga, the latter by Kalonzo Musyoka. KANU, which had campaigned with ODM against the draft constitution, in an ironic twist, threw its support behind Mwai Kibaki, as he sought to pursue a second term. KANU's leader, the unsuccessful presidential aspirant Uhuru Kenyatta, in a further twist, supported Mwai Kibaki, as did retired president Moi. Uhuru did not contest the election; KANU only fielded candidates for the member of parliament and councillor positions. Was it strategy, a decision not to challenge the president, a Kikuyu, for fear of splitting the vote? For what it was worth, it would eventually lead to Kenyatta being hauled before the International Criminal Court (ICC) after allegedly co-presiding over the worst ethnic violence that ever happened in Kenya.

Revisiting and expanding the ethnic angle: Bantus, Cushites, Nilotes and alliances

It's useful to revisit the constitutional review crisis and to unravel the alliance that was forged together in the crucible of the campaign for a new constitution. It is more useful to travel back to the pre-colonial period, to re-examine the different ethnic groups in Kenya (or Kenya and Uganda) to understand the shifting alliances, the concept of the "lesser evil" and the choices that the members of the different alliances made, in particular, the alliance among the Kalenjin, the Luhya and the Luo, in opposing Kibaki's second term, and the support that Kibaki received from both Kikuyu and Moi (rather than the Kalenjin), as a result of the quest for power within the Kalenjin community, given Moi's retirement five years previous. In particular, it is useful to examine how the Liberal Democratic Party faction of the NARC Alliance, which was heavily populated by Raila's Luo ethnic group, succeeded in creating a wider base by building a coalition with regional leaders from the Luhya in western Kenya, Kalenjin from the Rift Valley and Muslim leaders from Coast Province.

Returning to the ethnic groups' angle, it is useful to further explore Kenya's 42 ethnic groups and subdivide them into three broader groups. These are the Nilotes, the Bantu and the Cushites.[3] A pre-independence map of the East Africa region shows that Nilotic groups were roughly located in the area between Lake Victoria, up the Rift Valley, to Lake Rudolph (Lake Turkana); the Bantus were located in the central, east and southeast regions of Kenya (with some groups located near western Kenya); the Cushites, on the other hand, were located towards the northeastern area of Kenya, to the north going into Ethiopia and Somalia.[4] Some of the groups located in the present Kenya are further subdivided: among the Nilotes, there are the Luo (River Lake Nilotes), the Kalenjin (Highland Nilotes) and the Maasai, Turkana and Iteso (Plain Nilotes).[5]

The majority of the Nilotic communities have traditionally lived in western Kenya. Western Kenya was not always Kenya; "between 1894 and 1902", according to Ogula, "western Kenya was part of the Eastern Province of the Eastern Province of Uganda."[6] It later became the Kavirondo Province and, later, Nyanza Province. Isichei characterizes the greater East African language map as "dominated . . . by Eastern Nilotes, Eastern Cushites and, above all, Bantu."[7] Among the Cushites (Southern and Eastern Cushites, according to Okoth and Ndaloh, although the Southern Cushites have largely been subsumed into other groups, apart from the Dahallo), "include the Somali, Borana, Oromo (Galla), Rendille, Burji and Gabra."[8] The ethnic composition of these regions is much more complex than presented here; for example, the Mijikenda are classified as Bantu. However, Ehret writes that

> along the immediate interior of the East African coast, three major clusters of Bantu can be identified: the Sabaki-speakers, the Seuta-speakers and the Ruvu. The Sabaki language had three dialects, spoken along a very narrow strip of land behind the Kenyan coast. The ancestral Miji-Kenda dialect was spoken south of the River Tana.[9]

Some of the features of the groups' interactions as they migrated and settled included the displacement of communities and the adoption of some cultural practices (age-set systems and circumcision, for example, the practice of circumcision, thought to have been borrowed from the Southern Cushites by the Bantu). The groups also traded with neighboring communities, intermarried and influenced fighting tactics of other communities, exchanged technical skills (farming, e.g., Kwavi Maasai from the Kikuyu) and borrowed "institutions" (e.g., the Maasai Laibon from the Nandi Orkoiyot).[10] The Abaluyia, classified as Bantus, "are divided into 15 sub-tribes", which include the Bukusu, Idakho, Isukha, Kabras, Khayo, Kisa, Marachi, Maragoli, Nyala, Nyole, Samia, Tachoni, Tiriki, Tsotso, Wanga and Batura.[11] As much as the Western world was taken by surprise on account of breakup of Somalia, despite implied heterogeneity of the Somalis, Kenya's ethnic "tribes" are not as homogeneous. By some (different) accounts, the Abaluyia are believed to be constituted by anywhere between 18 and 19 sub-tribes, depending on who is counting and which of the sub-tribes are included. Often, these sub-tribes have "community leaders", and they can be leveraged to further divide, or forge alliances with other tribes. Thus, when Musalia Mudavadi was elevated to vice president, Moody Awori provided a counter-balance to split the larger tribe, splitting their allegiance to the opposition.

Thus, although different communities might appear to be homogeneous, speaking phonetically related languages (or the same, in the case of the Kikuyu), there are often in-group schisms that lead to splitting support for candidates during a general election, in addition to other variables in the domestic politics. The Kikuyus are, for instance, often split between the "Nyeri Kikuyu" (where Mwai Kibaki hails from), the "Mũrang'a Kikuyu" (where Kenneth Matiba and Peter Kenneth, presidential aspirant in 2013, hailed from) and the "Gatũndũ Kikuyu" (where Jomo Kenyatta and his son, Uhuru Kenyatta, call home). Elections in places where a presidential aspirant is running for parliament can exacerbate the ethnic schism; for example, most of Simeon Nyachae's votes in the 2002 elections came from the Kisii region. In some parliamentary constituencies, it is plausible that the people might elect a telephone pole if it identified itself with a particular political party. This has often been true of constituencies where presidents have stemmed from: elections were generally a mere formality. Thus, for the longest time, the Othaya constituency was represented by Mwai Kibaki, and he had just but a token of a challenge.

One other thing bears mentioning: the intersection of political parties and ethnicity. Although the freedom to form and espouse alternative political opinions was gradually stifled from the Kenyatta to the Moi years, the existence of a singular party meant that whoever was the head of the party effectively controlled the state, thus the question of ethnic division based on parties was moot. The multi-party era brought about a multiplicity of parties, none identifiable from the next based on ideology. Rather, the parties were based primarily on the leader and generally tended to coalesce around the individual and others who identified themselves as party members. Karega-Munene, for example, writes "that Kenya's political parties are devoid of ideologies, politicians find it easier to organise their voting blocks along ethnic lines."[12]

Yet even ethnicity, as the basis of political organization and party formation, can endure "crosscutting cleavages within groups and mutually self-serving relations between members of ethnic groups."[13] This is especially the case with the larger groups; (for example, the Kalenjin ethnic group consists of the Keiyo, Endorois, Kipsigis, Marakwet, Nandi, Pokot, Terik, Tugen, Sebei); often, the Kalenjin have a greater affinity to one of the members of the group rather than someone outside of the nine sub-groups. Outside of the sub-groups, inter-group cooperation has been evident in some instances; Karega-Munene gives an example of the Kalenjin cooperating with the Luhya during Kenya's colonization, considering themselves minorities and joining KADU.[14] Thus, the flux alliances seen in the 2005 referendum and the 2007 general election bore the hallmark of these cross-community relationships.

Although it may be folly to ascribe the voting patterns and thus the results of the constitutional review to specific communities, it is helpful to examine the correlation between where certain ethnic groups are located geographically and the patterns of voting in the referendum. Furthermore, by considering the settlement patterns based on the previously discussed Bantu, Cushitic and Nilotic communities, one can see specific patterns emerge. The Central Province, primarily inhabited by GEMA (Gikuyu, Embu and Meru and sometimes the Akamba), voted overwhelmingly (93.2 percent) to adopt the new constitution. Nairobi, whose population is most cosmopolitan, voted 56.8 percent against the new constitution, while Eastern Province, comprising of primarily Bantu peoples, voted 50.5 percent against, and 49.5 percent for (this was the closest vote). Coast Province, significantly populated not only by the Bantu (Mijikenda) and cosmopolitan Arab and Cushitic but also by mixed-ethnicity populations (see the discussion on the Likoni Clashes of 1997 and the cause thereof), had the second-highest "No" vote. North Eastern Province (Cushitic, but also less populated, with a total of about 51,000 votes), voted "No", while the Rift Valley, primarily inhabited by Nilotic peoples, voted 75.7 percent to reject the new constitution. The 24 percent vote might be attributed to other groups that may have included the Bantu groups. Nyanza, on the other hand, with the highest (87.8 percent) rejection rate, is primarily populated by Lake Nilotes. More important, this was beginning to set up the alliances for the 2007 election.

Post-referendum and campaigns for general elections: reorganization

The campaigns for the acceptance or rejection of the draft constitution were largely peaceful, as was the immediate period after the referendum, despite the recriminations surrounding the coalition, and the fact that some of the ministers affiliated with LDP opposed the adoption of the draft constitution. As Njogu notes, "Odinga's group (which was opposed to the adoption of the draft constitution) was mainly drawn from Nairobi, the expansive Rift Valley, Luo-Nyanza, Coast, Eastern and Western Provinces."[15] The opposition to the new constitution was joined by Uhuru Kenyatta, the then leader of KANU, perhaps more on principle.[16] After the loss, Kibaki dismissed his entire cabinet (ostensibly to replace those ministers who had opposed the constitution). More important, around the country, the reorganization of the political landscape started in earnest; as Kithinji, Koster and Rotich write, "the period after the 2005 referendum on the constitution witnessed major political realignments characterized by the disintegration of NARC and the rise of the Orange Democratic Movement (ODM) under Odinga and the Party of National Unity (PNU) led by President Kibaki."[17]

The defeat of the draft constitution also meant that the upcoming elections in December 2007 would be held under the framework of the old (independence era, with many amendments) constitution. Muli notes as much, writing that "every stage and step in the electoral cycle and process is governed by the law in a very detailed manner", including procurement of ballots, ballot materials, guarding polling centers, transport of ballot materials and even investigating instances of electoral violence and offences. However, this also meant, as Muli notes, that the electoral matters were governed by nine separate laws.[18] Electoral campaigns, following the thorough chastising of the NARC government, did little to bring the nation back together, or diminish the undercurrents of manifestly ethnic division in the country; indeed, they served to solidify the positions the protagonists had taken. The split of ODM into ODM and ODM-Kenya was an unfortunate disagreement of who would be on the ODM ticket, but the view as generally that Kibaki's first term was his last. Yet, Kenyatta's (and KANU's) decision to throw their lot in with Kibaki and PNU, after having helped defeat the proposed constitution, in no way benefitted the opposition: the numbers looked to be dwindling.

The different sides pulled out all the stops for the 2007 general election campaigns: helicopters criss-crossed the skies, money exchanged hands and over the airwaves, campaign rhetoric (or propaganda), spewed forth. Although Kenya's liberalization of the press has been less than a quarter-century in the making, and continues to suffer periodic interruptions and instances of intimidation (e.g., the third president's wife, Mrs. Lucy Kibaki, storming of Nation Center on 3 May 2005), there has been a proliferation of electronic and print media, but more important, TV and radio stations that magnify the ethnic divide, by providing programming in their target audience languages. As such, radio and TV stations broadcasting in practically all of Kenya's 43 languages can be heard and are often concentrated around the regions where the specific languages are spoken.

During the campaign period (as it later emerged), the media was deemed to have either abetted conditions that facilitated propaganda or transmission of ethnically driven electoral content (e.g., the Kass FM presenter Joshua Sang was one of the six individuals hauled before the ICC to answer charges of complicity in genocide and crimes against humanity) or failed, in many instances, to carry out their role to inform the public without bias. For example, Somerville observes that

> the state-owned KBC [Kenya Broadcasting Corporation] was criticized heavily by EU election monitors for failing "to fulfill even its minimal legal obligation as a public service broadcaster . . . its coverage demonstrating high degree of bias in favour of the Party of National Unity (PNU) coalition."[19]

It is perhaps useful to note that KBC has never been quite the poster child for independence, despite its national reach. Also, as a state-owned enterprise, KBC has long been plagued by inertia; as such, other newer broadcasters have carved out the most significant share of the listener and viewership markets because of dynamism. That said, Sommerville does note the general sentiment that "mainstream press and broadcasting organizations did not incite hatred but failed to prevent the dissemination of party propaganda and the violent rhetoric of many political leaders."[20]

The question of ethnic electoral violence, particularly in Kenya, is quite complex. Why were there no ethnic clashes in all the elections before 1992? (The easy answer might be that every elected official was theoretically a member of KANU). Perhaps the introduction of multi-party politics inevitably led to parties that were more aligned with ethnic groups than they were with ideology, but the structures of electoral reforms were so constituted as to favor the incumbent, and by exploiting ethnic divisions and grievances – whether legitimate or not – to ensure that the ruling party could afford to minimize its losses and maximize the potential for the loss of those in opposition. For example, the expulsion of the Kikuyu, Luhya and Luo from the Rift Valley simultaneously disenfranchised the internally displaced persons (IDPs), while denying opposition presidential candidates the 25 percent votes in at least five of the eight provinces. Thus, the deliberate constraints to the presidency were still in place. Had the constitutional review of 2005 succeeded, the winner of the presidential contest would have needed to obtain the specified 50 percent + 1 of all votes cast.

It is helpful to revisit Lynch and Anderson's discussion on what the shift to multi-party politics does, that is, "altered the identity cleavages around which political mobilization revolves."[21] Posner, studying Kenya and Zambia transitions and elections 15 years before Kenya's mayhem, argues that the shift "has caused ethnic conflict to be carried out in the name of different kinds of identities"[22] by altering "the dimension of ethnic cleavage around which political competition – violent or otherwise – takes place."[23] This is especially pertinent if the proper institutions are not part of the transition to multi-party politics. In the case of

Kenya and in terms of institutions, it is not clear that the appropriate institutions were in place prior to the 2007 general elections. One such institution, which bore the brunt of the wrath of the collective political spectrum, was the Electoral Commission of Kenya (ECK); the chairman was traditionally selected by the president, as were the commissioners. It thus bears reflection that one of the first institutions to be broken up was the ECK, even before Kenya's second attempt at a new constitution in 2010. The ECK's successor, the Interim Independent Electoral Commission (IIEBC) that conducted the 2010 Constitutional Referendum, was replaced by the Independent Electoral and Boundaries Commission (IEBC) in 2011, whose tenure and independence are guaranteed by the constitution. The importance of credible institutions was evident in 2016, when the Commissioners of the IEBC, accused of complicity in the "*Chickengate*" surrounding the elections of 2013, were bundled out of office.

Other institutional arrangements were particularly lacking. For example, the independence of parliament and the ability to determine its calendar was lacking; indeed, the president still retained the power to convene, prologue and dissolve parliament.[24] This challenged the notion of the independence and co-equality of the branches of government. There existed no constitutional provisions on the management of the elections, in terms of dispute resolution, filing grievances or even fundamental issues such as reporting and certifying the results. There was no guidance on periods between the general election, the certification of the results and any contest of the results, before the victorious (especially presidential) candidate was sworn into office. For example, in Kenya's 2007 election, which took place on 27 December, on 28 December, after Raila's electoral lead grew and then began to shrink late in the afternoon, allegations started flying, results stopped coming in. "President Kibaki pulled ahead and after some confusion and controversy at the headquarters of the National Elections Commission (ECK), Kibaki was quickly declared the winner and was sworn in approximately 45 minutes later."[25]

Further clouding the transparency and concept of "process" was the fact that

> [o]nly KBC could run the picture of S. Kivuitu[26] in the precincts of the Kenyatta International Conference Centre (KICC) and all the private television channels and radio stations could only retransmit the public station's signals and the ECK announcement.[27]

This gave the impression of a "staged" event, yet it appeared to indicate legitimacy since the president was announced as the winner and duly sworn in, at the State House grounds, with media (pictures and videos) made available. In contrast to the events in Kenya, it is well established in the case of the US that the elections for federal officers are held "the Tuesday next after the first Monday in the month of November"[28] while the inauguration is held on the 20 January each year. Such established institutional protocols were especially necessary but lacking in the case of Kenya.

The elections and the aftermath

Much has been written about the 2007 elections, and the aftermath. Since the goal of this volume is to demonstrate the socio-cultural, ethnic and sometimes economic (based on ethno-cultural) factors that help explain the history and contemporary conditions in Kenya that make elections almost necessarily a violent affair, the analysis of the elections and the post-election violence will only be contemplated in the context of the socio-cultural and ethnic dimensions that it produced. Nevertheless, it is useful to briefly highlight some of the issues around the elections, including the conditions that precipitated the ethnic violence; some of these have been discussed in the previous section.

Some brief backtracking here: in the 2007 Kenya general elections, nine candidates contested the presidency, and the turnout was 69 percent. Although the figures are contested, according to Semetko, incumbent president Mwai Kibaki (PNU) garnered 46.4 percent of the vote, Raila Odinga (ODM) 44.1 percent and Kalonzo Musyoka of ODM-Kenya 8.9 percent while other candidates garnered less than 1 percent.[29] Other scholars[30] argue that the there was widespread rigging and ECK had been compromised, an assertion supported by Maxon and Ofcansky.[31] The confusion surrounding the results was so significant, however, that the chairman of ECK was quoted as saying, "I don't know whether Kibaki won the election."[32] As often happens in many African countries and their elections, Raila declared himself the duly elected president of Kenya. Robbins moderates the language, writing that "while the opposition leader Raila Odinga claimed victory, the incumbent President Mwai Kibaki was declared the winner and sworn in on December 30, despite serious lingering questions about the election results."[33] It is important to note that the election process and the conduct of the elections are by themselves not widely questioned; what appeared to be problematic was the vote tallying.[34] By then, the conflict was ready to rage.[35]

Mayhem comes to town: who really won, and what caused the violence?

The subsequent mayhem followed predictable paths; predictable, in a sense, since it appeared to follow the voting patterns and the voting patterns were closely affiliated with ethnic communities. The voting in the 2007 elections followed decidedly ethnic lines, with significant guidance and direction from the presidential candidates. Maxon and Ofcansky, for example, write that "the published figures revealed a start ethnic pattern of voting: 95 percent of the rural Kikuyu, Embu and Meru supported Kibaki, while 99 percent of the Luo voted for Odinga, as did almost 85 percent of the Kalenjin (following Ruto's lead)."[36] Given Posner's finding that multi-party politics shifted the kind of ethnic identity and found a vehicle through which to propagate politics through ethnically oriented parties.

Indeed, it is useful to note Mutua's assertion that the "reality on the ground is that most African political parties are not communities of political ideology or philosophy; rather they are vehicles for ethnic nativism."[37] Thus, even the communities that were fighting were not doing so based on ideology but, rather, to support of their "candidate". The weaknesses of the parties according to Mwangi have been historical, perhaps because there was no opportunity for the parties to develop and have concrete ideologies. Mwangi argues that

> since independence, political parties in Kenya have been institutionally weak, thus rendering them functionally ineffective as democratic and democracy-promoting institutions in the political process. This has been primarily a function of poor doctrine, poor leadership, lack of effective programmes, lack of human and financial resources, and weak societal linkage.[38]

What Mwangi might have added is that other than KADU and KPU (for about three years), there has been but one legally sanctioned party in those 30 years. When the multi-party era returned, individuals who had risen to national prominence over the previous 30 years between independence and multi-party era became the embodiment of politics. Subsequently, they were able to hijack the party process to drive an ethnic agenda.

Interestingly, though, even in Kenya's pre-election season in 2007, polls showed that citizens were more likely to assess a candidate for the presidency based on "performance record", although "each of the main parties attracts a rather distinct ethnic profile in terms of support."[39] Voting, however, followed different patterns. One of the contentious points of departure between Raila and Uhuru concerns the exit polls, which generally showed Raila leading Kibaki. As such, any reversal, absent independent institutions such as a non-partisan electoral commission was nearly impossible to enforce. It may be the case though, that the respondents determined to appear non-ethnically inclined; self-reporting can be quite a constraint on finding out who an individual planned to vote for.[40] Roberts's account shows the three main ethnic groups involved in the 2007/8 post-election violence: these were the Kikuyus, Luos and Kalenjins and, although the Luhya voted overwhelmingly, as seen previously, with ODM for Raila Odinga, were not involved in the fighting.[41]

The post-election violence was both national in scope and localized in its execution, and the different perpetrators enjoyed support from diverse sources. Although the national dimension of the violence stemmed from the general election outcomes, the violence was localized. The violence exploited a range of grievances: from the electoral outcomes to the perception that the Kikuyus were monopolizing and had traditionally benefitted most from the "national cake" to historic land grievances to incitement by politicians and opportunists seeking to occupy land abandoned by the fleeing members of different ethnic groups; the catalysts were many and varied. The subsequent violence turned ordinary citizens, former peaceful neighbors and shadowy ethno-nationalist groups, aspects of government agencies, well-heeled elites and shadowy groups against each other in Kenya's worst ethnic bloodletting.

Shadowy groups

One of the least appreciated manifestations of Kenya's persistent ethnic conflict stems from the role of sub-national, ethnically-oriented armed groups that have existed in Kenya, which have often been proscribed but continued to enjoy patronage from different politicians. These groups have in the past included, for example, Mũngiki (Nairobi and Central Kenya), Chinkororo and Amachuma (Kisii and Nyanza), Baghdad Boys (Kisumu), Taliban (Kibera and Mathare slums, Nairobi), the Republican Force (Mombasa) and others not specifically affiliated with ethnic groups, including Jeshi la Mzee, Jeshi la King'ola, Jeshi la Mama and Kosovo Boys.[42] Other similar groups included, for example, the Sabaot Land Defence Forces, which had been active 15 years before the 2007 elections.

These shadowy groups have often leveraged underemployed youths who are often paid or otherwise incited in the entire spectrum of violence: from heckling political opponents to perpetrating violence against political opponents and their campaigns and, at the extreme, violence against "outsider communities". The primary reason for their existence, according to Katumanga, was the sheer need to survive.[43] In some instances, groups sought to legitimize themselves, by organizing themselves as business concerns. Firestone writes that "in the poorest slums of Nairobi, they provide jobs and hope in an otherwise bleak economic landscape. They also advocate a return to traditional beliefs and practices."[44] In most other cases, they were simply vigilante groups. Most scholarship identifies Mungiki as one of the largest of the vigilante groups. Firestone writes, "Established in 1995 by Maina Njenga, the Mũngiki [*mũingi, ki*][45] (literally 'multitude') refer to themselves as *thuna cia Mau Mau* (Mau Mau offshoot). . . . The fundamental principles of Mũngiki are cultural self-determination, self-pride and self-reliance."[46] Gecaga, on the other hand, shows Mũngiki to have more pan-Africanist and global outlooks: "the general objective of Mũngiki, as already indicated, is to restore dignity to black people."[47]

The post-election violence was not the first time that the vigilante groups locked horns: "in March 2002, after the confrontations that pitted two militia groups (the Kikuyu Mũngiki movement and the Luo Taliban) in Nairobi, all vigilant (sic) groups were banned by the Kibaki administration."[48] Their asking price was rather meager:

> [T]hese groups could be hired by politicians for around Kshs. 250 (US$4) to unleash violence on their opponents. Jeshi la Mzee was used to beat up civil society activists such as the Reverend Timothy Njoya, whilst Jeshi la Embakasi was deployed in land disputes in Nairobi.[49]

Between 2003 and 2005, the government undertook a crackdown especially on Mũngiki, leading to a number of disappearances, mass killings, extra-judicial killings of Mũngiki members, imprisonment of some of its adherents and even the conversion to Christianity of its "founder", Maina Njenga. Yet, even as it was under serious assault by the government, the group's activities continued underground.

The dangers posed by such groups were often underestimated by the state, but as Mueller notes, some of these groups in

> Murang'a, Meru, and the slums of Nairobi have become virtual shadow states. Increasingly, the state has lost or abrogated its monopoly on legitimate force and finds it difficult to maintain peace or order . . . politicians, having used gangs to gain or maintain power, now are themselves beholden to them or afraid of them.[50]

The state did, even before the groups turned on the general citizenry of the opposing political side, attempt to completely eradicate them: "before the 2007 election, government security forces killed a total of 500 members of Mũngiki around Nairobi as well as an estimate of 600 persons died during election campaigning."[51]

Initially, the post-election violence manifested itself, according to Nichols, as "violent protests in the streets within minutes of the elections results being announced",[52] but these quickly degenerated:

> mobs in Nairobi, Kisumu, Eldoret and Mombasa targeted the Kikuyu ethnic group because they were perceived to be loyal to Kibaki. In less than 24 hours, hundreds of persons from these areas had been killed. Property belonging to Kikuyu persons was burned, looted and vandalised and thousands of people forced to flee their homes.[53]

Dutton concurs, noting that some of the violence was spontaneous, while other aspects of the violence were "orchestrated by Odinga supporters against the ethnic groups that supported Kibaki."[54] The Kenyan police were also accused of contributing to the violence. It is still notable that the violence was initially directed at one ethnic group, despite the fact that other groups had also voted for Kibaki.

Next came the "organized phase", into which mix the police force was thrown. "Opportunistic elites used the election controversy to mobilise their own ethnic groups into violence against rival ethnic groups. Politicians, businessmen, religious leaders and tribal elders held meetings in town halls to organise the attacks, promising cash payments to those who participated in the violence."[55] The initial phase of this violence saw "thousands of Kalenjin youths brandishing machetes, bows, and poisonous arrows",[56] in a repeat of previous occurrences of ethnic violence, attack non-Kalenjin ethnic groups. This phase saw some of the worst attacks: the torching and massacre of 35 mostly Kikuyu women and children at the Kenya Assemblies of God Church in Kiambaa, outside Eldoret town on 1 January 2008.[57] The retaliations were swift and severe and leveraged the police forces and the hitherto proscribed groups, such as Mũngiki. For example, Nichols writes that

> from 24 to 28 January 2008, members of the Kikuyu ethnic group attacked the Rift Valley towns of Nakuru and Naivasha, targeting persons of the Kalenjin

> and Luo ethnicity. In one arson attack in Naivasha, 19 members of the Luo community were killed when they were trapped inside their burning homes.[58]

Even as the violence raged, some groups that "traditionally" have had grievances seemed to stay out of the violence: "Whilst Maasais maintained a neutral position, Kikuyus in Naivasha – in reaction to evictions of and violence against members of the Kikuyu community in western Kenya – retaliated against people perceived as not belonging to 'their' place."[59]

International Actions, Intervention and the Return of Reason in Resolving Kenya's PEV: *nusu mkate* government

Kenya benefitted from a number of interrelated factors, factors that at first glance may appear to be internally negative. First, although the country has experienced instances of ethnic violence, the violence has been mostly localized and has never risen to the level of a civil war, as has happened in many other African countries. Part of this, however, is due to the fact that different communities have settled in all parts of the country, and as such, any violence between any two (or more groups) was likely to affect them and their economic concerns. Second, because of the large number of ethnic groups in Kenya, it was often difficult to take sides. For example, the Maasai, who have traditionally claimed communal, pre-colonial ownership of the land located around Naivasha – and indeed, the whole of Nyandarua district, with places named Kinangop, Ol Kalou and such – largely stayed out of the conflict, even though in the elections, the Maasai-supported Raila Odinga and have traditionally been part of the KAMATUSA (Kalenjin, Maasai, Turkana, Samburu) alliance. Thus, other groups may have seen minimal benefit in the conflict and began applying pressure on the two leaders to come to an accommodation.

The stability Kenya has enjoyed since independence has produced not only an elite, wealthy class but also a significant, well-heeled middle class, comprising, for example, of Indians. These groups have traditionally bankrolled economic growth, employment and the generally successful Kenyan economy that grew at 7 percent between 2003 and 2007. Losing their economic power was untenable, and this class was able to apply pressure for an accommodation. Additionally, the strategic importance of Kenya, the need for the country to not fail, or produce another Rwanda, was imperative. Kenya houses the United Nations Office in Nairobi and, as such, was especially important strategically given the purposes of the United Nations. Furthermore, the importance of Kenya to the US war against terrorism cannot be gainsaid; as such, both the British and American governments saw the importance of compelling the two principals to compromise and applied as much pressure as was necessary, including threatening travel sanctions against the leaders and their associates.

Kenya also had the benefit of the lessons of ethnic conflict elsewhere: from the neighboring Somalia, a failed state since 1991 that produced the biggest refugee camps housed on Kenya's own territory, to the conflicts in Uganda, Sudan and farther away, in Rwanda, Congo and Burundi. Thus, the likelihood that the conflict was going to escalate, while always present, provided better odds for resolution. In retrospect, the speed with which the country and the two principals (Raila Odinga and Mwai Kibaki) reached an accommodation under the Government of National Unity (GNU) was remarkable. Unfortunately, while the immediate issues surrounding the latest flare-up of the conflict – that is, the electoral outcomes were addressed, the most significant issues remained unaddressed, including the historic grievances surrounding community land ownership claims.

Thus, although the environment surrounding elections often provides a pretext for the initiation of ethnic clashes (a discussion in the next chapter points to this), Kenya has continued to experience inter-ethnic violence that has more to do with the allocation of resources and that manifests itself as a replay (and sometimes extension) of pre-colonial conflicts that included communities raiding each other. For example, Jenkins notes that "already, in 2012 and early 2013, inter-communal clashes in parts of Kenya have claimed more than 477 lives. Another 118,000 people have been displaced."[60]

The ethnic dimension

The general election of 2002 showed a different side of Kenya: an ability of both the electorate and the candidates to overwhelmingly shun the ethnic orientation of politics, notwithstanding Posner's assertion regarding multi-party politics in ethnically divided societies. The country came together to accomplish a national goal that was larger than the ethnic angle. Perhaps the entire nation had decided to accept Kenya's sixth vice president's famous quote on sacrifice in 2002, when he stated that "there comes a time when the interests of the nation are more important than those of an individual."[61] No significant instances of ethnic violence occurred before or after the general election; in the multi-party era's five elections, this was one of the two that were pacific.

Yet, the next two cycles of events in which citizens expressed their preferences at the ballot box showed that the ghosts of ethnic conflict were not quite buried. In 2005, the constitutional review referendum rekindled the ethnic undercurrents of violence that had been so prevalent in 1992 and 1999. 2005 avoided open conflict between the different groups, but 2007 manifested the violence in ways that attracted international attention and intervention under the Responsibility to Protect doctrine. The conflicting sides in this case were the Luo versus Kikuyu but with the former having support from the Kalenjin community.

The huge loss of life (more than 1,100 reported deaths), internal displacement of between 650,000 and 1.5 million people, the international actions to stop the violence, and the subsequent investigation and prosecution of individuals bearing the greatest responsibility for the post-election violence left its mark: the next two instances of expression of voters' preferences (through the 2010 constitutional referendum and the 2013 elections) mimicked the previous pre-multi-party election season: a return to peaceful elections. It is helpful that there were institutional mechanisms in place for all the presidential candidates to pursue; indeed, Raila Odinga pursued the case that he was the next president of Kenya all the way to the Supreme Court in 2013, before the eventual inauguration of President Uhuru Kenyatta.

Political parties, though, have perfected the process of leveraging ethnicity and presenting it as an avenue for grievances; for example, given the 1992 clashes and the concept of the need to get rid of foreigners, it was easy to see the Kikuyus as "outsiders", and since Mwai Kibaki led the Democratic Party and Kenneth Matiba the FORD-Asili in the 1990s, it was quite easy to associate the opposition with Kikuyus. Thus, despite temporary alliances, there appears to be no permanent interests amongst the electors in ways that ensure that ideology is more important than the constantly shifting between the different groups.

Notes

1 David Fickling & Agencies. "Kenyans Say No to New Constitution." *The Guardian*. Tuesday 22 November 2005. (Web).
2 Bard Anders Andreassen & Arne Tostensen. "Of Oranges and Bananas: The 2005 Kenya Referendum on the Constitution." CMI Working Paper 2006: 13. (Bergen, Norway, 2005): 6.
3 Some scholars, for example, Okoth and Ndaloh, also add Semites; peoples of Arabic, Amharic, Tigrinya and Hebrew extraction, some found in the coastal cities of East Africa; see Assa Okoth & Agumba Ndaloh. *Social Studies: PTE Revision Series for Primary Teacher Education*. (Nairobi, Kenya: East African Educational Publishers, 2008): 114.
4 Elizabeth Isichei. *A History of African Societies to 1870*. Cambridge University Press, 121.
5 Paul A. Ogula. "Inter-Ethnic and Intra-Ethnic Interactions in Western Kenya up to 2000." In William Robert Ochieng, Ed. *Historical Studies and Social Change in Western Kenya: Essays in Memory of Professor Gideon S. Were*. (Nairobi, Kenya: East African Educational Publishers, 2002): 263. Okoth and Ndaloh add the Samburu and Njemps to the Plain(s) Nilotes group.
6 Ogula. "Inter-Ethnic and Intra-Ethnic Interactions in Western Kenya up to 2000." 263.
7 Isichei. *A History of African Societies to 1870*. 126–127.
8 Okoth and Ndaloh. *Social Studies*. 113.
9 Ehret. "Between the Coast and the Great Lakes." 481.
10 Okoth and Ndaloh. *Social Studies*. 113.
11 Erhard M. Winkler & Robert R. Sokal. "A Phenetic Classification of Kenyan Tribes and Subtribes." *Human Biology*, 59, No. 1 (February 1987): 12.
12 Karega-Munene. "Production of Ethnic Identity in Kenya." In Kimani Njogu, Kabiri Ngeta & Mary Wanjau, Eds. *Ethnic Diversity in Eastern Africa: Opportunities and Challenges*. (Nairobi, Kenya: Twaweza Communications, 2010): 42.
13 Cohen, John M. "Foreign Aid and Ethnic Interests in Kenya." In Milton J. Esman & Ronald J. Herring, Eds. *Carrots, Sticks, and Ethnic Conflict: Rethinking Development Assistance*. (Ann Arbor, MI: The University of Michigan Press, 2003): 91.
14 Karega-Munene. "Production of Ethnic Identity in Kenya." 42.
15 Koki Muli. "Reflections about the Events at Kenyatta International Conference Centre (KICC) on 27th–31st December 2007." In Kimani Njogu, Ed. *Defining Moments: Reflections on Citizenship, Violence, and the 2007 General Elections in Kenya*. (Nairobi, Kenya: Twaweza Communications, 2011): 14.
16 Michael M. Kithinji, Mickie M. Koster & Jerono P. Rotich. "Introduction." In Michael M. Kithinji, Mickie M. Koster & Jerono P. Rotich, Eds. *Kenya after 50: Reconfiguring*

Historical, Political, and Policy Milestones. (New York, NY: Palgrave Macmillan, 2016): 10.

17 Kithinji, Koster & Rotich. "Introduction." 10.

18 Muli. "Reflections about the Events at Kenyatta International Conference Centre (KICC) on 27th–31st December 2007." 16–17.

19 Keith Somerville. *Hatred: Historical Development and Definitions*. (New York, NY: Palgrave Macmillan, 2012). (eBook): n.p.

20 Sommerville. *Hatred*. n.p.

21 Gabrielle Lynch & David M. Anderson. "Democratization and Ethnic Violence in Kenya: Electoral Cycles and Shifting Identities." In Jacques Bertrand & Oded Haklai, Eds. *Democratization and Ethnic Minorities: Conflict or Compromise?* (New York, NY: Routledge, 2014): 84.

22 Daniel N. Posner. "Regime Change and Ethnic Cleavages in Africa." *Comparative Political Studies*, 40, No. 11 (September 2007): 1302.

23 Posner. "Regime Change and Ethnic Cleavages in Africa." 1302.

24 See, for example, Oscar G. Mwangi. "Political Corruption, Party Financing and Democracy in Kenya." *The Journal of Modern African Studies*, 46, No. 2 (June, 2008): 268.

25 Meredith Preston-McGhie & Serena Sharma. "Kenya." In Jared Genser & Irwin Cotler, Eds. *The Responsibility to Protect: The Promise of Stopping Mass Atrocities in Our Time*. (New York, NY: Oxford University Press, 2012): 1926.

26 The chairman of the Electoral Commission of Kenya.

27 Brice Rambaud. "Caught between Information and Condemnation: The Kenyan Media in the Electoral Campaigns of December 2007." In Jérôme Lafargue, Ed. *The General Elections in Kenya, 2007*. (Dar es Salaam, Tanzania: Mkuki na Nyota Publishers, 2009): 94.

28 The Library of Congress. "Statutes at Large, 1789–1875: Volumes 1 to 18." (Web). Accessed on 12/3/2016, from: https://memory.loc.gov/ammem/amlaw/lwsllink.html

29 Holli A. Semetko. "Election Campaigns, Partisan Balance, and the News Media." In Pippa Norris, Ed. *Public Sentinel: News Media and Governance Reform*. (Washington, DC: The World Bank, 2010): 167.

30 Kimani Njogu. "A Prologue to Ethnic Diversity in Eastern Africa." In Kimani Njogu, Kabiri Ngeta & Mary Wanjau, Eds. *Ethnic Diversity in Eastern Africa: Opportunities and Challenges*. (Nairobi, Kenya: Twaweza Communications, 2009): vii–xvii.

31 Robert Maxon & Thomas P. Ofcansky. *Historical Dictionary of Kenya*. (Lanham, MD: Rowman & Littlefield, 2014): 118.

32 Mara J. Roberts. "Conflict Analysis of the 2007 Post-Election Violence in Kenya." In Akanmu Gafari Adebayo, Ed. *Managing Conflicts in Africa's Democratic Transitions*. (Lanham, MD: Lexington Books, 2012): 141.

33 Jeffrey Robbins. *Radical Democracy and Political Theology*. (New York, NY: Columbia University Press, 2011): 55.

34 Nichols notes that "initial results over the first three days of counting suggested an Odinga victory, but on 30 December 2007, the Electoral Commission of Kenya ('ECK') declared that Kibaki had prevailed by just over 200,000 votes. . . . Some members of the ECK admitted that there were serious problems with the vote tallying and its chairman later claimed to have been subjected to intense pressure from ruling political elites" (Lionel Nichols. *The International Criminal Court and the End of Impunity in Kenya*. (New York, NY: Springer, 2015): 49).

35 In 2016, Uganda's opposition candidate, Kiiza Besigye, after a fraudulent election, attempted to illustrate the difficulty of winning rigged elections and was promptly arrested for suggesting that he was the duly elected president. According to the United States Institute of Peace (USIP), "Besigye escaped house arrest on May 11 to be "sworn in" as president by Forum for Democratic Change (FDC) colleagues during a mock inauguration ceremony, and shortly thereafter was arrested and charged with treason." Elizabeth Murray, Berouk Mesfin & Stephanie Wolters. "Weak Ugandan Democracy,

Strong Regional Influence." United States Institute of Peace & Institute for Security Studies. *Peaceworks*, No. 120 (September, 2016): 11.
36 Maxon & Ofcansky. *Historical Dictionary of Kenya*. 119.
37 Makau Mutua. *Kenya's Quest for Democracy: Taming Leviathan*. (Boulder, CO: Lynn Rienner, 2008): 22.
38 Oscar Gakuo Mwangi. "Political Corruption, Party Financing and Democracy in Kenya." *The Journal of Modern African Studies*, 46, No. 2 (June, 2008): 269.
39 Gabrielle Lynch. *I Say to You: Ethnic Politics and the Kalenjin in Kenya*. (Chicago, IL: The University of Chicago Press, 2011): n.p.
40 See, for example, Feldman (2003) and Houghton (2015).
41 Roberts. "Conflict Analysis of the 2007 Post-Election Violence in Kenya." 147.
42 Musambayi Katumanga. "Kenya: Imagined Closed Spaces of the Political Economy of Violence." In Mbugua wa Mungai & G. M. Gona, Eds. *(Re)membering Kenya: Identity, Culture and Freedom*. (Nairobi, Kenya: Twaweza Communications, 2010): 140 and Margaret Gathoni Gecaga. "Religious Movements and Democratisation in Kenya: Between the Sacred and the Profane." In Godwin R. Murunga & Shadrack W. Nasong'o. *Kenya: The Struggle for Democracy*. (New York, NY: Zed Books, 2007): 80.
43 Musambayi Katumanga. "A City under Siege: Banditry & Modes of Accumulation in Nairobi, 1991–2004." In Rita Abrahamsen, Ed. *Conflict and Security in Africa*. (Rochester, NY: James Currey, 2013): 187.
44 Matthew Firestone, Stuart Butler, Paula Hardy & Adam Karlin. *Kenya: Lonely Planet*, (Melbourne, Australia: Lonely Planet, 2016, eBook): 32; see also Gecaga. "Religious Movements and Democratisation in Kenya." 80.
45 My explanation, square brackets.
46 Firestone, Butler, Hardy & Karlin. *Kenya*. 32.
47 See, for example, Gecaga, "Religious Movements and Democratisation in Kenya." 75; although this view can be disputed if, as argued elsewhere, Mũngiki's purpose is specifically the empowerment of the Kikuyu people and the promotion of the Kikuyu cultural traditions in ways that exclude other black people.
48 Lafargue. *The General Elections in Kenya, 2007*. 44.
49 Katumanga. "A City under Siege." 187.
50 Susanne D. Mueller. "Dying to Win: Elections, Political Violence, and Institutional Decay in Kenya." In David Gillies, Ed. *Elections in Dangerous Places: Democracy and the Paradoxes of Peacebuilding*. (Montreal, CA: North-South Institute, 2011): 115.
51 Sultan Juma Kakuba. "Political Violence in Plural Democracies: A Comparative Study of Uganda and Kenya." In Şefika Şule Erçetin, Ed. *Chaos, Complexity and Leadership 2014*. (Heidelberg, Switzerland: Springer International Publishing AG Switzerland, 2016): 122.
52 Nichols. *The International Criminal Court and the End of Impunity in Kenya*. 49.
53 Nichols. *The International Criminal Court and the End of Impunity in Kenya*. 49.
54 Dutton. *Rules, Politics, and the International Criminal Court*. 146.
55 Nichols. *The International Criminal Court and the End of Impunity in Kenya*. 49–50.
56 Nichols. *The International Criminal Court and the End of Impunity in Kenya*. 50.
57 See Tim Cocks. "Mutilated Bodies Found a Week after Kenya Massacre." *Reuters World News*. Tuesday 8 January 2008; Xan Rice. "One Year after Massacre, the Dead Lie Unburied in Village without Roofs." *The Guardian*. Friday 26 December 2008 and Robyn Dixon, "Kenyans Recall the Screams of the Dying in Burning Church." *LA Times*. 3 January 2008.
58 Nichols. *The International Criminal Court and the End of Impunity in Kenya*. 50.
59 Britta Lang & Patrick Sakdapolrak. "Belonging and Recognition after the Post-Election Violence: A Case Study on Labour Migrants in Naivasha, Kenya." *Erdkunde*, 68, No. 3 (July–September, 2014): 189.
60 Sarah Jenkins. "Kenya: Kenya's Legacy of Violent Ethnic Politics and the 2007–2008 Postelection Crisis." In Joseph R. Rudolph, Jr., Ed. *Encyclopedia of Modern Ethnic Conflicts*, 2nd Ed. [2 volumes]. (Santa Barbara, CA: ABC-CLIO): 320.

61 Joe Khamisi. *The Politics of Betrayal: Diary of a Kenyan Legislator*. (Bloomington, IN: Trafford Publishing, 2011): 17.

References

Andreassen, Bard Anders & Arne Tostensen. "Of Oranges and Bananas: The 2005 Kenya Referendum on the Constitution." CMI Working Paper 2006: 13. Bergen, Norway, 2005): 6. Accessed on 11/28/2016 from: www.cmi.no/publications/file/2368-of-oranges-and-bananas.pdf

Cocks, Tim. "Mutilated Bodies Found a Week after Kenya Massacre." *Reuters World News*. Tuesday 8 January 2008. Accessed on 12/3/2016 from: www.reuters.com/article/us-kenya-violence-church-idUSL0847034820080108

Cohen, John M. "Foreign Aid and Ethnic Interests in Kenya." In Milton J. Esman & Ronald J. Herring, Eds. *Carrots, Sticks, and Ethnic Conflict: Rethinking Development Assistance*. Ann Arbor, MI: The University of Michigan Press, 2003.

Dickinson, Torry D. & Robert K. Schaeffer. *Transformations: Feminist Pathways to Global Change*. New York, NY: Routledge, 2016.

Dixon, Robyn. "Kenyans Recall the Screams of the Dying in Burning Church." *LA Times*. 3 January 2008. Accessed on 12/3/2016 from: http://articles.latimes.com/2008/jan/03/world/fg-church3

Dutton, Yvonne. *Rules, Politics, and the International Criminal Court: Committing to the Court*. New York, NY: Routledge, 2013.

Ehret, Christopher. "Between the Coast and the Great Lakes." In Djibril Tamsir Niane, Ed. *General History of Africa, IV: Africa from the Twelfth to the Sixteenth Century*. Paris, France: UNESCO, 1984. Ch. 19, pp. 481–497.

Feldman, Jan Lynn. *Lubavitchers as Citizens: A Paradox of Liberal Democracy*. Ithaca, NY: Cornell University Press, 2003.

Fickling, David & Agencies. "Kenyans Say No to New Constitution." *The Guardian*. Tuesday 22 November 2005. (Web). Accessed on 11/28/2016 from: www.theguardian.com/world/2005/nov/22/kenya.davidfickling

Firestone, Matthew, Stuart Butler, Paula Hardy & Adam Karlin. *Kenya: Lonely Planet*, Melborne, Australia: Loney Planet, 2016 (eBook).

Gecaga, Margaret Gathoni. "Religious Movements and Democratisation in Kenya: Between the Sacred and the Profane." In Godwin R. Murunga & Shadrack W. Nasong'o. *Kenya: The Struggle for Democracy*. New York, NY: Zed Books, 2007.

Houghton, David Patrick. *Political Psychology: Situations, Individuals, and Cases*. New York, NY, Routledge, 2015.

IEBC. "The Independent Electoral Boundaries Commission." (Web). Accessed on 12/3/2016 from: www.iebc.or.ke/

Isichei, Elizabeth. *A History of African Societies to 1870*. New York, NY: Cambridge University Press, 1997.

Jenkins, Sarah. "Kenya: Kenya's Legacy of Violent Ethnic Politics and the 2007–2008 Postelection Crisis." In Joseph R. Rudolph, Jr., Ed. *Encyclopedia of Modern Ethnic Conflicts*, 2nd Ed. [2 volumes]. Santa Barbara, CA: ABC-CLIO, 2015.

Kakuba, Sultan Juma. "Political Violence in Plural Democracies: A Comparative Study of Uganda and Kenya." In Şefika Şule Erçetin, Ed. *Chaos, Complexity and Leadership 2014*. Heidelberg, Switzerland: Springer International Publishing AG Switzerland, 2016. Ch. 12, pp. 119–130.

Karega-Munene. "Production of Ethnic Identity in Kenya." In Kimani Njogu, Kabiri Ngeta & Mary Wanjau, Eds. *Ethnic Diversity in Eastern Africa: Opportunities and Challenges*. Nairobi, Kenya: Twaweza Communications, 2010.

Katumanga, Musambayi. "A City under Siege: Banditry & Modes of Accumulation in Nairobi, 1991–2004." In Rita Abrahamsen, Ed. *Conflict and Security in Africa*. Rochester, NY: James Currey, 2013. Ch. 12, pp. 179–194.

Katumanga, Musambayi. "Kenya: Imagined Closed Spaces of the Political Economy of Violence." In Mbugua wa Mungai & George M. Gona, Eds. *(Re)membering Kenya: Identity, Culture and Freedom*. Nairobi, Kenya: Twaweza Communications, 2010.

Khamisi, Joe. *The Politics of Betrayal: Diary of a Kenyan Legislator*. Bloomington, IN: Trafford Publishing, 2011.

Kithinji, Michael Mwenda, Mickie M. Koster & Jerono P. Rotich. "Introduction." In Michael Mwenda Kithinji, Mickie Mwanzia Koster & Jerono P. Rotich, Eds. *Kenya after 50: Reconfiguring Historical, Political, and Policy Milestones*. New York, NY: Palgrave Macmillan, 2016.

Lang, Britta & Patrick Sakdapolrak. "Belonging and Recognition after the Post-Election Violence: A Case Study on Labour Migrants in Naivasha, Kenya." *Erdkunde*, 68, No. 3 (July–September 2014): 185–196. Accessed on 12/3/2016 from: www.jstor.org/stable/24365231

The Library of Congress. "Statutes at Large, 1789–1875: Volumes 1 to 18." (Web). Accessed on 12/3/2016 from: https://memory.loc.gov/ammem/amlaw/lwsllink.html

Lynch, Gabrielle. "Courting the Kalenjin: The Failure of Dynasticism and the Strength of the ODM Wave in Kenya's Rift Valley Province." *African Affairs*, 107, No. 429 (October 2008): 541–568. Accessed on 12/3/2016 from: www.jstor.org/stable/27667069

Lynch, Gabrielle. *I Say to You: Ethnic Politics and the Kalenjin in Kenya*. Chicago, IL: The University of Chicago Press, 2011.

Lynch, Gabrielle & David M. Anderson. "Democratization and Ethnic Violence in Kenya: Electoral Cycles and Shifting Identities." In Jacques Bertrand & Oded Haklai, Eds. *Democratization and Ethnic Minorities: Conflict or Compromise?* New York, NY: Routledge, 2014. Ch. 5, pp. 83–102.

Mueller, Susanne D. "Dying to Win: Elections, Political Violence, and Institutional Decay in Kenya." In David Gillies, Ed. *Elections in Dangerous Places: Democracy and the Paradoxes of Peacebuilding*. Montreal, CA: North-South Institute, 2011. Ch. 7, pp. 105–126.

Muli, Koki. "Reflections about the Events at Kenyatta International Conference Centre (KICC) on 27th–31st December 2007." In Kimani Njogu, Ed. *Defining Moments: Reflections on Citizenship, Violence, and the 2007 General Elections in Kenya*. Nairobi: Twaweza Communications, 2011.

Murray, Elizabeth, Berouk Mesfin & Stephanie Wolters. "Weak Ugandan Democracy, Strong Regional Influence: United States Institute of Peace & Institute for Security Studies." *Peaceworks*, No. 120 (September, 2016). (Web). Accessed from: www.usip.org/sites/default/files/PW120-Weak-Ugandan-Democracy-Strong-Regional-Influence.pdf

Mutua, Makau. *Kenya's Quest for Democracy: Taming Leviathan*. Boulder, CO: Lynn Rienner Publishers, 2008.

Mwangi, Oscar Gakuo. "Political Corruption, Party Financing and Democracy in Kenya." *The Journal of Modern African Studies*, 46, No. 2 (June, 2008): 267–285. Accessed on 12/3/2016 04:28 UTC from: www.jstor.org/stable/30225924

Nichols, Lionel. *The International Criminal Court and the End of Impunity in Kenya*. New York, NY: Springer, 2015.

Njogu, Kimani. "A Prologue to Ethnic Diversity in Eastern Africa." In Kimani Njogu, Kabiri Ngeta & Mary Wanjau, Eds. *Ethnic Diversity in Eastern Africa: Opportunities and Challenges*. Nairobi, Kenya: Twaweza Communications, 2009.

Ogula, Paul A. "Inter-Ethnic and Intra-Ethnic Interactions in Western Kenya up to 2000." In William Robert Ochieng, Ed. *Historical Studies and Social Change in Western Kenya: Essays in Memory of Professor Gideon S. Were*. Nairobi, Kenya: East African Educational Publishers, 2002.

Okoth, Assa & Agumba Ndaloh. *Social Studies: PTE Revision Series for Primary Teacher Education*. Nairobi, Kenya: East African Educational Publishers, 2008.

Posner, Daniel N. "Regime Change and Ethnic Cleavages in Africa." *Comparative Political Studies*, 40, No. 11 (September, 2007): 1302–1327. Doi:10.1177/0010414006291832

Preston-McGhie, Meredith & Serena Sharma. "Kenya." In Jared Genser & Irwin Cotler, Eds. *The Responsibility to Protect: The Promise of Stopping Mass Atrocities in Our Time*. New York, NY: Oxford University Press, 2012. Ch. 13, pp. 279–297.

Rambaud, Brice. "Caught between Information and Condemnation: The Kenyan Media in the Electoral Campaigns of December 2007." In Jérôme Lafargue, Ed. *The General Elections in Kenya, 2007*. Dar es Salaam, Tanzania: Mkuki na Nyota Publishers, 2009.

Rice, Xan. "One Year after Massacre, the Dead Lie Unburied in Village without Roofs." *The Guardian*. Friday 26 December 2008. Accessed on 12/3/2016 from: www.theguardian.com/world/2008/dec/27/kiambaa-church-massacre-kenya-survivors

Robbins, Jeffrey. *Radical Democracy and Political Theology*. New York: Columbia University Press, 2011.

Roberts, Mara J. "Conflict Analysis of the 2007 Post-Election Violence in Kenya." In Akanmu Gafari Adebayo, Ed. *Managing Conflicts in Africa's Democratic Transitions*. Lanham, MD: Lexington Books, 2012.

Semetko, Holli A. "Election Campaigns, Partisan Balance, and the News Media." In Pippa Norris, Ed. *Public Sentinel: News Media and Governance Reform*. Washington, DC: World Bank, 2010. Ch. 7, pp. 163–192.

Somerville, Keith. *Hatred: Historical Development and Definitions*. New York, NY: Palgrave Macmillan, 2012. (eBook).

Winkler, Ehret M. & Robert Reuven Sokal. "A Phenetic Classification of Kenyan Tribes and Subtribes." *Human Biology*, 59, No. 1 (February, 1987): 121–145. Accessed on 11/29/2016 from: www.jstor.org/stable/41463855

6 Resolving Kenya's complex socio-historical contestations

Descent into chaos and a global SOS

As soon as the violence began, the international community began to express alarm and call for quick resolution, beginning with the United Nations Secretary-General, Ban Ki-moon, on the day after the commencement of the violence.[1] In quick succession, the Nobel laureate, South Africa's Archbishop Desmond Tutu; then US secretary of state for African affairs, Jendayi Frazer; and the Panel of Eminent Persons (former presidents Benjamin Mkapa [Tanzania], Joaquin Chissano [Mozambique], Ketumile Masire [Botswana] and Kenneth Kaunda [Zambia]) were joined by the then African Union (AU) chair John Kufuor (Ghana) for rather fruitless mediation talks.

By 10 January, Kofi Annan, the former UN secretary-general; Graca Machel; and Tanzania's Benjamin Mkapa, who were acceptable as negotiators to the Party of National Unity (PNU) and Orange Democratic Movement (ODM) sides, led the discussions that ultimately led to the agreement of 28 February 2008, establishing the Government of National Unity (GNU). The talks and negotiations were perhaps urged along by the promise (perhaps threat), such as that of Bernard Kouchner, the French foreign and European affairs minister's statement, which simultaneously appealed to the United Nations Security Council (UNSC) to invoke the Responsibility to Protect (R2P) protocols to quickly resolve the situation in Kenya.[2] Importantly, the agreement created three commissions: the Commission of Inquiry on Post-Election Violence (CIPEV); the Truth, Justice and Reconciliation Commission (TJRC); and the Independent Review Commission on the General Elections.[3]

GNUs are not new, or unique, to Kenya. Mukuhlani notes that they have been around in countries including Israel, Greece, Italy, United Kingdom, and Luxembourg[4] and in Nepal, Lebanon, Italy, Hungary, Croatia, Canada and Sri Lanka. There has been perhaps no speedier resolution of post-election violence anywhere than there was in Kenya. The post-election conflicts that occurred in Zimbabwe (2008–2009), producing a "marriage of convenience"[5] and Ivory Coast (28 November 2010–11 April 2011) took much longer, and, in the case of the latter, intervention by France, to compel the resolution of the crisis. Kenya's conflict began in, on or about 30 December and lasted through 28 February 2008, two months.

The National Accord and Reconciliation Act (also sometimes referred to as the Kenya National Dialogue and Reconciliation Accord of February 28, 2008)[6] that was assented to and commenced on 29 March set out the operative terms of GNU, the coalition government or, as Kenyans derisively called it, "*nusu mkate*" (half a loaf of bread). In this half-loaf arrangement, each of the sides involved in the post-election dispute (PNU and ODM) that led to the Post-Election Violence got "half" of government, including appointments to cabinet positions, parastatals and other publicly appointed positions but, most important, provided for the position of a prime minister with some executive power.[7] Rather remarkably, though, the cabinet that Mwai Kibaki named on 8 January 2008 filled only 17 positions, of a future 42 cabinet positions; as such, it was easy to fit in the ODM ministers appointed into the government.

In addition to securing peace for the time being, and incorporating a majority of the parties that had contested the 2007 elections, the new GNU set about completing the work that had remained outstanding, including the implementation of significant political reforms, beginning with the disbanding and reconstitution of the Electoral Commission of Kenya (ECK). The coalition government "did oversee the drafting and ratification of a new constitution in the face of divided public and political opinion."[8] The appointment of a prime minister further served to upend the balance of power; the constant question of who, between the prime minister and the vice president, ranked higher was the constant staple of the news and, to some extent, reflected ethnic persuasions.

On one hand, the vice president, Kalonzo Musyoka, had quickly joined government after Kibaki was declared president; on the other hand, the National Dialog and Reconciliation Act had the force of an international agreement, and the prime minister clearly appeared to favor the argument that the office was co-principal to that of the president. There were questions, for example, of the size of the motorcade, the sitting positions (and arrival sequence to major events); it appeared that these issues had not been addressed. The power-sharing agreement, unfortunately, also institutionalized ethnic division as a legitimate method of coming into government. The division of cabinet positions, appointments to parastatals and other commissions saw the officers of government appoint people from their ethnic groups to different positions in the civil service.

CIPEV: or the Waki Commission and the ICC process

The National Accord and Reconciliation Act included the constitution of CIPEV, which was led by Appeal Court Justice Philip Waki and was generally referred to as the Waki Commission. One of its recommendations was for the establishment of a Special Election Violence Tribunal,[9] with international participation[10] and both Kibaki's and Odinga's December 2008 agreement to implement the commission's recommendation was rejected by Parliament in February 2009. The commission's recommendations' implementation and the requirement to establish the local tribunal was expected to have occurred by March 2009, but "on July 30, the Kenyan Cabinet announced that it would not establish a special tribunal, but would instead convene a 'Truth, Justice and Reconciliation Commission' (TJRC)"[11] but without the mandate to prosecute the post-election violence crimes.

The Waki Commission's report was also submitted to the Kenya chief peace mediator, former UN secretary-general Kofi Annan, with "the envelope" containing names of individuals thought to have borne the greatest responsibility for either starting, promoting, organizing, coordinating or funding the post-election violence.[12] Importantly, the commission had a "trigger mechanism": if the proposed Special Election Violence Tribunal (or a similar mechanism) was not established in Kenya, the envelope was going to be handed over to the International Criminal Court (ICC), for investigation and eventual prosecution of those individuals. Kenya went through the motions of trying to establish a local mechanism, including debating whether or not a special division of the High Court of Kenya could be established to prosecute those accused of the crimes, but internal wrangling prevented that from happening.

There were concerted, significant efforts to frustrate, stall or altogether ensure that a tribunal would not be established, but the ICC kept abreast of the process, and in July 2009, the prosecutor met in the Netherlands with Kenyan government officials. The delegation "informed the special prosecutor that a special tribunal or other judicial mechanism should be adopted by the Kenyan parliament to investigate and prosecute those responsible for the 2008 violence",[13] yet this occurred more than six months after the expiry of the original deadline and the extension. Helpfully, according to Olásolo, Moreno-Ocampo suggested an ICC process, national proceedings to deal with other perpetrators (including prosecution in courts) and a TJRC.[14] On 9 July 2009, Kenya's delay and/or inability to constitute a domestic mechanism to address the post-election violence caused

> Kofi Annan – the mediator to the Kenyan conflict and the custodian of the Waki Commission evidence – to hand the envelope containing the names of the suspected masterminds of the PEV and the evidence collected by the Waki Commission to ICC Prosecutor Luis Moreno-Ocampo.[15]

At this point, there was still hope that the Kenyan parliament might still come through with a domestic process to prosecute the violence; however, it was increasingly clear that Kenya faced terrible options; it was now a question of the "least-worst option".

The delays were no redeeming quality for Kenya's lethargy, and the government inaction after the proposed constitutional amendment necessary to estabilish the tribunal was soundly defeated. "In November 2009 the ICC Prosecutor took the unprecedented step of investigating the violence in Kenya without a referral from a member state or the Security Council",[16] ultimately summoning six individuals to The Hague, after determining that they had cases to answer; they would later be referred to as "the Ocampo Six". A year and a half later, on 10th December 2010, the ICC prosecutor unveiled the six names of individuals who would face prosecution for allegedly bearing the greatest responsibility in the prosecution of the violence. They included William Samoei Ruto, Henry Kosgey and Joshua Sang (Case 1) and Uhuru Kenyatta, Francis Muthaura and Mohammed Ali",[17] with confirmation of the charges in the cases of William Ruto and Joshua Sang (Case 1) and Uhuru Kenyatta and Francis Muthaura (Case 2).[18] According to Höhn, "all six were charged with murder, forcible transfer and persecution. The government's suspects (Case 2) were additionally charged with rape and other inhuman acts."[19]

Understanding Kenya's non-referral: (in)justice for victims

The complexity of the ICC process and the case were evident to Kenya and the disparate ethnicities, but perhaps not so with both the ICC and international partners. Although the Waki Commission had established that "a total of 1,133 people were killed in the post-election violence, with most of these deaths concentrated in the Rift Valley, Nyanza and in Nairobi Province",[20] the overwhelming sentiment favored not just some punishment but also reconciliation. For those who had been displaced, the general preference was to be able to return to their property and some form of compensation. While prosecution might bring about some justice, it would not resolve the underlying issues and causes of violence. Thus, the preference was for the Truth, Justice and Reconciliation Commission fashioned after South Africa or Rwanda's format. From the perspective of an ethnically divided nation, it made sense that the parliament, and the government, made no significant effort to establish a local mechanism to prosecute the violence.

In retrospective analysis, it appears that Kenya's government officials pursued strategies that were consistent with their appreciation of the complex ethnic picture in the country. For starters, the government appeared to be approaching rapprochement, with GNU. Did it make strategic sense to reopen old wounds by appearing to send some members of different communities to ICC? How would that be interpreted by the communities to which the suspects belonged? If parliament passed a constitutional act mandating a tribunal or other mechanism, there was still a possibility for its interpretation along ethnic (read party) lines. As such, the "do nothing" strategy would force foreign entities (Kofi Annan, ICC or the Security Council) to compel some action, thus giving the government an "out" in that the prosecution could be attributed to "foreigners". Indeed, as the cases went to trial, this became the rallying cry: a neo-colonial bent, using the "Court for Africans" (i.e., ICC), to further persecute "our people" without regard to the organized violence that occurred.

The "do nothing" strategy also served as a catalyst for the unlikeliest of allies: by being bound to a very public trial in a far-off country, which in time became a trial against the president and the deputy president (who, ironically, had been on opposing sides of the post-election violence), the joint persecution led to that Churchillian maxim: "the enemy of my enemy is my friend". Thus, the government and parliament, by compelling Moreno-Ocampo to institute the cases, escaped any illusion of complicity in the prosecution. This was a positive outcome for inter-ethnic relations; the communities focused less on each other and more on ICC. Prayers were held, sometimes joint prayers by the Ocampo Six, thus uniting them in the face of the charges at ICC. The "healing" value of this team of rivals may be underestimated, but the "prayer rallies" that occurred almost every weekend turned the six not into villains but into victims.

The third outcome approximated "buyer's remorse": when it appeared that Kenyan authorities were either unwilling or unable to implement the recommendations of the Waki Commission, particularly to establish a Special Tribunal on Electoral Violence, the nation resigned itself to the possibility that The Hague (ICC) provided the only real possibility of impartial prosecution of those in Waki's infamous envelope. As the country waited for a year and a half while the ICC carried out its investigations, nearly every politician was on edge, and the rumor mill worked overtime. Questions of whether Kenya would, or should, cooperate with the ICC became a major issue, even as questions were raised whether or not Kenya would be better off attempting the Rwanda-like Gacaca[21] courts and focus on the reconciliation aspect of justice rather than the retributive aspect, since the neighbors would have to live with each other. As ICC prosecutes the individuals who "bear greatest responsibility" for the commission of crimes against humanity, questions lingered surrounding whether or not the two principals, Kibaki and Raila, whose supporters were fighting, were in some way complicit in the conditions that contributed to the post-election violence.

Institutional reforms, truth, justice and reconciliation: TJRC

It is reasonable to take the view that the agreement entered into between Raila Odinga and Mwai Kibaki on 28 February 2008, in many ways, intimated a requirement to do the difficult work of rebuilding the country and, therewith, establish several institutions and mechanisms, some of which would succeed, while the impact of others was not so significant. Although the proposed establishment of some judicial mechanism to prosecute violators identified by the Waki Commission did not happen, in other areas, significant changes were made, including the promulgation of a new constitution for the second republic,[22] a feat that had not quite succeeded in 2007. In 2008, the Political Parties Bill was passed; this guaranteed that political parties would be funded by the government, and funding would be allocated based on parties' legislative strength.[23] Other successful changes included the establishment of CIPEV – or the Waki Commission, the Independent Review Commission on the General Elections (also called the Kriegler Commission) as well as TJRC. While both deserve a look, TJRC was quite interesting, given what it aimed to do and, ultimately, did, or did not, do.

TJRC was seen in some quarters as an avenue through which the persistent historical injustices, going all the way back to independence. This would facilitate inclusion of events such as the 1984 Wagalla massacre, the numerous "forced disappearances" of individuals, the unresolved murders, such as those of Tom Mboya, Pio Gama Pinto, J. M. Kariuki, Robert Ouko, Father Kaiser, among others. It would also seek to uncover the causes of the land clashes of the early 1990s in the Rift Valley and Likoni later in the same decade. More importantly, it would investigate the sources and perpetrators of ethnic Post Election Violence conflict immediately after the 2007 General Election. According to Young,

> the mandate of the TJRC included a requirement that the commission 'inquire into and establish the reality or otherwise of perceived economic marginalisation of communities and make recommendations on how to address the marginalisation" and "the root causes of ethnic tensions and make recommendation on the promotion of healing, reconciliation and co-existence among ethnic communities."[24]

Ojielo concurs: "the TJRC would document historical and systemic factors underlying the inability of the state to deal with the previous cases of impunity and the role of state institutions in exacerbating or perpetuating violence."[25] Then, it was expected not only to propose a mechanism to remedy past issues but also to propose expectations for state officials' conduct as well as provide a template for a fairer, just society.

The question of who would head such a commission was first and foremost in the national deliberations: considering that many of the well-respected public officials had served in the oppressive Moi government, who among them was fit to cast the first stone? The task fell to Ambassador Bethuel Kiplagat, a seasoned diplomat, who had served as Kenya's special envoy to Somalia's peace process, ambassador to France, high commissioner to Britain and a permanent secretary in the Ministry of Foreign Affairs, in addition to many other government positions. Although TJRC convened in 2009, soon, it would be embroiled in major disagreements, particularly over its chairman's alleged role in the 1984 Wagalla Massacre; this did indeed make sense, given that these historical injustices fell under the purview of the TJRC's mandate.

The Wagalla Massacre, for purposes of clarification, was a 1984 incident in which

> security forces rounded up several thousand men from the Degodiya clan in a purported disarmament operation and forced them to remove their clothes and lie down on the Wagalla airstrip for up to five days in the sun, while beating and torturing them.[26]

It was further claimed in Parliament in 2001, that "their clothes (were) set ablaze. Their personal effects and valuables like watches and money were looted by these security forces."[27] Other accounts suggest that "the men were subject to security force brutality, which included being burned, beaten, and shot."[28] Estimates of the death toll vary, from 300[29] to 380[30] to 2,000,[31] and the episode earned the dubious distinction of being "the worst human rights violation in Kenya's history",[32] according to Ron Slye, a TJRC commissioner. In particular, the commission's leadership by Kiplagat was questioned, with allegations suggesting that he was dictatorial and partisan but especially that he was complicit in some of the atrocities he would be investigating, since he was the permanent secretary in the Ministry of Foreign Affairs and International Co-operation from 1983 to 1991, during which the Wagalla Massacre occurred (February 1984):[33] that "as the PS for foreign affairs, had attended a meeting in Wajir in February 1984 at which some say a decision was made to round up all the Degodiya men in the area for interrogation",[34] leading to the subsequent massacre. Kiplagat's alleged complicity did not stop there: while he was still PS in the Ministry of Foreign Affairs, his then boss, Robert Ouko, the minister for foreign affairs, "disappeared" and was found murdered in February 1990 at Got Alila. Kiplagat was further implicated in the Ndũng'ũ Report as "someone who benefitted from irregular land allocations under President Moi."[35] Given the mandate of TJRC and the pressure that Kiplagat was under, in November 2010 he stepped aside to end the paralysis of TJRC. Although he was reinstated in 2012, the damage to his reputation and the potential findings of TJRC had been done.

By the time its work was done and a report submitted to the president and the prime minister, close to 50,000 statements, memoranda and other interactions had taken place between TJRC and especially the indigenous peoples. The release of its final report, in several volumes, was the anti-climax, and the report itself was met with allegations of political manipulation,[36] rendering it rather underwhelming. Markedly, its release was accompanied by a statement of dissent by the three international commissioners, Ronald C. Slye, Berhanu Dinka and Gertrude Chawatama, protesting everything from the leadership, conduct and final production of the report and subsequent amendments not agreed to by the commissioners.[37] Perhaps it was not surprising: the history of Kenya, the complicity of Kenya's public officials and their implication in some of these issues made it nearly impossible for the report to see the light of day without major modifications.

Still, the report provided a depository and chronicle of some of Kenya's worst atrocities. For example, in the summary report, the following account, regarding one of the many "disarmament" activities (such as the one that resulted in the Wagalla Massacre); the account was provided by a witness to the Lotiri Massacre in West Pokot, February to May 1984 (about the same time as the Wagalla Massacre):

> Mzee Atoligole Losute became the first person to surrender his gun, but when he tried to raise the certificate, the helicopter dropped down and then he was told: because you are good person, we will take you round to be an example to other people . . . his wives saw him go inside the helicopter and after going round, he was seen hooked or tied on his neck to the helicopter and then he was flown off and went round [with] the helicopter and after 30 minutes, that old man died. He was thrown away at the border of Kenya and Uganda.[38]

The report did point out the significant issues and occurrences of massacres, torture, political assassinations, extrajudicial killings and enforced disappearances, detention, torture and ill treatment, sexual violence, land/conflict, economic marginalization and violation of socio-economic rights, grand corruption and economic crimes, marginalization of women and poor history of women's rights, minority and indigenous peoples' marginalization and perennial ethnic tensions.[39]

In its report's closing, TJRC considered the question of the implementation of its recommendation, calling for the report to "be widely disseminated and accessible to the Kenyan public,"[40] full implementation of the recommendations, with specific frameworks and responsible parties. Rather helpfully, the report was released in May 2013, one month after the inauguration of the first government of the Second Republic. The new government had the opportunity to demonstrate its commitment to the rule of law, but given that the president and the deputy president's case at ICC were still ongoing, the argument for the imprudence of such action can be credibly made. It is not clear that there have been any specific moves to implement the recommendations. For example, although the commission called for the implementation of the 1967 Arusha Agreement between Kenya and Somalia, all the publicly available copies of the agreement are held by Stanford University's Keesing's Record of World Events. Thus, the TJRC report was ultimately destined to go the way of many other commissions in Kenya: even when the reports see the light of day, there is generally lethargy in their implementation. This might have future implications for the nation, particularly given the unresolved issues and the knowledge of the past atrocities.

2010 constitution and devolution: finally "Majimbo"

One of the urgent tasks of the coalition government was the drafting and the ratification of a new constitution, one that would check the previous excesses of the executive. This was accomplished in two years; on 4 August 2010, the second referendum was held, asking citizens.[41] The result was an overwhelming "Yes" vote, with 68.6 percent of the voters approving, while the "No" vote was approximately 31.5 percent. The requirement for the constitution's passing was a simple majority, and at least 25 percent of all votes in five of the eight provinces. Among the supporters of the new constitution were the president and prime minister; the vice president; the two deputy prime ministers (Uhuru Kenyatta and Musalia Mudavadi); the first Jubilee vice president, also indicted by the ICC; William Ruto; and Daniel arap Moi remained opposed. The church, too, opposed the proposed constitution new, on account of the recognition of *Kadhi* courts and abortion.[42] Yet, when the results were tallied, the results were clear: in at least six provinces, the new constitution was approved with over 76 percent of the vote, with a 72 percent voter turnout. Unlike the results of the previous referendum, the vote in Central Province was 84.4 percent, while in Nyanza, it was 92.04 percent.[43] On 27 August 2010, a new constitution was promulgated, hailed as one of the most progressive in Africa, if not the world.[44]

The concentration of executive power at the level of the national government had been long identified as one of the sources of dictatorial tendencies; as such, distribution of this power (along the lines of the short-lived independence-era devolution) was finally accomplished.[45] The 2010 constitution introduced and

> distinguishe[d] the functions of the national government from those of county governments . . . county governments have legislative authority "to make

> any laws that are necessary for, incidental to the effective performance of the functions and exercise the powers of the county governments under the Fourth Schedule."[46]

Furthermore, the 2010 constitution's Article 174 lists nine principles (objectives) of devolution. These principles include the promotion of democracy and accountability, fostering national unity under diversity, enabling self-governance of the people towards their interrogation of the state, recognition of communities' right to self-management and development. Others are protecting and promoting the rights and interests of minorities and marginalized groups, promoting socio-economic development, ensuring equitable sharing of national and local resources, rationalizing further decentralization of state organs and enhancing checks and balances.[47] The 2010 constitution thus clipped part of the powers of the presidency, including being president and holding another office, determining the size of the cabinet, appointing members of parliament as cabinet secretaries (unless they resign first), determine the election calendar and dissolve parliament.[48]

Yet it must be understood that the problem with Kenya (and many African countries), was not the absence of legislation and constitutions that specified the rights, privileges and immunities of the citizens: rather, it is the ability of the state to violate them, to use state apparatus to suppress their rights, including leveraging violence to achieve political ends as had happened in Kenya after the introduction of the multiparty system. Thus, even as the new constitution made significant changes and altered the power structure, for example, introducing the long-desired "Majimbo", couched as "devolution" based on 47 counties; some issues remained unaddressed, as did the implementation of the changes. Sharma, in particular, notes that

> certain elements of Agenda 4 were doomed to fail because of an inherent tension . . . for instance, by addressing the underlying causes of the violence, one of the principal aims of Agenda 4 was to end impunity and ensure accountability for the crimes committed during the post-election period,[49]

yet this might have implied establishing the mechanisms required by the Waki Commission, which was not done, as it might have to prosecute members of the coalition government. Cheeseman notes that "although commissions of inquiry into the 'Kenya crisis' were established and delivered damning verdicts, the high number of veto players within the government of national unity ensured that few reform efforts were carried through."[50]

As the first elections under the new 2010 constitution approached, another issue gained more and urgent attention: one of orderly power transition from Kibaki's administration to the next presidency. Notwithstanding the general trends elsewhere in Africa with change-the-constitution movements and incumbents hanging on to power, it was generally never expected that Mwai Kibaki was going to extend his rule beyond the two five-year terms, particularly given his previous statements and the state of the country. As such, the institutional practice started by Moi in 2002 was favored to continue in 2013. This was especially important, given several factors, including his remarks at inauguration in 2002, promising a nation ruled by law, not "roadside pronouncements and directives"; the detrimental outcomes of the 2007 general election, a (newly) promulgated constitution in 2010, the international involvement in Kenya's affairs, spanning both the High Panel of Eminent Persons and the ICC's (then) ongoing cases, the general national mood and the legacy that he was likely to bestow on the country, upon his departure from office.

Heroes or villains: Uhuruto

History is littered with heroes and heroines, and in the context of the post-election violence 2007 and the events of 2016, a mere six years later when two of the accused were elected to office. It is useful to review the peculiar cases of Kenyatta and Ruto but, before doing so, to recognize how history has often assigned the labels of "hero" "freedom fighters" and/or "terrorist". While an inexhaustive list, examples abound: the British considered George Washington a traitor and rebel; Nelson Mandela was considered a pest to the apartheid government, while considered founding fathers of their nations, the British considered Ben Gurion and Jomo Kenyatta as terrorists. In Myanmar, Aung San Suu Kyi spent years under house arrest – the pattern repeats throughout history and around the world, giving rise to the notion that 'they are freedom fighters if they are yours, terrorists if they are on the other side'. Uhuru's and Ruto's cases are especially pertinent: both were accused of fomenting violence by their respective communities and against the others' community, yet several years later they were touring the country in pursuit of "ICC-Ocampo prayers", uniting slightly later on, to form the winning coalition for the 2013 general elections.

This duo would also produce one of the greatest ironies of the investigation and indictment of the "Ocampo Six" and the subsequent prosecution of a subset of four at ICC. Uhuru Mũigai Kenyatta, one of the "villains", teamed up with William Samoei Ruto; the former as a presidential candidate and the latter as his running mate, for the 2013 elections, under the auspices of the Jubilee Alliance, formed in January 2013.[51] Despite that this newfound amity caused consternation particularly over Ruto, "who many Kikuyu voters blamed for orchestrating election-related violence in 1992, 1997 and 2007"[52] in which the Kikuyu suffered significant losses in life and limb, the duo ran in the 2013 presidential election. The attraction of Uhuru Kenyatta, a Kikuyu and the son of Kenya's first president, would potentially be the fourth president of the republic. Gachigua writes that

> Uhuru Kenyatta and William Ruto, the two most prominent politicians among the accused, used the platform afforded by the ICC's indictment to form a political merger that saw them mount a highly choreographed anti-ICC campaign leading to their election as Kenya's president and deputy president in March 2013.[53]

Soon after their indictment, the six often appeared together in prayer rallies, in political rallies and in strategy sessions, where they railed individually and jointly against ICC and its practice of singling out Africans for prosecution at ICC. Perhaps, after all, there were no permanent enemies in Kenyan politics, only two groups of Kenyans: the *wenye nchi* and *wana-nchi.*[54] It was abundantly clear who was what.

The ethnic dimension: old foes, new friends

The five-year period between the elections of 2007 and the new government elected in 2013 saw near-seismic shifts in the ethnic relations between communities in Kenya. From a renewal of the old rivalries, complete with armed conflict and widespread death and mayhem. Returning to the old, familiar pre-election and post-election routine, the Rift Valley became a hotspot for ethnic conflict, with especially the Kikuyus bearing the brunt of the conflict. What was generally considered to be a protest of the election violence especially by members of the Luo community in major urban centers was quickly hijacked by other groups, particularly the Kalenjin, where the atrocities approximating genocide and crimes against humanity began to occur. At that point, it was unclear clear if the violence was organized, or systematically targeted one or more ethnic groups. A short while after the election, the Kamba allied themselves with the government and were 'rewarded' with the appointment of Kalonzo Musyoka as the vice president.

Ethnic violence, especially between the Kikuyu and the Kalenjin, had been evident especially in the era of one-party state. However, there had never been any systematic violence between the Kikuyu and the Luo, save for the sporadic, but non-targeted protests and the accompanying violence following the assassination of Tom Mboya on 5 July 1969 and the Kisumu Massacre in October 1969, where it can be expected the passions were still high. Generally, the communities were content to ignore each other outside of the vigorously contested political space through elections. Such was the initial phases of the post-election violence. The losing side in the election, headed by Raila Odinga and supported by William Ruto, benefitted from a continuation of the pre-election pact, but perhaps now in a violently destructive direction.

This time, however, the Kikuyus did not just flee: after the worst of the atrocities, such as the Kiambaa Massacre on New Year's Day, they retaliated in places where "others" could be found: such places included most of Central Province and majority Kikuyu areas, including Naivasha, where 19 members of the Luo community were torched. The return of the shadowy groups including Mũngiki was evident: Mũngiki was accused of, in some instances, collaborating with the government in singling out members of other communities for attack (or they incurred no sanction). Thus, although animosities might have been in the undercurrents of inter-ethnic relations elsewhere, the Kikuyu, Luo and Kalenjin were the most affected, and involved, in the atrocities. The Maasai, who have in the past asserted land claims to places like Kajiado and Naivasha, stayed out of the melee.

Although the peacemaking and reconciliation efforts were subsumed to the other significant events – the creation of the three commissions per the agreement of 28th February 2008 – the involvement of the ODM side in GNU helped the diminish the benefits for continuing with conflict. Both Raila Odinga, the leading figure in the Luo community, and William Ruto, the rising "leader" of the Kalenjin, were incorporated into government, with the former as the prime minister and the latter as the minister of agriculture. The power-sharing agreement was also beneficial in many ways to all communities and particularly the communities involved in the conflict; Raila and the ODM faction were able to nominate individuals for appointment to the cabinet and the civil service, especially to the lifetime appointments to constitutional commissions, thus alleviating the pressure and accusations of nepotism benefitting the Kikuyu. As coalition partners, the different communities did benefit by having "their people" appointed to government, negating one of the major complaints on the domination of government by the Kikuyu.

Towards the promulgation of the new constitution, the flux in (ethnic) alliances was remarkable and developed quickly. Nyanza, the stronghold of ODM, voted 92 percent "Yes" for the adoption of the new constitution. Common interest in seeing the new constitution promulgated by the coalition partners appeared to bind the Luo and the Kikuyu together, particularly given their earlier conflict. Rift Valley Province, on the other hand, the home of KAMATUSA (Kalenjin, Maasai, Turkana, Samburu; and some of the participants in the post-election violence) rejected the constitution by nearly 40 to 60 percent margin. While William Ruto continued with his opposition to the new constitution, Moi, the septuagenarian that KANU wouldn't let go, was in favor of the new constitution. Even as the power play was going on nationally, the Kalenjin were having an old-generation, new-generation contest.

The 2010 constitutional review process and referendum were peaceful; subsequently, the 2013 election demonstrated that pre- and post-election conflicts could be avoided. Having a bigger target for collective national anger was helpful: Raila Odinga, presidential candidate, was contesting against Uhuru Kenyatta and William Ruto, both indicted by ICC. Just as the alliance that was crafted in 1966 in the face of a resurgence of opposition (Kenya People's Union, by Jaramogi Oginga Odinga), where Jomo Kenyatta appointed a Kalenjin legislator, Daniel arap Moi as vice president, Uhuru Kenyatta's running mate would be another Kalenjin "leader", William Ruto. The entire process had come full circle. On 4 March, Kenya elected its third Kikuyu president and elevated the second Kalenjin vice (deputy) president.

Notes

1 United Nations. "Statement Attributable to the Spokesperson for the Secretary-General on Kenya." New York. 31 December 2007. (Web): n.p.
2 ICRtoP. "The Crisis in Kenya." The International Coalition for the Responsibility to Protect. (Web): n.p.
3 ICRtoP. "The Crisis in Kenya." n.p.
4 Treda Mukuhlani. "Zimbabwe's Government of National Unity: Successes and Challenges in Restoring Peace and Order." *Journal of Power, Politics & Governance*, 2, No. 2 (June, 2014): 170.
5 Mukuhlani. "Zimbabwe's Government of National Unity." 170.

6 ICTJ. "The Kenyan Commission of Inquiry into Post-Election Violence." International Center for Transitional Justice. 26 April 2011. (Web): n.p.
7 National Council for Law Reporting. "The National Accord and Reconciliation Act." 2008, pp. 5
8 Sarah Jenkins. "Kenya: Kenya's Legacy of Violent Ethnic Politics and the 2007–2008 Postelection Crisis." In Joseph R. Rudolph, Jr., Ed. *Encyclopedia of Modern Ethnic Conflicts*, 2nd Ed. [2 volumes]. (Santa Barbara, CA: ABC-CLIO, 2016): 317.
9 OECD, African Development Bank, United Nations Economic Commission for Africa. *African Economic Outlook 2009 Country Notes: Volumes 1 & 2*. (Paris, France: OECD, ADB & UN-ECA, 2009): n.p.
10 Alexis Arieff, Rhoda Margesson & Marjorie Ann Browne. *International Criminal Court Cases in Africa: Status and Policy Issues*. (Washington, DC: Congressional Research Service, 2010): 24.
11 Arieff, Margesson & Browne. *International Criminal Court Cases in Africa*. 24.
12 OECD, ADB & UN-ECA. *African Economic Outlook 2009 Country Notes*. n.p.
13 Héctor Olásolo. *Essays on International Criminal Justice*. (Portland, OR: Hart Publishing, 2012): 52.
14 Olásolo. *Essays on International Criminal Justice*. 52.
15 Abel S. Knottnerus. "The AU, the ICC, and the Prosecution of African Presidents." In Kamari Clarke, Abel S. Knottnerus & Eefje de Volder, Eds. *Africa and the ICC: Perceptions of Justice*. (New York, NY: Cambridge University Press, 2016): 188.
16 Sabine Höhn. "New Start or False Start? The ICC and Electoral Violence in Kenya." In Gerhard Anders & Olaf Zenker, Eds. *Transition and Justice: Negotiating the Terms of New Beginnings in Africa*. (Malden, MA: Wiley-Blackwell, 2015): 184.
17 Lorraine Smith-van Lin. "Non-Compliance and the Law and Politics of State Cooperation: Lessons from the *Al Bashir* and *Kenyatta Cases*." In Olympia Bekou and Daley Birkett, Eds. *Cooperation and the International Criminal Court: Perspectives from Theory and Practice*. (Leiden, The Netherlands: Koninklijke Brill NV, 2016): 118.
18 Smith-van Lin. "Non-Compliance and the Law and Politics of State Cooperation." 118.
19 Höhn. "New Start or False Start? The ICC and Electoral Violence in Kenya." 184.
20 Triestino Mariniello. "'One, No One and One Hundred Thousand': Reflections on the Multiple Identities of the ICC." In Triestino Mariniello, Ed. *The International Criminal Court in Search of Its Purpose and Identity*. (New York, NY: Routledge, 2015): vi.
21 For more on Gacaca courts and process, see for example, Paul Christoph Bornkamm. *Rwanda's Gacaca Courts: Between Retribution and Reparation*. (New York, NY: Oxford University Press, 2012) and Phil Clark. *The Gacaca Courts, Post-Genocide Justice and Reconciliation in Rwanda: Justice without Lawyers*. (New York, NY: Cambridge University Press, 2010).
22 Maxon and Ofcansky. *Historical Dictionary of Kenya*. 55.
23 OECD. African Development Bank, United Nations Economic Commission for Africa. *African Economic Outlook 2009 Country Notes*. n.p.
24 Laura A. Young. "A Challenging Nexus: Transitional Justice and Indigenous Peoples in Africa." In Ridwan Laher & Korir Sing'oei, Eds. *Indigenous People in Africa: Contestations, Empowerment and Group Rights*. (Pretoria, South Africa: Africa Institute of South Africa, 2014): 135.
25 Ozonnia Ojielo. "Justice versus Reconciliation: The Dilemmas of Transitional Justice in Kenya." In Kenneth Omeje & Tricia Redeker Hepner, Eds. *Conflict and Peacebuilding in the African Great Lakes Region*. (Bloomington, IN: Indiana University Press, 2013): 124.
26 Ben Rawlence. *'Bring the Gun or You'll Die': Torture, Rape, and Other Serious Human Rights Violations by Kenyan Security Forces in the Mandera Triangle*. (New York, NY: Human Rights Watch, 2009): 14.
27 Kenya National Assembly. *Official Record, (Hansard) Apr 25, 2001*. (Nairobi, Kenya: Government Printer, 2001): 581.

28 Hannah Whittaker. *Insurgency and Counterinsurgency in Kenya: A Social History of the Shifta Conflict, c. 1963–1968*. (Leiden, The Netherlands: Koninklijke Brill NV, 2011): 139.
29 Hussein A. Mahmoud. "Conflicts and Constraints to Peace among Pastoralists in Northern Kenya." In Mwesiga Laurent Baregu, Ed. *Understanding Obstacles to Peace: Actors, Interests, and Strategies in Africa's Great Lakes Region*. (Kampala, Uganda: Fountain Publishers, 2011): 156.
30 Rawlence. *'Bring the Gun or You'll Die'*. 14.
31 Whittaker. *Insurgency and Counterinsurgency in Kenya*. 139.
32 Kim Foulds. "The Somali Question: Protracted Conflict, National Narratives, and Curricular Politics in Kenya." In Denise Bentrovato, Karina V. Korostelina & Martina Schulze, Eds. *History Can Bite: History Education in Divided and Postwar Societies*. (Göttigen, Germany: V&R unipress GmbH, 2016): 147.
33 Mayesha Alam. *Women and Transitional Justice: Progress and Persistent Challenges in Retributive and Restorative Processes*. (New York, NY: Palgrave Macmillan, 2014). (eBook): n.p.
34 Gabrielle Lynch. "Bringing the Audience Back in: Kenya's Truth, Justice and Reconciliation Commission and the Efficacy of Public Hearings." In Shirin M. Rai & Janelle Reinelt, Eds. *The Grammar of Politics and Performance*. (New York, NY: Routledge, 2015): 177.
35 Lynch. "Bringing the Audience Back in." 177.
36 Young. "A Challenging Nexus: Transitional Justice and Indigenous Peoples in Africa." 137.
37 Ronald C. Slye, Berhanu Dinka & Gertrude Chawatama. *Dissent: Statement by International Commissioners*. The Final Report of the Truth Justice and Reconciliation Commission of Kenya, 2013. 5 February 2013. (Web).
38 TJRC (Truth, Justice and Reconciliation Commission). *The Final Report of the Truth Justice and Reconciliation Commission of Kenya (2013)*. (2013). (Web): 4.
39 TJRC. *The Final Report of the Truth Justice and Reconciliation Commission of Kenya (2013)*. 11.
40 TJRC. "The Final Report of the Truth Justice and Reconciliation Commission of Kenya (2013)", pp. 8
41 The 2010 Referendum questions read as follows: *Do you approve the proposed new Constitution?* The Swahili version read as follows: *Je, unaikubali katiba mpya inayopendekezwa?*
42 Sung Kyu Park. *Christian Spirituality in Africa: Biblical, Historical, and Cultural Perspectives from Kenya*. (Eugene, OR: Pickwick Publications, 2013): 156.
43 African Elections Database. "National Election Results: Kenya Detailed Election Results. 4 August 2010 Constitutional Referendum." (Web). Accessed on 12/4/2016 from: http://africanelections.tripod.com/ke_detail.html#2010_Constitutional_Referendum
44 See, for example, Dennis Ben Mosota. "Chapter Two: Constitutionalism and the Rule of Law under the New Constitutional Order." In Patrick L. O. Lumumba, Morris K. Mbondenyi & Steve O. Odero, Eds. *The Constitution of Kenya: Contemporary Readings*. (Nairobi, Kenya: LawAfrica Publishing, 2013). Ch. 2: 45–60; Michael Amoah. *Nationalism, Globalization, and Africa*. (New York, NY: Palgrave Macmillan, 2011): 126 and Westen K. Shilaho. "Third Time Lucky? Devolution and State Restructure under Kenya's 2010 Constitutional Dispensation." In Carl A. LeVan, Joseph Olayinka Fashagba & Edward R. McMahon, Eds. *African State Governance: Subnational Politics and National Power*. (New York, NY: Palgrave Macmillan, 2015): 152.
45 Barrett defines *devolution* as "the transfer of public authority, resources, and personnel from the national level to subnational jurisdictions." Sam Barrett. "Subnational Adaptation Finance Allocation: Comparing Decentralized and Devolved Political Institutions in Kenya." *Global Environmental Politics*, 15, No. 3 (2015): 119.
46 Shilaho. "Third Time Lucky? Devolution and State Restructure under Kenya's 2010 Constitutional Dispensation." 156.

47 Othieno Nyanjom. "Devolution in Kenya's New Constitution: Society for International Development (SID)." Constitution Working Paper Series No. 4. (Web). 10. Paraphrased and abbreviated.
48 Stephen Mutula, Wilson K. Muna & Geoffrey P. Koma. "Leadership and Political Corruption in Kenya: Analysis of the 2010 Constitutional Provisions on the Presidency." *The Journal of Social, Political, and Economic Studies*, 38, No. 3 (Fall, 2013): 265.
49 Serena K. Sharma. *The Responsibility to Protect and the International Criminal Court: Protection and Prosecution in Kenya*. (New York, NY: Routledge, 2016): 65.
50 Nic Cheeseman. "Kenya." In Andreas Mehler, Henning Melber & Klaas Van Walraven, Eds. *Africa Yearbook, Vol. 5: Politics, Economy and Society South of the Sahara in 2008*. (Leiden, The Netherlands: Koninklijke Brill NV, 2009): 327.
51 Mariniello. "'One, No One and One Hundred Thousand'." vi.
52 Cheeseman. "Kenya." 327.
53 Sammy G. Gachigua. "Discursive Reconstruction of the ICC-Kenyan Engagement through Kenyan Newspapers' Editorial Cartoons." In Kamari Clarke, Abel S. Knottnerus & Eefje de Volder, Eds. *Africa and the ICC: Perceptions of Justice*. (New York, NY: Cambridge University Press, 2016): 188.
54 *Wenye nchi*: literally, "the owners of the country"; *wana-nchi*: "citizens".

References

African Elections Database. "National Election Results: Kenya Detailed Election Results. 4 August 2010 Constitutional Referendum." (Web). Accessed on 12/4/2016 from: http://africanelections.tripod.com/ke_detail.html#2010_Constitutional_Referendum

Alam, Mayesha. *Women and Transitional Justice: Progress and Persistent Challenges in Retributive and Restorative Processes*. New York, NY: Palgrave Macmillan, 2014. (eBook).

Amoah, Michael. *Nationalism, Globalization, and Africa*. New York, NY: Palgrave Macmillan, 2011. p. 126.

Arieff, Alexis, Rhoda Margesson & Marjorie Ann Browne. *International Criminal Court Cases in Africa: Status and Policy Issues*. Washington, DC: Congressional Research Service, 2010.

Barrett, Sam. "Subnational Adaptation Finance Allocation: Comparing Decentralized and Devolved Political Institutions in Kenya." *Global Environmental Politics*, 15, No. 3 (August 2015): 118–139.

Bornkamm, Paul Christoph. *Rwanda's Gacaca Courts: Between Retribution and Reparation*. New York, NY: Oxford University Press, 2012.

Brown, Stephen & Chandra Lekha Sriram. "The Big Fish Won't Fry Themselves: Criminal Accountability for Post-Election Violence in Kenya." *African Affairs*, 111, No. 443 (2012): 244–260. Doi:10.1093/afraf/ads018

Cheeseman, Nic. "Kenya." In Andreas Mehler, Henning Melber & Klaas Van Walraven, Eds. *Africa Yearbook, Vol. 5: Politics, Economy and Society South of the Sahara in 2008*. Leiden, The Netherlands: Koninklijke Brill NV, 2009.

Clark, Phil. *The Gacaca Courts, Post-Genocide Justice and Reconciliation in Rwanda: Justice without Lawyers*. New York, NY: Cambridge University Press, 2010.

Foulds, Kim. "The Somali Question: Protracted Conflict, National Narratives, and Curricular Politics in Kenya." In Denise Bentrovato, Karina V. Korostelina & Martina Schulze, Eds. *History Can Bite: History Education in Divided and Postwar Societies*. Göttigen, Germany: V&R unipress GmbH, 2016. pp. 45–60.

Gachigua, Sammy G. "Discursive Reconstruction of the ICC-Kenyan Engagement through Kenyan Newspapers' Editorial Cartoons." In Kamari Clarke, Abel S. Knottnerus & Eefje de Volder, Eds. *Africa and the ICC: Perceptions of Justice*. New York, NY: Cambridge University Press, 2016.

Höhn, Sabine. "New Start or False Start? The ICC and Electoral Violence in Kenya." In Gerhard Anders & Olaf Zenker, Eds. *Transition and Justice: Negotiating the Terms of New Beginnings in Africa*. Malden, MA: Wiley-Blackwell, 2015.

ICRtoP. "The Crisis in Kenya." The International Coalition for the Responsibility to Protect. (Web). Accessed on 12/3/2016 from: www.responsibilitytoprotect.org/index.php/crises/crisis-in-kenya

ICRtoP. "Statement Made by Bernard Kouchner on the Situation in Kenya." The International Coalition for the Responsibility to Protect. 31 January 2008. (Web). Accessed on 12/3/2016 from: http://responsibilitytoprotect.org/index.php/component/content/article/129-africa/1501-violence-in-kenya-statement-made-by-french-foreign-and-european-affairs-minister-bernard-kouchner

ICTJ. "The Kenyan Commission of Inquiry into Post-Election Violence." International Center for Transitional Justice. 26 April 2011. (Web). Accessed on 12/3/2016 from: www.ictj.org/publication/kenyan-commission-inquiry-post-election-violence

Jenkins, Sarah. "Kenya: Kenya's Legacy of Violent Ethnic Politics and the 2007–2008 Postelection Crisis." In Joseph R. Rudolph, Jr., Ed. *Encyclopedia of Modern Ethnic Conflicts*, 2nd Ed. [2 volumes]. Santa Barbara, CA: ABC-CLIO, 2016.

Kenya National Assembly. *Official Record, (Hansard) Apr 25, 2001*. Nairobi, Kenya: Government Printer, 2001.

Knottnerus, Abel S. "The AU, the ICC, and the Prosecution of African Presidents." In Kamari Clarke, Abel S. Knottnerus & Eefje de Volder, Eds. *Africa and the ICC: Perceptions of Justice*. New York, NY: Cambridge University Press, 2016.

Lynch, Gabrielle. "Bringing the Audience Back in: Kenya's Truth, Justice and Reconciliation Commission and the Efficacy of Public Hearings." In Shirin M. Rai & Janelle Reinelt, Eds. *The Grammar of Politics and Performance*. New York, NY: Routledge, 2015.

Mahmoud, Hussein A. "Conflicts and Constraints to Peace among Pastoralists in Northern Kenya." In Mwesiga Laurent Baregu, Ed. *Understanding Obstacles to Peace: Actors, Interests, and Strategies in Africa's Great Lakes Region*. Kampala, Uganda: Fountain Publishers, 2011. Ch. 4, pp. 146–169.

Mariniello, Triestino. *The International Criminal Court in Search of Its Purpose and Identity*. New York, NY: Routledge, 2015.

Mosota, Dennis Ben. "Chapter Two: Constitutionalism and the Rule of Law under the New Constitutional Order." In Patrick L. O. Lumumba, Morris K. Mbondenyi & Steve O. Odero, Eds. *The Constitution of Kenya: Contemporary Readings*. Nairobi, Kenya: LawAfrica Publishing, 2013. Ch. 2, pp. 45–60.

Mukuhlani, Treda. "Zimbabwe's Government of National Unity: Successes and Challenges in Restoring Peace and Order." *Journal of Power, Politics & Governance*, 2, No. 2 (June, 2014): 169–180. Accessed from: http://jppgnet.com/journals/jppg/Vol_2_No_2_June_2014/9.pdf

Mutula, Stephen, Wilson K. Muna & Geoffrey P. Koma. "Leadership and Political Corruption in Kenya: Analysis of the 2010 Constitutional Provisions on the Presidency." *The Journal of Social, Political, and Economic Studies*, 38, No. 3 (Fall, 2013): 263–286.

National Council for Law Reporting. "The National Accord and Reconciliation Act." No. 4 of 2008. Kenya Law Review Commission. Accessed on 12/3/2016 from: http://kenyalaw.org/kl/fileadmin/pdfdownloads/Acts/NationalAccordandReconciliationAct_No4of2008.pdf

Nyanjom, Othieno. "Devolution in Kenya's New Constitution." Society for International Development (SID). Constitution Working Paper Series No. 4. (Web): 10. Accessed on 12/4/2016 from: www.sidint.net/sites/www.sidint.net/files/docs/WP4.pdf

OECD, African Development Bank, United Nations Economic Commission for Africa. *African Economic Outlook 2009 Country Notes: Volumes 1 & 2*. Paris, France: OECD, ADB & UN-ECA, 2009.

Ojielo, Ozonnia. "Justice versus Reconciliation: The Dilemmas of Transitional Justice in Kenya." In Kenneth Omeje & Tricia Redeker Hepner, Eds. *Conflict and Peacebuilding in the African Great Lakes Region*. Bloomington, IN: Indiana University Press, 2013.

Olásolo, Héctor. *Essays on International Criminal Justice*. Portland, OR: Hart Publishing, 2012.

Onyiego, Michael. "Landmark Moment as New Kenyan Constitution Takes Effect." VOA. (Web). 26 August 2010. Accessed on 12/4/2016 from: www.voanews.com/a/kenyas-new-constitution-signed-into-law-101632883/124592.html

Park, Sung Kyu. *Christian Spirituality in Africa: Biblical, Historical, and Cultural Perspectives from Kenya*. Eugene, OR: Pickwick Publications, 2013.

Rawlence, Ben. *'Bring the Gun or You'll Die': Torture, Rape, and Other Serious Human Rights Violations by Kenyan Security Forces in the Mandera Triangle*. New York, NY: Human Rights Watch, 2009.

Sharma, Serena K. *The Responsibility to Protect and the International Criminal Court: Protection and Prosecution in Kenya*. New York, NY: Routledge, 2016.

Shilaho, Westen K. "Third Time Lucky? Devolution and State Restructure under Kenya's 2010 Constitutional Dispensation." In A. Carl LeVan, Joseph Olayinka Fashagba & Edward R. McMahon, Eds. *African State Governance: Subnational Politics and National Power*. New York, NY: Palgrave Macmillan, 2015.

Slye, Ronald C., Berhanu Dinka & Gertrude Chawatama. "Dissent: Statement by International Commissioners." The Final Report of the Truth Justice and Reconciliation Commission of Kenya, 2013. 5 February 2013. (Web). Accessed on 12/4/2016 from the Seattle University School of Law Digital Commons. Accessed from: http://digitalcommons.law.seattleu.edu/cgi/viewcontent.cgi?article=1007&context=tjrc

Smith-van Lin, Lorraine. "Non-Compliance and the Law and Politics of State Cooperation: Lessons from the *Al Bashir* and *Kenyatta Cases*." In Olympia Bekou & Daley Birkett, Eds. *Cooperation and the International Criminal Court: Perspectives from Theory and Practice*. Leiden, The Netherlands: Koninklijke Brill NV, 2016.

TJRC. "The Final Report of the Truth Justice and Reconciliation Commission of Kenya (2013)." TJRC Report (Abridged Version). Seattle University School of Law Digital Commons. 26 May 2013. Accessed on 12/4/2016 from: http://digitalcommons.law.seattleu.edu/cgi/viewcontent.cgi?article=1009&context=tjrc

United Nations. "Statement Attributable to the Spokesperson for the Secretary-General on Kenya." New York. 31 December 2007. (Web). Accessed on 12/3/2016 from: www.un.org/sg/en/content/sg/statement/2007-12-31/statement-attributable-spokesperson-secretary-general-kenya

Whittaker, Hannah. *Insurgency and Counterinsurgency in Kenya: A Social History of the Shifta Conflict, c. 1963–1968*. Leiden, The Netherlands: Koninklijke Brill NV, 2011.

Young, Laura A. "A Challenging Nexus: Transitional Justice and Indigenous Peoples in Africa." In Ridwan Laher & Korir Sing'oei, Eds. *Indigenous People in Africa: Contestations, Empowerment and Group Rights*. Pretoria, South Africa: Africa Institute of South Africa, 2014.

7 Contemporary Kenya

First half-century and opportunities

Kenya's storied history, for the first half-century of its existence as an independent state (1963 to 2013), has, like most of its African peers, been one with more challenge than opportunity. For the most part, it has been pacific, but occasionally, it descends into general melee, attempting to imitate its neighbors Uganda, Somalia and Ethiopia. While its social, political and economic contestations have been violent, they have not risen to that level, and Kenya continues to host close to a million refugees. Apart from the challenges of social and economic development, Kenya struggled with the gamut of issues prescient in the global South: two coup attempts, a reversal in democracy, adoption of one-party rule and becoming a reluctant partner in the third wave of democratization. It went through "aid conditionalities" by the international finance institutions (IFIs), participated in inter-state war (against the Shifta bandits in the Northern Frontier District bordering Somalia), and even entertained the proposition of a civil war. For the first six years of independence, the Polity IV score (level of democracy) was at 2 (3 years), then at 0 (3 years), and then stayed in the negative digit until 2012 (thus, close to 40 years). Throughout most of its electoral history, elections were synonymous with ethnic violence, which has continued to manifest itself since before independence.

The blame cannot solely be laid at the feet of Kenya's leaders: conditions existed before independence that sowed the seeds of these outcomes, beginning with the decision to turn Kenya into an "export-oriented colony", deliberate denial of educational opportunities, ability to organize and/or carry out other social organizational activities that provide the genesis of a functioning society. One might surmise that the British departed, leaving a FUBAR situation; Kenya's independence and subsequent leaders did not do much to regulate it. Statistics that the new, independent Kenya government inherited were measly: shortly after independence, life expectancy was 50.5 years, gross domestic product (GDP) per capita (current US$) was $122, and enrolment in primary education was 1.35 million. By the end of the first half-century of an independent Kenya, life expectancy had risen by (a mere) 10 years on average, GDP per capita (current US$) stood at $1261.1 while enrollment in primary education, both sexes stood at 8.1 million.[1]

A more complex issue was the concept of government in the newly independent Kenya. Prior to 1963, the general experience of and with government for most

African countries was primarily negative: that is, the colonial government. Thus, despite the great celebrations surrounding independence, it is not evident that Kenyans knew, or were prepared, for the challenges that came along with independence. It might have been too much to hope, to expect that after 68 years of occupation by the British, initially, for 25 years as the British East Africa Protectorate and later, for 43 years as the Kenya Colony, for Kenya to suddenly up and turn into a liberal democracy with rights, privileges and immunities such as those found in the advanced industrial democracies. This is especially true, since Kenya lacked even the most basic infrastructure, such as social systems.

Democracy as tyranny of numbers

One of the remarkable, but little remarked upon, realities of Kenya is that despite the limitations on political activities that endured between 1969 and 1991, there were fewer instances of ethnically driven conflict. Even the contested 1988 "*Mlolongo*" elections did not produce inter-ethnic conflict; yet, the pre- and post-election periods in 1992, 1997 and 2007 showed remarkable degrees of ethnic conflict. One must then pose the question, Is stability in ethnically divided societies than a nobler purpose, more than the ability for different individuals to run for office? Here, avoiding the use of *democracy* is intentional: it is necessary that the "form" of African democracy, or, more accurately, multi-party politics, be distinguished from the universal definition of democracy.

Rather ironically, the introduction of multi-party politics did not necessarily provide an avenue for the articulation of differences in ideologies, much as one would expect between Democrats, Republicans and Libertarians in the US or Conservatives, Liberals and the Labour Parties in the UK. Thus, Kenya's "democracy" provided a multiplicity of potential contestants for legislative positions and the presidency, rather than a forum for competing ideologies. Thus, it is not clear that multiparty politics have necessarily expanded the possibility of accommodating preferences and differences, much as they have the number of contestants. And rather unfortunately, the basis of contestation is ethnicity, not ideas. In the context of Africa's mostly ethnically divided societies, it is useful to revisit the concepts of democracy. Assuming that democracy is universal and identifiable where it manifests or that all polities are capable of being democratic has not shown itself to be a valid position.

Whereas the history, definition, application, articulation and contestations of democracy are sufficient to fill many volumes, even libraries, this section does not delve into the entire range of nuance. Still, questions abound, whether democracy (liberal democracy) is primarily a "Western concept" that best manifests itself in societies that value individualism rather than collective, social systems. Especially since democracy has almost never shown success in African countries, why this is the case continues to engage scholars, leaders and citizens alike. In its suggested form and application to Africa (and globally), democracy is as much about the process of deliberative decision-making as it is the numbers of those that make the decisions, their motivations, their values and their intended outcomes.

Although democracy has existed for close to several centuries, beginning in Athens, its practical applications, rather than its theoretical definition, has occupied even well-known statespeople. The most basic definition of democracy stems from a combination of words: *demos* (people) and *krates* (rule) to form *democracy*, or "rule by the people." So, in a democracy, the idea is that people rule. They are sovereign, meaning that they are the highest authority in the land.[2] These ideas are echoed by Morrell, who argues that "there is a promise inherent in democracy: before a society makes decisions that it will use its collective power to enforce, it will give equal consideration to everyone in the community."[3] Perhaps not everyone: the question of who gets to participate in the decision-making, even in those symbolic, antecedent democracies such as Athens, excluded certain peoples: slaves, women and children. There are all kinds of questions about even the basic constitutive words: what is rule (the extent of issues to be deliberated), who are "people" (e.g., men, women, prisoners, youth or, in the case of 17th- and 18th-century US, African Americans and slaves) and questions of participation (requirements, ease, incentives, punishments, frequency). The questions extend to whether or not to consider direct democracy, or representative democracy.

So there is not only an unsettled question of the definition of democracy; there exist remarkable differences between the theory and practice: Dahl's notion of pure democracy is premised on all citizens' participation as political equals with the rights to formulate preferences, signify preferences to fellow citizens and government individually and through collective action and have the preferences weighed equally in the conduct of government, without discrimination.[4] Held helpfully attempts to shed some light on the question of "rule by the people", by outlining the seven ideas that generally supplant Dahl's criteria. These include involvement of all in legislating/governing (broadly conceived) and application of laws in government administration; personal involvement in 'crucial decision-making' – general laws and policies; that there should be accountability of rulers to the ruled (justification of selected courses of action), and should be removable by the ruled.[5] Further, that there should be accountability of rulers to the representatives of the ruled; that rulers ought to be chosen by the ruled; that rulers should be chosen by the representatives of the ruled; and finally, that the rulers act in the interests of the ruled.[6]

For most polities flirting with the idea of collective participation in decision-making, the question then (except perhaps for Switzerland) is whether or not to employ direct democracy or republicanism. This is the question that Madison, one of the US's foremost thinkers on democracy, sought to parse. Madison, according to Fishkin, deliberated on a "pure democracy" – that is, a direct democracy, versus a "republic", which "employs representatives". According to Madison, a republic held greater capacity to "refine and enlarge the public views by passing them through a chosen body of citizens", thus producing greater deliberation[7] but perhaps greater aggregation which also stood to subsume citizens – preferences, particularly if they were not considered mainstream. Madison's view of the strength of the republic stemmed from the notion that "you take in a greater variety of parties and interests; you make it less probable that a majority of the whole will have a common motive to invade the rights of other citizens."[8] But what if the parties and interests deliberated in the republic format, by the representatives, were necessarily skewed against groups of citizens who could not contest the same, for example, the allocation of resources towards specific groups while excluding others.

Madison's view was that there was less likelihood of a tyranny of the majority in a republic that used representatives since they would take into account these disparate interests. Yet, the potential fallacy of this argument is discussed in the next section by Bohman: perhaps Madison was altruistic (despite proposing the Three Fifths Compromise and owning more than 100 slaves) and held that the representatives would pursue interests based on the common good. Perhaps it was his argument against direct democracy that is of special importance; his was made in the context of small, direct democracies. Yet, the possibilities of tyrannical rule, where "the passions of the people can be immediately aroused",[9] has manifested itself repeatedly in African countries transitioning into democracies, tyrannies that often presided over the near annihilation of entire ethnic groups, despite the appearance of being representative democracies.

Thus, that representative democracies were less likely to be a tyranny is not necessarily supported in especially ethnically divided societies that have attempted to democratize. A specification of the limits of the interests that a democracy should support would have limited the legitimacy of ethnically driven ideas masquerading under the guise of "preferences". For although there ought to be respect for personal property as one of the foundations of a republic, what happens when the "formulation of preferences and signaling of preferences" leads to the dispossession of such private property (land, in the Rift Valley); would this then count as a legitimate expression of preferences? It may have been as well: Madison might not have considered ethnically divided societies as being capable of the higher form of government.

In the case of Kenya, Bohman's critique especially of the conditions and articulation of democracy, through political parties, is useful to highlight. Bohman notes that

> current arrangements undermine the most important principles of democracy: contemporary political practices are based on a politics of self-interest that produces social fragmentation, they permit an unequal distribution of social and economic power that persistently disadvantages the poor and the powerless, and they presuppose institutions that depend almost entirely upon merely aggregative, episodic and inflexible forms of decision-making and that leave deep structural problems of social and economic renewal resolved.[10]

Thus, although there have been some systemic changes, for example, from single-party politics to multiparty politics, this perhaps does not count as a change in democratic systems. Take, for example, representative democracy. Individuals elect their representatives to congress, parliament or other deliberative bodies. In the event that the public is unhappy about legislation, they have some options – for example, judicial recourse, public protests or perhaps recalling the legislators (this is not always a possibility). Often, there exists no mechanism to change the democratic systems; for example, how does a system go from representative democracy to direct democracy?

More recent literature on democracy trends towards democracy as (a method for) deliberation, although as scholars quickly note, especially quoting Freeman, "there is no settled and commonly accepted account of the central features of a deliberative democracy among political scientists and theorists."[11] To illustrate the state of the unsettled debate, Guttmann and Thompson's definition trends towards the Madisonian concept of the republic, writing that "most fundamentally, deliberative democracy affirms the need to justify decisions made by citizens and their representatives."[12] They note that both representatives and citizens should justify their decisions and positions to each other; they add that "not all issues, all the time, require deliberation"[13] but that the deliberative process provides opportunity for various forms of negotiation, such as negotiation, bargaining and such. Deliberation is useful in dealing with substantive questions, some which can be exceedingly complex. For example, should a country go to war just because a majority supports war? Deliberative democracy might stand a better chance of arriving at fair decisions, rather than simply procedural decisions as would be the case in purely majoritarian and election-driven decision-making political arrangements. Yet, Guttmann and Thompson's view of deliberative democracy already imposes the notion that the decision-making arrangements include representatives, who must be chosen in some deliberative format (so far, this has tended to favor election); selecting the "deliberators" thus falls into the same trap of determining how to organize politically to select the representatives. Bohman and Rehg's definition holds that "deliberative democracy refers to the idea that legitimate lawmaking issues from the public deliberation of citizens. As a normative account of legitimacy, deliberative democracy evokes ideals of rational legislation, participatory politics and civic self-governance."[14]

Lafont agrees with most of the previously highlighted literature, but is more nuanced on whether deliberation is a process by the individuals in a society, or whether it is both individuals organized into some form of political body, making decisions together. Lafont writes:

> according to the ideal of a deliberative democracy, political decisions should be made on the basis of a process of public deliberation among citizens including, in my view, on whether the political arrangements include direct democracy, or that there should be representatives. Thus, political decision-making procedures should be both democratic and deliberative.[15]

Yet Lafont points out that deliberation and democracy are not necessarily mutually exclusive. Also, the process of deliberation can produce outcomes antithetical to what might be thought to be right; for example, in 2005, under the political organization name "Change and Reform", Hamas organized, fielded candidates and in a democratic election, won a plurarity of the seats in the Palestinian National

Authority legislature. Deliberation in commonly accepted ways had led to the elevation of a "terrorist group", according to the US Government, to power in Gaza.

Kenya's democracy, the constitution and practical matters

The introduction of multi-party politics in Kenya and most African countries, imagined to possibly bring about greater opening in political space and thus perhaps lead to greater deliberation, was assumed to be the step towards democratization. But what did democratization mean? What was the utility of multi-party politics, and increased space for self-expression, particularly if the requisite institutions that should support democracy, were not reformed? Did the citizens have sufficient knowledge about their preferences, about economic policy, foreign affairs and other aspects necessary to fully participate in a democracy? And even if they did, what constraints did they face in the new "democratic dispensation"?

It is not evident that the necessary social, economic and political structures were in place to support expanded democratic space or that citizens were sufficiently informed of their alternatives, given that especially the government still controlled the media and publication, that laws banning publication of "sedition" where free-speech items often found themselves so classified. Indeed, it is useful to question whether or not improving the conditions antecedent to democracy, such as free speech, access to publications and other forms of information, might have had different outcomes for democracy in Kenya. As it was, it was easy to appeal to the ethnic angle, to deliberate based on the principal preferences, which turned out to be, in many cases, the ethnic affiliation.

If politics is about "who gets what, when and how", and if "the influential are those who get the most of what there is to get" and "those who get the most are *elite*; the rest are *mass*",[16] then it follows that given the scarcity of resources, the elite will necessarily be fewer but have the most, as has been shown by the discussions of the 1 percent versus the 99 percent, while the mass will be the most but have the least. To legitimate the distribution – in effect to actualize "who gets what, when and how", elites will generally recruit the assistance of the masses, who determine who gets into office. This is often done through a range of strategies: aligning their preferences with those of the masses (or articulating the masses preferences in a way that the latter believe their welfare to be tied to that of the elites) and through appealing to shared experiences (cultural, linguistic or ethnic) or historic (appealing to commonly shared history and sense of injustices, including by previous and/or existing governmental authorities), among other perceived shared experiences.

As unrepresentative as one-party, autocratic rule might be, democratic, multiparty politics can be equally autocratic and non-responsive to the wishes of the majority, especially where the elite has a stranglehold on different aspects of the country and the citizenry has no recourse other than to the same government, democratic institutions notwithstanding – or where the said institutions are beholden to the elites as they represent the interests of the elites. This is especially true where democracy is measured based on whether or not elections are held, rather than the robustness of institutions; for as Stalin is said to have astutely observed, in one variant or another, "it doesn't matter who votes. What matters is who counts the votes" – and this was true in the Kenyan elections of 2007 and, allegedly, many other elections before that. It is plausible, too, that the citizenry may not be well informed, may vote against their interests or may not form/articulate their preferences independent of those of the elites.

Paradoxically, multi-party politics in a country as ethnically divided as Kenya have been characterized by both promise and peril almost in equal measure, in determining who gets into office to share the "what". Even as multi-party politics and elections are not synonymous with democracy, they ought to lead to deliberative processes, since none of the political parties, generally identifiable through their leaders and thus ethnic groups, are large or popular enough by themselves to form a government, and have a need for their other countrymen to do so. Recall the ethnic distribution of the population of Kenya: its 2016 population was estimated to be near 47 million. The largest ethnic groups are the Kikuyu 22 percent, Luhya 14 percent, Luo 13 percent, Kalenjin 12 percent, Kamba 11 percent, Kisii 6 percent, Meru 6 percent and the other approximately 36 groups account for approximately 15 percent, with a negligible 1 percent for non-African populations.[17] To win the presidency, considered the ultimate political prize,[18] none of the ethnic groups, not even the Kikuyus, could have mustered the 25 percent vote in each of the five provinces and a majority of the vote, per the system that was in place before the promulgation of the second post-independence constitution in 2010.

Even in the era of the new constitution, sometimes referred to as the Second Republic, to win the presidency, the community would still have needed to collate all their votes and cast them for one candidate and elicit the support of at least two other larger communities, and even then it wasn't guaranteed; for example, an alliance among the Kikuyu (22 percent), the Luhya (14 percent) and the Kalenjin (13 percent), assuming each of the communities was equally represented in the eligible voting population, only came to 49 percent of the vote. If, as was the case in 1992, 1997, 2002, 2007 and 2013, the Kikuyu community fielded several candidates, even the three largest communities could still have lost the presidency. Thus, by necessity, multi-party politics and election to the presidency required the collaboration of different groups, thereby rendering ethnic origin an asset, rather than a liability. To elicit the support of a different ethnic community, the questions of who, where, what and when would need revisiting.

Historically, there have been specific attempts to engineer political arrangements designed to foster national unity, at the expense of what one might consider democratic principles and practices. After the fall of Saddam Hussein during the 2003 Iraq war, the question of how to involve the Sunnis, who suddenly lost not only the presidency but also the military, high-ranking positions in the civil service and considerable influence, thus making them more sympathetic to the "Sunni insurgency", occupied the Coalition Provisional Authority, up to the drafting of the new constitution and the first free elections. Although the initial agreements were characterized by boycotts and the whole range of opposition, more recent arrangements have shown the possibilities of integrating democracy into a power-sharing agreement. As a compromise during the 2014 negotiations for a new government, the prime minister's position was filled by a Shiite prime minister (with Kurdish and Sunni deputies) and the presidency by a Kurd, while the Speaker of the Parliament was generally filled by a Sunni. As a negotiated settlement, Rubin and Al-Sahly note that this became the tradition: "by custom, a Sunni holds the position of speaker; a Kurd has the presidency, and a Shiite is prime minister."[19]

Consociational democracy in Kenya

It is nigh impossible to combine the concepts of democracy arrived at through formulation of preferences and expression of such preferences through elections: it cannot be coincidence that the Shiites will nearly always have a majority in parliament, and as long as Iraq is a parliamentary democracy, there will be a Shiite prime minister. This is the simple tyranny of numbers as the foundation of a democracy that puts individuals into office through elections. It is no less of a coincidence that three of Kenya's four presidents, as of 2017, have been from the majority ethnic Kikuyu group. A 22 percent ethnic majority is sufficiently significant to ensure that any president elected in Kenya will most likely have to have the backing of the Kikuyu, unless there is an alliance of the anti-Kikuyu, as happened during the 2005 constitutional review referendum. As Oloo notes, after the re-introduction of multi-party politics, and the angling that followed, for Jaramogi Oginga Odinga to be the flag bearer for the opposition, the Kikuyu elite "recognized that ethnicity was a dominant factor and calculated that due to the demographic advantage Kikuyus had over other Kenyan communities, they could always count on their numbers to grab the ultimate political prize."[20]

The Kikuyu dominance of government started much earlier: from opposing the colonial authority through the Mau, the imprisonment of Jomo Kenyatta, and the implicit support from the West of a non-socialist leader, the foundation was set. At the same time,

> the state was not seen as a neutral arbiter standing above different ethnic groups; it was a prize to be captured. Thus, when Kenyatta was succeeded by Daniel arap Moi in 1978, patronage shifted abruptly from the Kikuyu to the Kalenjin and other ethnic groups supporting Moi.[21]

After Moi's term ended in 2002, it was easy to see how the re-emergence of a Kikuyu president ensured that the patronage would be seen to shift back to the community, while in 2007, the failure of Kibaki to concede what was considered a lost election most decidedly played into the notion of "entitlement" and the denial of opportunity for the "sharing of national cake" as the issue is often referred to in the nation's press.

Kenya's ethnic considerations could have been much helped by institutions that ensured that ethnicity did not disadvantage members of other ethnic groups, by ensuring equal and equitable distribution of resources (although, the question of the role of women remained unaddressed). By utilizing patronage as the basis for support, every group would want to have access to the state, in effect, effecting "state capture". Unfortunately, this had the effect of setting up contestation based not on ideology but on the "winner-take-all" approach to politics. A consociational democracy was most likely the best approach to assure that the who gets what, when and how was not going to depend on ethnicity but on equal distribution of resources, and the presence in government of elites who would ensure that their communities were adequately represented. To some extent, this did occur: in the history of Kenya since independence, the top two positions were never once occupied by members of the same ethnic group, yet because the president had the power to appoint government officers, including the vice president, such officers were beholden to the president, and personal interest limited the extent of their intervention on behalf of the community.

Consociational democracy arises from the idea of consociational theory, which "seeks to explain the existence of political stability in certain countries with deeply fragmented political cultures. It comprises of a set of propositions concerning the two main aspects of such political systems: their political sociology and the nature of their political elites' behavior."[22] Lijphart adds that "the leaders of the rival subcultures may engage in competitive behavior and thus further aggravate mutual tensions and political instability, but they may also make *deliberate efforts to counteract the immobilizing and unstabilizing effects of cultural fragmentation*",[23] achieving the kind of unity that was seen in Kenya in 2002, 2010 and 2013 during major electoral and constitutional review political contests. Bolte, quoting Lijphart, defines consociational democracy "as a model with four characteristics: executive power-sharing or 'government by a grand coalition', a high degree of segmental autonomy, proportionality as the standard of political representation, and mutual veto rights."[24]

Luther further articulates characteristics of the elites in such democracies: "socio-political segmentation, i.e. the existence of vertically encapsulated and mutually hostile political subcultures";[25] given the ethnic and political violence that certain "outsider" groups have been subjected to in Kenya, ethnic differences can be seen in this light. As suggested earlier, considering that none of the ethnic groups have a majority vote or ability to form a government without some form of coalition, one would expect that "the replacement of segmental loyalties by a common national allegiance appears to be a logical answer to the problems posed by a plural society",[26] Lijphart considers that they may firm up the cohesions within the groups, and further promote the inter-ethnic conflicts, as has happened in Kenya since 1992.

In further explaining these types of regimes, Lijphart, a quarter-century after proposing the theory acknowledges the existence of countries that fit into this schema: as "fragmented but stable democracies", which "violates the principle of majority rule, but [it] does not deviate very much from normative democratic theory"[27] since some institutions of the democratic variety have arisen notwithstanding. The theoretical premises of consociationalism are further justified in the context of the coalition governments formed in even homogenous countries such as Sweden, during World War II, and in the idea that "the formation of a grand coalition cabinet or an alternative form of elite cartel is the appropriate response to the internal crisis of fragmentation into hostile subcultures."[28] Would Kenya have benefitted from such institutional arrangements, codified in the law, as much as other aspects of the national subcultures were integrated into the constitution, for example, the codification of Kadhi's courts?

Kenya struggles with the question of "who gets what, when, where and how" as much as the next country: even the premier democracies – including Polity IV 10 score such as Norway – struggle with challenges such as inequality. It is widely recorded that as of 2016, a woman in the US workforce was earning 79 cents to the dollar for every man, a figure that has not budged since 2000.[29] In Kenya's case, the issues ranged from polygamy to property inheritance to legislative representation. For example, in the 2010 constitution, Part 2 – Rights and Fundamental Freedoms, Article 27, sections (3) specifies that "women and men have the right to equal treatment, including the right to equal opportunities in political, economic, cultural and social spheres". Section (4) adds that: "The State shall not discriminate directly or indirectly against any person on any ground, including race, sex, pregnancy, marital status, health status, ethnic or social origin, colour, age, disability, religion, conscience, belief, culture, dress, language or birth"; while section 8 directly addresses the legislative questions, especially specifying the "two-thirds gender rule". To wit, section (8) reads as follows: "in addition to the measures contemplated in clause (6), the State shall take legislative and other measures to implement the principle that not more than two-thirds of the members of elective or appointive bodies shall be of the same gender."[30]

To give this section meaning and implementation, the government set aside, in National Assembly, 47 positions for women representatives, to be nominated by the political parties based on their representation in parliament and to represent each of the 47 counties in the country. In addition to several women elected to office, the total number of women members of parliament rose to 69. Interestingly, the number of constituencies rose from 210 to 290. Prior to the increase in the number of constituencies, the percentage of women in Kenya's National Assembly stood at about the same number. Now, even with the increase in the number of constituencies and the additional 47 nominated positions, a total of 337, the 69 women represent a paltry 19.71 percent of all elected representatives.[31] Of course, other countries struggle with the question of representation: citizens will not just vote for a candidate because she is a woman and will not fail to vote for her on the account of being a woman, yet encouraging participation by women faces other constraints that have nothing to do with democracy, direct, representative or otherwise.

In some ways then, Kenya is already implementing the concepts inherent in consociational democracy: in its history, the presidency ensured that a member of an ethnic group different from the president filled the number two slot. Further, just as the number of parliamentary constituencies was set by an act of parliament, consideration for the number of cabinet positions (cabinet secretaries, formerly ministers) should have been provided for in the constitution, without the ability to change the number save in a national referendum. Their appointees, suitably qualified, would be appointed from each of the different communities on rotating basis format. For example if there were 21 cabinet positions, with an equal number of deputy cabinet secretary position (or permanent secretary), the occupancy of these positions would rotate per each complete-period election, given that some cabinet positions are deemend "key", e.g. Foreign Affairs, Defense and Trade. The non-political, Permanent Secretary positions would also be assigned on rotating basis, such that no one community holds on to, for example, a cabinet portfolio for two consecutive presidential terms, or two cabinet positions – given that there might be 21 slots but 42 communities, or through an approach similarly arrived at – through the deliberative process.

Such an approach would not necessarily be novel or unprecedented, except that it would be provided for in the law. After all, between 2008 and 2013, the country operated under a government of national unity (GNU) as a result of the post-election violence of 2007–2008. The subsequent constitution, supported by more than 65 of the country, recognized the chronic underrepresentation of women, persons living with disabilities youth, and other minorities, and made special provisions for them. The constitution did not deliberate on the question of a rotational executive, which might have worked as in the case of Switzerland, with a presidential council, in ways that would offer the other ethnic groups an opportunity to chair the council, and decreasing the importance of the presidency as a "winner-take-all" prize. Additionally, it would have given other groups an opportunity to demonstrate leadership in ways that the country has not done in the more than half-century of independence. After all, the elements of a consociational democracy are in place, except for the consideration of a rotating presidency and/or a prime minister.

Ethnicity and consociational democracy

The end of the Cold War and the collapse of the Soviet Union heralded quickly the beginnings of what Huntington (and Diamond) considers the third wave of democracy. In just two years, multi-party politics became the norm; political prisoners were freed, freedom of the press and of association flourished, and the world was moving towards the proverbial democratic peace theory. Many countries were beginning to select their leaders not based on "birth, lot, wealth, violence, cooptation, learning, appointment or examination."[32] New leadership was instituted according to the tried-and-tested hypotheses advanced by western scholars, elected officials and even the World Bank and International Monetary Fund, which had been co-opted into threatening to withhold foreign aid unless political changes were made and political systems overhauled, with evidence that such overhaul occurred in the shortest time possible. Never mind that the same proponents for democracy had instigated wars, denied civil rights to their populations, and colonized large swathes of the future Global South.

As the Cold War thawed and ultimately ended, "democracy" was the new catchword; politically expedient alliances with economically marginalized regions were no longer attractive; it was about governance. As Huntington further notes, the emphasis was fidelity to democratization, western-style: "the central procedure of democracy is the selection of leaders through competitive elections by the people they govern."[33] The view of democracy as "institutional arrangement for arriving at political decisions in which individuals acquire the power by any means of a competitive struggle for the people's vote"[34] simultaneously gained prevalence, yet there was little concern of the development of institutions – or lack thereof, given the history of the state in Kenya, Africa and elsewhere.

Of particular concern, not much attention was paid to the ethnic factionalization and division that had in some instances been sowed as a way to contain collective action against imperialism, and subsequently exploited by tin-pot dictators often robustly supported by western powers, as long as they did not see red. How would these institutional arrangements, which required demonstration of loyalty to some unifying attribute, manifest themselves in these ethnically divided countries? It was short-sighted to hope that ethnicity would not play a part, or that elections would be free, fair and guided by notions of collective good. Given to surviving, the formerly autocratic nations quickly made superficial changes and held elections. It did not matter that even in some of the bastions of democracy, for example, the US, it took nearly 100 years to free slaves, another 100 years to give voting rights to the former slaves and 150 years for women to acquire the franchise – all conditions that met the "institutional" threshold. The wheel had been invented a few thousand years ago, and did not need reinventing – neither did democracy. But, was there a reasonable expectation that countries with little to no history of democracy, fewer than 5 to 10 years of multi-party democracy – nations that were forged at the sunset of European empires – could become liberal democracies under the drive-thru schedule that had been imposed by the west?

The result of the requirements to overhaul the systems and transition to democratization produced what Fareed Zakaria has labeled as "illiberal democracy". The tenets of illiberal democracy that arose from Huntington's own characterization of polities that carry out elections, yet after elections, the manifestation of "constitutional liberalism coming apart", even as elections are held, is spreading. To paraphrase Huntington, "governments produced by elections may be inefficient, corrupt, shortsighted, irresponsible, dominated by special interests, and incapable of adopting policies demanded by the public good. These qualities make such governments undesirable but they do not make them undemocratic."[35]

Thus, equating democracy with elections, without the gradual development of institutions necessary to underwrite democracy, can be considered "shortsighted". In 1997, Zakaria further wrote that after elections,

> popular leaders like Russia's Boris Yeltsin and Argentina's Carlos Menem bypass their parliaments and rule by presidential decree, eroding basic constitutional practices. The Iranian parliament elected more freely than most in the Middle East imposes harsh restrictions on speech, assembly, and even

> dress, diminishing that country's already meager supply of liberty. Ethiopia's elected government turns its security forces on journalists and political opponents, doing permanent damage to human rights (as well as human beings).[36]

Yet, Hamid poses an interesting theoretical (and sometimes practical) question: "[W]hat if Tunisians, Egyptians, Libyans, Yemenis or Syrians decide, through democratic means, that they *want* to be illiberal?"[37] Thus, as Hamid intimates, individuals and collectives can elect to be illiberal, and that ought to be a choice to the extent that their selections do not infringe on others' freedoms. As mentioned before, the plurality of the seats won by Hamas in Gaza in 2006, or by the Islamic Salvation Front which won elections in Algeria in 1992, showed the folly of democracy: it can produce unintended consequences. Indeed, increasingly and in many countries, the procedures that outwardly characterize the desired liberal democracies – mainly elections – happen with regular frequency. Yet, given the contending realities in some of the countries: inadequacy of institutions, strong executives, weak legislatures and judiciaries, the election of and in theocracies or theocratic-leaning polities (e.g., Iran and Saudi Arabia and Egypt with the Muslim Brotherhood), liberal democracy is unlike to manifest widely any time soon.

Perhaps the more pertinent question is whether governments produced out of consensus and deliberation must be liberal democracies in order for both the process and outcome to be valid. This is especially true, given that while some countries move towards "illiberal democracy", some have continued to liberalize; for example, the former communist countries of Eastern Europe have generally climbed in rankings, in terms of both civil and political liberties and the Freedom House (and Polity IV) scores. Kenya, then, toys with being illiberal democracy or according to Levitsky and Way, a polity that exhibits competitive authoritarianism, also described as a hybrid regime or incomplete democracy. Indeed, while the conditions in Kenya have significantly changed, and Kenya's Polity IV polity 2 variable score has averaged between 8 and 9 save for 2007, 2008 and 2009, the years following the post-election violence, Kenya was defined as a competitive authoritarian regime, where "formal democratic institutions are widely viewed as the principal means of obtaining and exercising political authority. Incumbents violate those rules so often and to such an extent, however, that the regime fails to meet conventional minimum standards for democracy."[38]

As democratization and democratic stability go, beyond the 2007 post-election violence, which dented Kenya's polity 2 score variable by 1 point, Kenya's democratic stability appears to be holding. Especially for an African country outside of the usual suspects – Botswana, South Africa, Tanzania, Ghana, Senegal (to an extent) and Zambia, for the most part, which have maintained constitutional governance for significant periods and increased the civil and political liberties – 12 years is impressive but in no way suggests that a democratic reversal is impossible. Since this volume concerns itself with Kenya, it is still useful to consider the issues that remain unresolved, the weaknesses of institutions, the unaddressed grievances, historic issues, land allocation, national cohesion – or the absence thereof – rule of law and institutional robustness, in order to ensure the viability of democracy and gradual tendency towards liberal democracy, rather than the (current) iterations of democracy.

Doing the same thing the same way . . . 2013 to the present

In a meeting between Zambia's leading government ministers and World Bank officials in 2000, ostensibly to assess Zambia's progress first with the Structural Adjustment Programs and later with the Poverty Eradication and Growth Facility, the country director for the World Bank stated,

> Today, Zambia is at the Crossroads. Nine years of reforms have had mixed results. Growth has been uneven, and on average, below economic growth. Worst of all, poverty is still very high and key social indicators have stagnated. On the other hand, economic indicators have improved. To achieve a permanent reduction in poverty, Zambia needs to continue with its reform program in four key areas.[39]

These prescriptions for economic reforms, which admittedly had not had the intended outcomes, could as easily be paraphrased and "economic" changed to "democracy", Zambia to Kenya.

They were the latest in a trend that saw solutions and prescriptions to social, economic, political and technological challenges for Africa as coming from the West, notwithstanding the potential pitfalls of the notion of path development. Thus, replacing Zambia with Kenya, one would have arrived at a statement similar to this one:

> [T]oday, Kenya is at the Crossroads. Fifteen years of [democratic] reforms have had mixed results. [Institutionalization] has been uneven, and on average, below [fidelity to liberal constitutionalism]. Worst of all, [nepotism, electoral violence, autocratic tendency] is still very high and key [democratic] indicators have stagnated. On the other hand, [the frequency of holding elections and number of parties] have [increased].

On paper, Kenya's democratic indicators have improved, but on the ground, the 2007 post-election violence demonstrated that Kenya is not out of the woods yet. In 2007, the worst bloodletting, with 1,133 deaths and close to a million internally displaced, yet the polity score was a 7. Freedom House paints a different picture: the political rights (PR) have stagnated in the 20s (rising from 21 to 22 in the last three years up to 2016), while civil liberties (CL) have gradually declined, from 36 in 2012 to 29 in 2016. Thus, despite the incongruence of the statistics by both Freedom House and the Center for Systemic Peace's (CSP's) Polity IV project, it appears that reconciliation is in order: Is Kenya becoming more democratic, as CSP's data suggests, or is it becoming less tolerant and taking away especially civil liberties, as Freedom House suggests? Adding the Fragile States Index (a revision from the Failed States Index), Kenya's 98.3 score, its "alert" status and its placement (20th out of 178) leads one to question the interpretation of the mixed data. Thus, just as the Zambia report shows, data, figures and statistics rarely tell the whole story.

Even through great peril, Kenya has pulled back from the brink, as the resettlement in Molo and Nakuru areas showed, after 1992, and after the 2007/8 post-election violence. Yet, the facts cannot be glossed over: an ethnically divided society was on the brink of sweeping violence and potential long-term instability. International intervention helped; as did Kenya's diversity, which, in this instance, was a boon for stopping the violence (either one had too many enemies or no enemies, but their lot still suffered). After the International Criminal Court (ICC) indictments, the Ocampo Six toured the country, subsuming their ethnic identities, cooperating and collaborating to defeat the ICC process, even eliciting other African countries to take a go at ICC, accusing it of being "the court for Africans." Months on end, "prayers" for the indicted were held across the country. Although it was not clear that divine intervention was in the works, the sight of all the accused juxtaposed against the internally displaced persons (IDPs) was stark: yet all of them, three Kalenjin, two GEMA (Gikuyu, Embu and Meru Association, sometimes the Akamba) and one Somali, served to minimize (although not necessarily heal) the schisms occasioned by the elections.

Indeed, the question of prosecution of Kenyans by "foreigners" is illustrated by a report about one of the accused: the then police commissioner suggested that "the activists had sold out to foreigners by setting up the 'Ocampo Six' to stand prosecution before the ICC for crimes against humanity."[40] At the same time, there was a broad 'us versus them', in this case western powers, that saw the most unlikely alliances: "13 Cord MPs broke ranks with their opposition colleagues and attended Saturday's thanksgiving ceremony for the Kenyans previously charged at the International Criminal Court (ICC), referred to as the 'Ocampo Six'".[41] ICC was often painted as a greater threat to Kenya, and the accused Kenyan leaders often found friends among the opposition, indicating the tenuous – and sometimes durability in the nature of the political alliances, even against individuals accused of crimes against humanity. Other Kenyans appeared to quickly put the events of 2007/8 behind them: in 2010 they overwhelmingly promulgated a new constitution, while in 2013 they elected to the presidency and vice presidency two of those indicted by ICC for crimes against humanity against each other's ethnic group.

It is clear that ethnicity in Kenya has been used as stick-and-carrot: stick to punish certain groups for perceived transgressions, ranging from appropriation of ancestral land, to failure to support the "right candidate" during elections. It has been used as a carrot, primarily by elites, when they seek votes to assume the highest office. Thus, Kenya's citizens would be well served to remember that there are only two tribes in the country – *wenye nchi* and *wananchi* – and that they have never seen *wenye nchi* fight among themselves. Ethnicity can be a good thing and can also be the foundation for a consociational democratic order. Perhaps 2017 will be a repeat of 2010 and 2013. One hopes.

Notes

1 The World Bank. "World DataBank: Kenya." (Web). 2016.
2 Alex Woolf. *Systems of Government: Democracy*. (Milwaukee, WI: World Amanac Library, 2006): 4.
3 Michael E. Morrell. *Empathy and Democracy: Feeling, Thinking, and Deliberation*. (University Park, PA: The Pennsylvania State University Press, 2010): 1.
4 Robert Dahl. *Polyarchy: Participation and Opposition*. (New Haven, CT: Yale University Press, 1971): 2.
5 Which, in effect, suggests and/or includes a form of representative, rather than direct democracy, a point emphasized in the idea of being chosen by the representatives of the ruled.
6 David Held. *Models of Democracy*. (Stanford, CA: Stanford University Press, 2006): 2.
7 James S. Fishkin. *Democracy and Deliberation: New Directions for Democratic Reform*. (New Haven, CT: Yale University Press, 1991): 16.
8 Fishkin. *Democracy and Deliberation*. 16.
9 Fishkin. *Democracy and Deliberation*. 17.
10 James Bohman. *Public Deliberation: Pluralism, Complexity, and Democracy*. (Cambridge, MA: The MIT Press, 2000): 1.
11 See, for example, Harsanyi, 2010: 18; Morrell, 2010: n.p.
12 Amy Guttmann & Dennis Thompson. *Why Deliberative Democracy?* (Princeton, NJ: Princeton University Press, 2004): 3.
13 Guttman & Thompson. *Why Deliberative Democracy*. 3.
14 James Bohman & William Rehg. "Introduction." In James Bohman & William Rehg, Eds. *Deliberative Democracy: Essays on Reason and Politics*. (Cambridge, MA: The MIT Press, 1997): ix.
15 Christina Lafont. "Is the Ideal of a Deliberative Democracy Coherent?" In Samantha Besson & José Luis Martí, Eds. *Deliberative Democracy and Its Discontents*. (Burlington, VT: Ashgate, 2006): 3.
16 Harold D. Laswell. *Who Gets What, When, How*. Excerpt. n.d. (Web): 295.
17 CIA World Factbook. *Kenya*. (Web). 2016, n.p.
18 See Goldsworthy, *Tom Mboya*. 269 and Oloo. "The Contemporary Opposition in Kenya." 104.
19 Alissa J. Rubin & Suadad Al-Salhy. "Iraqi Parliament Elects Speaker in Effort to Form New Government." *New York Times*. 15 July 2014. (Web): n.p.
20 Oloo. "The Contemporary Opposition in Kenya." 104.
21 Francis Fukuyama. *Political Order and Political Decay: From the Industrial Revolution to the Globalization of Democracy*. (New York, NY: Farrar, Strauss and Giroux, 2014): 331.
22 Kurt Richard Luther. "A Framework for the Comparative Analysis of Political Parties and Party Systems in Consociational Democracy." In Kris Deschouwer & Kurt Richard Luther, Eds. *Party Elites in Divided Societies: Political Parties in Consociational Democracy*. (New York, NY: Routledge, 1999): 2.
23 Arend Lijphart. "Consociational Democracy." In Robert Alan Dahl, Ian Shapiro & Jose Antonio Cheibub, Eds. *The Democracy Sourcebook*. (Cambridge, MA: The MIT Press, 2003): 142.
24 Patrick Bolte. *Consociational Democracy in Multiethnic Societies*. (Nordenstedt: GRIN Verlag, 2004): 3.
25 Luther. "A Framework for the Comparative Analysis of Political Parties and Party Systems in Consociational Democracy." 2.
26 Arend Lijphart. *Democracy in Plural Societies: A Comparative Exploration*. (New Haven, CT: Yale University Press, 1977): 24.
27 Lijphart. "Consociational Democracy." 142.

28 Lijphart. "Consociational Democracy." 142.
29 Lauren Leader-Chivee & Karl Weber. *Crossing the Thinnest Line: How Embracing Diversity – from the Office to the Oscars – Makes America Stronger*. (New York, NY: Hachette Book Group, 2016): 212; see also: US Congress, Joint Economic Committee. *Invest in Women, Invest in America: A Comprehensive Review of Women in the U.S. Economy*. December 2010. (Washington, DC: U.S. Government Printing Office, 2011): 10.
30 Kenya Law Reports. "The Constitution of Kenya." National Council for Law Reporting. 2010. (Web): 24–25.
31 Inter-Parliamentary Union. *Kenya National Assembly*. 2016. (Web): n.p. Accessed on 12/11/2016 from: http://www.ipu.org/parline/reports/2167.htm
32 Samuel P. Huntington. *The Third Wave: Democratization in the Late 20th Century*. (Norman, OK: University of Oklahoma Press, 1991): 6
33 Huntington. *The Third Wave*. 6
34 Huntington. *The Third Wave*. 6
35 Fareed Zakaria. "The Rise of Illiberal Democracy." *Foreign Affairs*, 76, No. 6 (1997): 24–25.
36 Zakaria. "The Rise of Illiberal Democracy." 24.
37 Shadi Hamid. *Temptations of Power: Islamists and Illiberal Democracy in a New Middle East*. (New York, NY: Oxford University Press, 2014): 26–27.
38 Levitsky & Way. "Elections without Democracy." 52.
39 Shantha Bloemen. T-Shirt Travels. (Video). Produced by Shantha Bloemen (New York, NY: Filmakers Library, 2001), 57 mins.
40 Nation Reporter. "Ex-Police Boss Confronts Human Rights Lawyer over ICC Issue." *Nation Newspapers*. Sunday 24 April 2016. (Web): n.p.
41 Francis Mũreithi & Nelcon Odhiambo. "Opposition MPs Break Ranks with Cord to Show Support for 'Ocampo Six'." *Nation Newspapers*. Monday 18 April 2016. (Web): n.p.

References

Bloemen, Shantha. T-Shirt Travels. (Video). Produced by Shantha Bloemen (New York, NY: Filmakers Library, 2001), 57 mins.

Bohman, James. *Public Deliberation: Pluralism, Complexity, and Democracy*. Cambridge, MA: The MIT Press, 2000.

Bohman, James & William Rehg. "Introduction." In James Bohman & William Rehg, Eds. *Deliberative Democracy: Essays on Reason and Politics*. Cambridge, MA: The MIT Press, 1997.

Bolte, Patrick. *Consociational Democracy in Multiethnic Societies*. Nordenstedt: GRIN Verlag, 2004.

Bowden, Rob. *Kenya*. London, UK: Evans Brothers, 2007.

CIA. "CIA Word Factbook: Kenya." (Web). 2016. Accessed on 12/11/2016 from: www.cia.gov/library/publications/the-world-factbook/geos/ke.html

Fishkin, James S. *Democracy and Deliberation: New Directions for Democratic Reform*. New Haven, CT: Yale University Press, 1991.

Fukuyama, Francis. *Political Order and Political Decay: From the Industrial Revolution to the Globalization of Democracy*. New York, NY: Farrar, Strauss and Giroux, 2014.

Fund for Peace. Fragile States Index 2016 Report. *Fund for Peace*. 2016. (Web). Accessed on 12/12/2016 from: http://fsi.fundforpeace.org/rankings-2016

Goldsworthy, David. *Tom Mboya: The Man Kenya Wanted to Forget*. New York, NY: Africana Publishing, 2008.

Guttmann, Amy & Dennis Thompson. *Why Deliberative Democracy?* Princeton, NJ: Princeton University Press, 2004.

Hamid, Shadi. *Temptations of Power: Islamists and Illiberal Democracy in a New Middle East*. New York, NY: Oxford University Press, 2014.

Harsanyi, Doina Pasca. *Lessons from America: Liberal French Nobles in Exile, 1793–1798*. University Park, PA: The Pennsylvania State University Press, 2010.

Held, David. *Models of Democracy*. Stanford, CA: Stanford University Press, 2006.

Huntington, Samuel P. *The Third Wave: Democratization in the Late 20th Century*. Norman, OK: University of Oklahoma Press, 1991.

Inter-Parliamentary Union. Kenya National Assembly. (Web). Accessed on 12/11/2016 from: www.ipu.org/parline/reports/2167.htm

Kenya Law Reports. "The Constitution of Kenya." National Council for Law Reporting. 2010. (Web). Accessed on 12/11/2016 from: www.kenyaembassy.com/pdfs/the%20 constitution%20of%20kenya.pdf

Lafont, Christina. "Is the Ideal of a Deliberative Democracy Coherent?" In Samantha Besson & José Luis Martí, Eds. *Deliberative Democracy and Its Discontents*. Burlington, VT: Ashgate, 2006.

Laswell, Harold D. *Who Gets What, When, How*. Excerpt. n.d. (Web). Ch. 1: Elite. Accessed on 12/11/2016 from: www.policysciences.org/classics/politics.pdf

Leader-Chivee, Lauren & Karl Weber. *Crossing the Thinnest Line: How Embracing Diversity – from the Office to the Oscars – Makes America Stronger*. New York, NY: Hachette Book Group, 2016.

Levitsky, Steven & Lucan A. Way. "Elections without Democracy: The Rise of Competitive Authoritarianism." *Journal of Democracy*, 13, No. 2 (2002): 51–65. doi:10.1353/jod.2002.0026

Lijphart, Arend. "Consociational Democracy." In Robert Alan Dahl, Ian Shapiro & Jose Antonio Cheibub, Eds. *The Democracy Sourcebook*. Cambridge, MA: The MIT Press, 2003.

Lijphart, Arend. *Democracy in Plural Societies: A Comparative Exploration*. New Haven, CT: Yale University Press, 1977.

Liljas, Per. "Iraq Approves New Unity Government, Sets the Stage for Combatting ISIS." *Time Magazine*. 9 September 2014. (Web). Accessed on 12/11/2016 from: http://time.com/3307624/iraq-approves-new-unity-government-sets-the-stage-for-combatting-isis/

Luther, Kurt Richard. "A Framework for the Comparative Analysis of Political Parties and Party Systems in Consociational Democracy." In Kris Deschouwer & Kurt Richard Luther, Eds. *Party Elites in Divided Societies: Political Parties in Consociational Democracy*. New York, NY: Routledge, 1999.

Møller, Jørgen. *Post-Communist Regime Change: A Comparative Study*. New York, NY: Routledge, 2009.

Morrell, Michael E. *Empathy and Democracy: Feeling, Thinking, and Deliberation*. University Park, PA: The Pennsylvania State University Press, 2010.

Mũreithi, Francis & Nelcon Odhiambo. "Opposition MPs Break Ranks with Cord to Show Support for 'Ocampo Six'." *Nation Newspapers*. Monday 18 April 2016. (Web): n.p. Accessed on 12/12/2016 from: www.nation.co.ke/news/politics/Future-of-Cord-shaky-as-13-MPs-attend-Nakuru-prayers/1064-3163810-mqlybv/index.html

Nation Reporter. "2016 Ex-Police Boss Confronts Human Rights Lawyer over ICC Issue." *Nation Newspapers*. Sunday 24 April 2016. (Web): n.p. Accessed on 12/12/2016 from: www.nation.co.ke/news/1056-3173484-723iaoz/index.html

Oloo, Adams G. R. "The Contemporary Opposition in Kenya: Between Internal Traits and State Manipulation." In Godwin R. Murunga & Shadrack W. Nasong'o, Eds. *Kenya: The Struggle for Democracy*. New York, NY: Zed Books, 2007.

Rubin, Alissa J. & Suadad Al-Salhy. "Iraqi Parliament Elects Speaker in Effort to Form New Government." *New York Times*. 15 July 2014. (Web). Accessed on 12/11/2016 from: www.nytimes.com/2014/07/16/world/middleeast/iraq.html?_r=0

US Congress, Joint Economic Committee. *Invest in Women, Invest in America: A Comprehensive Review of Women in the U.S. Economy*. December 2010. Washington, DC: U.S. Government Printing Office, 2011.

Woolf, Alex. *Systems of Government: Democracy*. Milwaukee, WI: World Amanac Library, 2006.

The World Bank. "World DataBank: Kenya." (Web). Accessed on 12/4/2016 from: http://databank.worldbank.org/data/reports.aspx?source=2&series=NY.GDP.PCAP.CD&country=#

Zakaria, Fareed. "The Rise of Illiberal Democracy." *Foreign Affairs*, 76, No. 6 (1997): 22–43. Accessed from: www.jstor.org/stable/20048274

8 Concluding thoughts

2017: lessons of 2007, 2010 and 2013

There are days, months, years, places and events that live in the collective history of a nation, whatever nation that might be. Some are celebratory, while others are, in Roosevelt's words, days that will live in infamy. The years of World War II are etched in every Jewish person's memory as they are in the collective conscience of the world. Places such as Abbottabad, Auschwitz, Chernobyl, Hiroshima, Nagasaki, Nanking, Pearl Harbor, Tranquility Base, Verdun and Waterloo – they all carry meaning. In Kenya, 20 October 1952, 1 June 1963, 12 December 1963, 7 July 1969, 1 August 1982, Saba Saba J. M. Kariuki, Nyayo House, Got Alila, Burnt Forest, Salgaa and 7 August 1998 – all these have meanings that are specific to the Kenyan experience.

In particular, 1992, 1997, 2002, 2007, 2005, 2010 and 2013 were years marked by some electoral activity, during which violence ensued (1992, 1997 and 2007). Statistically, during the multi-party politics era, Kenya's record with electoral violence is dismal: in three of the seven electoral activities (this includes voting to adopt or reject a new constitution in 2005 and 2010), there was some manifestation of violence, that is, 43 percent of the time. The next general election is slated for 8 August 2017. What is to be expected in the period before an election, in the context of previous electoral experiences, the perennial candidates for the office of the president, and the previous involvement of the international community in Kenya's internal conflict? It is useful to reflect on Kenya's record as a haven for peace, interspersed with periodic episodes of political violence.

History and the numbers of Kenya's conflicts

To consider the history of Kenya and the conflicts which have occurred, data from the Center for Systemic Peace Polity IV project and the Armed Conflict Location & Event Data (ACLED) are used. ACLED data, which cover 1997 to 2015, study different conflicts on the African continent. In the period covered, ACLED records a total of 5,041 conflicts, with a total fatality count of 9,129. ACLED's classification of the conflicts is unique; the database records all instances of violence, including "strategic development" and "violence against civilians" incidences; thus, 1,270 (or 25 percent) of the conflicts consisted of violence against civilians, sometimes carried out by the police forces. More specifically, 1,913 (or

38 percent) of the conflicts were classified as "riots", which involved actors as diverse as the Catholic Group, students and farmers, among others. The events with the highest number of casualties were terrorist attacks, include the bombing of the US embassy on 7 August 1998 (213) in Nairobi, Kenya, the Al-Shabaab attack on Garissa University in 2015 (148) and the Westgate Mall siege (more than 68). Only three of the conflicts were against a foreign entity; military forces of Kenya fought and displaced the Oromo Liberation Front from areas of northern Kenya in 2010 with no loss of life.[1]

Conflicts have outcomes, and some of those outcomes are internally displaced persons (IDPs) and when these cross international boundaries, become refugees. The 2007/8 post-election violence was seen as quite destructive in terms of population disruption: in addition to the 1,133 deaths recorded (identified elsewhere in this volume), violence in 1992/3 and 1997 displaced almost an equal number of persons. Kenya's situation is rather paradoxical: it has served as a safe haven for refugees from Somalia, Ethiopia and South (then) Sudan, hosting some of the largest contingents of refugees. Yet, the data from the Center for Systemic Peace on "Forcibly Displaced Populations, 1964–2008" paint an interesting picture for Kenya. Of special interest are three variables: SOURCE (denoting the number of refugees in thousands, who originate from Kenya), the IDP variable (which denotes the number of IDPs in thousands, originating from Kenya) and the HOST variable (denoting the number of refugees, in the thousands, who are hosted Kenya); all figures were premised on 2008. The figures, respectively, are 55,000 refugees, 4.07 million IDPs and 4.8 million refugees.[2]

Other statistics on inter-state war show that Kenya has not been involved in many of these – other than the 1964 Shifta war against Somali-backed "bandits", its participation in and membership of the Anti Piracy Task Force in the early years of the 21st century, peacekeeping mission in South Sudan and the military action initiated in Somalia in 2011. Kenya's source of instability is internal; it follows almost predictable patterns, particularly around elections. Other unusual events include high mass-casualty events such as terrorist attacks, some because it offers "soft targets" and poor security infrastructure, compounded by graft in all sectors of society. Thus, Kenya is not quite the haven of peace it is painted to be, except in the context of civil wars, internal conflicts, insurrections, cross-border conflict and providing haven for rebel groups, which elevate the levels of violence in other, neighboring countries. The implications of these conflicts, this violence, are important as the next elections loom, particularly since there has not been concerted action to resolve the issues that have generally led to conflict.

Containing the possibility of future conflict

Nothing in the internal politics of Kenya, or any other country, necessitates that violence be part of the political landscape, the conduct of elections or the relationships between ethnic groups. Rather, the degree to which conflict happens can be a function of the role of elites and their pursuit of self-interest and political power, maintenance of the status quo and concealment of prior misdeeds that might otherwise be prosecuted by incoming governments. To do this, elites often recruit their ethnic group members, appealing to perceived traditional grievances, past slights and generally, "othering" groups perceived to be the source of their marginalization, even when they share commonalities, such as membership and citizenship of a polity. Whereas states are taken to be sovereigns, beginning 2005, the landscape and the extent of sovereignty have been challenged and states' functions redefined. While Kenya's post-election conflict in 2007/8 did not rise to the level of requiring international intervention under the Responsibility to Protect (R2P) concept, it will be recalled that the French Ambassador, as Bernard Kouchner intimated that the UN should consider R2P intervention in Kenya.

Revisiting the basic principles of R2P, which changed the concept of sovereignty, and required that states not only exercise the traditional functions and authority of the state: establishment and regulation of economic, political and cultural norms, the regulation of currencies, economic flows, population migrations, legal norms, cultural values and so forth,[3] states have found themselves required to protect their citizens from some of the very concerns which they visit upon their citizens. The two basic principles undergirding R2P are (a) state sovereignty implies responsibility, and the primary responsibility for the protection of its people lies with the state itself, and (b) where a population is suffering serious harm, as a result of internal war, insurgency, repression or state failure, and the state in question is unwilling or unable to halt or avert it, the principle of non-intervention yields to the international responsibility to protect.[4] The R2P report was adopted during the sixtieth session of the United Nations General Assembly meeting under the auspices of the 2005 World Summit Outcome; three years later, the United Nations secretary-general appointed a special adviser on the prevention of genocide.

Even prior to the adoption of the R2P report, beginning 1996, the United Nations had commissioned work on an international criminal tribunal, culminating in a treaty signed in Rome, 17 July 1998, resulting in the adoption by a 120–7 vote (with 21 abstentions) of the Rome Statute of the International Criminal Court (ICC). Rather interestingly, the US voted against the statute, which came into force in 2002. It is useful to note that Kenya supported both the R2P project and was a signatory to the Rome Statute, thus becoming a member of the Assembly of State Parties and bound to the principles of ICC.[5] The twinship between the Rome Statute establishing ICC and the International Commission on Intervention and State Sovereignty outlining R2P effectively both changed the concept of state sovereignty from absolute power and ability to preside over all that happens within the jurisdiction of the state, to one of actively presiding over the well-being of the subjects.[6]

Naturally, if one were to consider Rousseau's concept of sovereignty, a wholly different meaning, one that is closer to the intentions of sovereignty according to R2P. Rousseau writes: "I hold then that sovereignty, being nothing less than the exercise of the general will",[7] although Rousseau subsequently admits that individuals' preferences are guided by private will, while general will is derived from consensus; thus, "while it is not impossible for a private will to coincide with the general will on some point or other, it is impossible for such a coincidence to be regular and enduring."[8] Yet, if it is the general will, if men come together and give up private violence in favor of state regulation of violence (e.g., in Kenya, regulating and resolving the question of land ownership in the Rift Valley, alleged to be dominated by Kikuyus), it follows then that such violence could be visited on the members of the community who live outside "their areas".[9] Therefore, general will dictate that for purposes of the greater benefit, harm would come to the private regulation of land ownership. It is then in the interest of individuals and communities to not just live harmoniously but to also shun those activities that would invite the intervention of outside forces, when people discard the collective violence resolution mechanisms and the state is unable or unwilling to intervene in case of an outbreak of violence.

Long before the debates on Libya, Syria, Ivory Coast and other disparate places, Kenya's post-election violence especially in 2008, the coordinated, well-funded, organized and planned attacks attracted the attention of international leaders. As Badescu notes,

> Desmond Tutu and Francis Deng, the UN Special Adviser on the Prevention of Genocide, were the first to make references to R2P in relation to the 2007 post-election violence in Kenya. . . . The UN Secretary-General reminded the Kenyans of their legal and moral responsibility to protect the lives of their citizens, regardless of ethnic, racial, or religious origin, and to prevent future violence.[10]

Badescu further adds that "collective efforts in early 2008 brought this [carnage and ethnic cleansing] to a halt, and showed the beneficial effects of rapid and consolidated international action."[11]

Formally established in 2002, ICC had had begun its work to prosecute crimes against humanity with perhaps one of Africa's worst cases of genocide and crimes against humanity: on the Ugandan government's referral by a state party to the Rome Statute, invited the ICC prosecutor, Luis Moreno-Ocampo, to investigate the restive Lord's Resistance Army;[12] in 2005 an inquiry began in July of the same year, naming

> Joseph Kony, the LRA's commander in chief; Vincent Otti, vice chairman and second in command of the LRA; Okot Odhiambo, deputy commander and brigade commander of Trinkle and Stocktree Brigades of the LAR; Dominic Ongwen, brigade commander of the LRA's Sinia Brigade; and Raska Lukiya, deputy army commander.[13]

Thus, with the start of the conflict in Kenya, and the activities that were going on next door, the individuals who might be considered to "bear the greatest responsibility for crimes against humanity and crimes of genocide" had an existing template; it was not a template any of the elites were keen to risk. Perhaps this risk was sufficient to lead to a step back, to encourage the principals to negotiate and bring about some settlement to the conflict. Ferris argues that "the international community's response to election violence in Kenya in early 2008 is held up by R2P advocates as the only successful instance of the application of R2P to date",[14] even though the threat of prosecution was sufficient to change the potentially catastrophic outcomes.

A roadmap to a peaceful and prosperous Kenya

Having gone through several elections that exposed her darker side, there is great hope that 2017 will be a repeat of 2013 and 2010 and will avoid the errors of 2007. Before reviewing some of the intended governmental actions, the sources that international partners can offer, the (lack of) need for civic and voter education, potential peace conferences and agreements between previously hostile communities, it is useful to revisit the question of electoral violence, its occurrence, the manifestation and the actions that the current Kenyan government is undertaking to insure that it retains its +8 polity score rating, emerge from the Freedom House's "Partly Free" classification and reclaim its place as the once-touted "island of peace" in a sea of conflict.

Fisher defines electoral violence as "any random or organized act or threat to intimidate, physically harm, blackmail or abuse a political stakeholder in seeking to determine, delay or to otherwise influence an electoral process."[15] It is neither new, unique to Kenya or Africa; it has a long history there and elsewhere, including some of Africa's now stable and peaceful democracies – Ghana – in 1956 and 1978.[16] Indeed, Jarstad notes that pre-election peace accords, similar to post-election peace accords, often end up in violence – 17 out of 38 accords.[17] The conflicts are attributed to "complex histories; they exhibit multiple and multidimensional causes, courses and consequences."[18] These complex histories and multidimensional causes have been increasingly parsed and widely debated and have included ethno-religious causes, for example, the Hindu–Muslim violence in India;[19] inconclusive democratic transitions resulting "in polarized local identities and unprecedented incidents of sectarian cleansing";[20] weak institutions; and the flouting of the rule of law.[21] Other explanations rely on the more generalized, economic-based rational-choice theory and outcomes: "if expected gains from violent conflict exceed the costs, then individuals will choose to take up arms."[22]

In other countries, electoral violence can be caused by a multitude of failures. One such example was Ghana's 1992 election; Gyimah-Boadi argues that a collection of failures – inadequate preparation by the national electoral body and voter registers; unreliable population data; time constraints on voter education, including the electoral staff on rules, laws and equipment; mistrust over neutrality of the electoral body; and logistical problems on election day[23] resulted in a sham election. For Ghana, none of the violence was directly attributable to the ethnic divisions. More benign and global-level explanations of such violence assert factors such as younger democracies (born in the third wave of democratization), whose income was low, and which were just coming out of colonialism and the Cold War.[24] Other generalist explanations include, for example, the expectation that inequality correlates (produces) discontent. Under this thesis, inequality is an insufficient but necessary condition[25] for political violence. Thus, "when violence does occur, it takes place only under the condition of high inequality."[26] Owing their attributes to other potential variables not tested by Muller, "Pakistan, Taiwan, Panama, and Iraq represent extreme positive errors of prediction, while Costa Rica and Brazil have political-violence scores that are much less than predicted on the basis of their level of income inequality."[27] Put differently , the levels of political violence in Pakistan, Taiwan, Panama and Iraq far exceed what should be expected based on the inequality, while the other two have much less violence than would be expected, pointing to other causes.

More generally, electoral violence can also be seen to stem from one, several or all of a variety of factors. They include gerrymandering, manipulation of the electoral poll or voters' registers, misallocation of electors to voting districts, manipulation of nomination process, manipulation of the local polling stations or polling booths, arrest and detention of political parties' opponents by the government, manipulation of ballot papers and ballot boxes on the polling day.[28] In addition to the other vast array of sources. Thus, in younger, less affluent democracies in transition without a long history of liberal democratic tradition, respect for the rule of law and individual (and collective) property and those with histories of autocracy, ethnic cleavages and electoral violence, and in taking into account Kenya's history, the probability of the next election being violent is better than 43 percent, probably higher.

The early campaign periods in the run-up to the 2017 Kenya general elections have begun illuminating a path that might mimic 2013 more than 2007. For starters, the pre-election violence that characterized some of the previous elections is largely absent. The president and the government have made all the appropriate assurances and exhortations for the election to be peaceful, fair and transparent. In a nod/wink to the 2016 US elections that were marred by allegations of foreign – read Russian – interference, warned the "foreign countries" against interfering with the upcoming elections.[29] Kenya's transparent, plastic ballot boxes do not necessarily lend themselves to the US–Russia-type hacking; traditionally, "interference" in the case of Kenya has generally referred to the pre-election civic education activities, elections monitoring processes, support for one party or the other, particularly the opposition, provision of equipment such as helicopters and campaign material and other similar contributions.

Simultaneously, the country's leadership has begun to emphasize the importance of conducting elections peacefully. For example, speaking both the head of state and a past visitor to ICC, Kenyatta impassioned his fellow countrymen:

> I do not have to remind you what disunity looks like . . . we know all too well what happened the last time we failed to treat each other as one family. So I will close by asking every Kenyan one single thing: in 2017, I ask you to be your brother's keeper.[30]

Perhaps a more durable approach would have been to emphasize the Tanzania-esque *Ujamaa* ideal of being one's brother's keeper all the time, rather than just during elections. Yet even as the country looks to the general elections, the nominations have been no less than chaotic: several clashes and conflicts have been reported, and the possibility of such conflict expanding and extending to the elections cannot be ignored.

Conducting peaceful elections and accepting the outcome of the elections will demonstrate Kenya's commitment to the rule of law and to being considered a gradually and progressively maturing democracy. For unlike trends in other parts of the continent, Kenya is surrounded by countries that have the Stalin-esque elections, where leaders have changed constitutions to facilitate the incumbent's stay in power forever (Uganda, Rwanda, the Democratic Republic of the Congo, Burundi), and where leaders refuse to accept the results of the popular vote. In contrast, apart from the Ivory Coast's 2011 situation, West African countries, including surprisingly, The Gambia, have shown willingness to concede elections (at least temporarily, in the case of The Gambia, one of the countries with the longest democratic tradition in Africa until 1994); Ghana's incumbent president lost the 2016 and gracefully conceded. As Kenya's perennial presidential candidate opined, it is possible that democracy is finally coming to Africa, and Africa into its own.

Resolving Kenya's perennial *Nyũmba ya Mũmbi* problem

Kenya, whether it likes it or not, whether the issue is acknowledged or swept under the rug every election year and after every conflict, has a "'House of Mũmbi'[31] Question." Did the British create the Kikuyu hegemony over Kenyan politics, both by design and by accident? Kenya's House of Mũmbi was most unwittingly contributed to by a combination of factors, some preceding colonialism, others exacerbated by it, and others post-colonialism, particularly with the formation of the first independence government, which was packed with Kikuyu ministers and ringed by the Family/the Kikuyu Mafia. As for the conditions of the Kikuyu people before colonialism, the group's main economic activity revolved around agriculture, growing crops that included sorghum, millet, beans, peas, yams and bananas. They occupied the region around Central Kenya, surrounding Mount Kenya.

Page writes that "after British colonial rule was established in the late nineteenth century, land policies were implemented to disenfranchise the Kikuyu of the prime highland soil. In addition, the Kikuyu were relegated to living in overcrowded tribal reserves while working on European plantations."[32] The Kikuyu experience with colonialism was different from that of other communities, initially for climatic reasons: they occupied the most fertile soils, with regular rainfall, areas that were prime for planting coffee and tea and other cash crops such as pyrethrum, all of which were in great demand in Britain, Europe and the New World. The British settlers made clear that they had no intention to depart from the White Highlands and were keen to turn it into another South Africa.

For the British, appropriating land in the fertile Kenya Highlands was a no-brainer; it was the area with the greatest potential for economic productivity and the most temperate weather and was considered grossly underutilized due to subsistence farming. Rather unfortunately, the British failed to recognize the relationship between the Kikuyus and land: "the Kikuyus believe in a special connection with the land and soil. They not only believe that they must own land, but all Kikuyus believe that they must build a home on that land";[33] thus, dispossession ran deeper than just the arable dirt. In order to more easily conquer and displace a numerically superior people, apart from the more lethal technology (guns), the British colonial authorities instituted a policy commonly known as "divide and rule", through which they "implemented indirect rule based on local leaders. They set out to divide the population and create ethnically homogeneous entities out of what in fact were fuzzy entities."[34]

The ultimate result of this was that the British "invented" new tribes, while others suffered "the imposition of a sharp boundary that divided previously united, or at least affiliated, people."[35] For the Kikuyu, being agriculturalists was also a disadvantage: settled peoples were easier to conquer. Contrasting with the Maasai, who were pastoralists, or the Kalenjin, who were pastoralists with some limited agricultural activity, or the Kamba, who occupied a rather semi-arid region of Kenya, and the agriculturally fertile western banks of the Rift Valley (the climate was hot, humid and mosquitoes were abundant), thus the Kikuyu bore the brunt of the worst excesses of colonialism. Chafing under colonialism, dispossessed of land, unable to access educational opportunities other than simple "hands-on" education that led to jobs such as carpentry, the Kikuyus sought to establish both independent schools and churches, which would provide opportunities for the Kikuyu people. The banning of ethnic Kikuyu associations such as the Young Kikuyu Association, and the Kikuyu Central Association (KCA), led to even more discontent. Ultimately, the Kikuyus would start the Kenya Land and Freedom Army (KLFA), which was popularly known as Mau Mau.

At the same time, to relieve some of the pressure due to loss of the White Highlands, "the Kikuyu . . . moved into the Rift Valley Province during the colonial period and after independence."[36] A British-educated Kikuyu and author of *Facing Mount Kenya*, Johnstone Kamau, later known as Jomo Kenyatta, the first president, would be accused of leading the organization, jailed for seven years and hard labor. By the time Kenya was becoming independent, it was not inevitable, but extremely likely, that Kenyatta would become the leader of independent Kenya. As Fitzpatrick, Brewer and Firestone argue, "due to the influence of Jomo Kenyatta, Kenya's first president, the Kikuyu today are disproportionately represented in government."[37]

Soja notes that part of the domination of the Kikuyu of post-independence Kenya had much to do with geography (proximity) and the shift in focus from the coastal strip, which had been the center of trade with the Far East and Europe, to Nairobi, the new capital, facilitated by the building of the Uganda Railway, completed in 1902. Soja writes that "the importance of just one factor-geographical position-should be emphasized; proximity to the major centers of European population, particularly Nairobi, may have been the required catalyst behind the rapid change of mobilization and change among the Kikuyu."[38] Of the four post-independence Kenyan presidents, three have been ethnic Kikuyus. According to

Fitzpatrick, Brewer and Firestone, "this has proved to be a source of ongoing friction with other groups, and a stumbling block on Kenya's path to national integration."[39] Further illustrating the dominance and the perception of the Kikuyu by other ethnic groups, Hummel writes that "Kikuyus also see themselves as the dominant tribe in Kenya, and as a result they tend to look down on other communities, which, understandably creates resentment."[40]

It is indeed illuminating to muse on the perception of the leaders surrounding Jomo Kenyatta and Kibaki; under Kenyatta, the Kikuyu elites who were closest to him were referred to as "the Family" – a clear Mafia inflection, while those who surrounded Kibaki were derisively referred to as the "Mount Kenya Mafia."[41] It makes sense then, that the Kalenjin would have attempted to both reduce the presence of the Kikuyu in the Rift Valley and use the tools of government, once Moi was in power in 1978, to rectify some of these egregious conditions. Even the campaigns surrounding the third wave of democracy were viewed with suspicion: "to the Kalenjin, the re-introduction of multi-party politics was aimed at getting Moi and the Kalenjin out of political power. They thus picked up the land question and used it launch a Majimboist campaign once again."[42]

Thus, the confluence of the perfect storms of British appropriation of the traditional ancestral land of the Kikuyu and turning it into the White Highlands, dispossession that led to immigration and settlement in the Rift Valley, the precolonial demographic numbers (Kikuyus were still the most numerous group), the British colonial policy of "divide and rule", collaborating with the church to introduce rudimentary education for Africans, the favorable climate for agriculture and settlement, the proximity of the Kikuyus to the metropolitan Nairobi area and the business acumen that Kikuyus pursued led to the domination of Kenya's social, political, economic and to some extent, cultural landscape[43] of Kenya.

Can there be a solution to the "Nyũmba ya Mũmbi" question? In the past, the Kikuyus have done what was most expedient: it can be absolutely explained through rational choice theory (RCT). The community has generally acted in a unitary fashion but looked out for its best interests, per RCT. RCT holds that actors have to make a decision with or without complete information, but that they have choices; among these choices they have preferences that can be ordered transitively: A ➔ B; B ➔ C. Actors then formulate and consider valid alternatives, always maximizing their utility, that is, computation of their optimal decision. They do a cost–benefit analysis (e.g., support one candidate over the other, oppose government *en masse*) and then make their preferences known.

It is difficult to get anyone to give up power;[44] it is certainly not easy to get the Kikuyu to *not* pursue business opportunities, land, power, influence or political office, especially given their involvement in the process of building the Kenyan nation, beginning with colonization, during independence and in the post-independence period. Yet, as much as they might pursue power, such pursuit has generally followed conventional means – especially persuasion – and the tyranny of numbers. Indeed, the only almost-successful coup d'état was attempted by individuals from the Luo ethnic group. One might almost assert "manifest destiny" of the Kikuyu people in their exercise of influence over Kenya's business and leadership.

The Kikuyu (non-)response

There is a Swahili "saying" that goes thus: *msiba wa kujitakia hauna kilio*, which roughly translates into "one should not complain/rue self-inflicted wounds (tragedies)." One of the issues that confront the Kikuyu hegemony is, in part, the diminished understanding of and the lack of sympathy regarding the impact of the community's domination of Kenya's landscape. Additionally, some positions taken by the community's leaders and their public pronouncements often unmask a deep-seated self-aggrandization and determination to continue dominating other groups. For example, during Kenyatta's succession battles, the "Kikuyu Mafia", also called "the Family", was well known to have opposed Moi's potential to succeed Kenyatta based on the then constitutional provisions, including potential constitutional amendments. In 1969, surrounding the disbanding of the Kenya Peoples' Union, it was alleged that the "Kiambu Mafia" around Kenyatta had "vowed not to let *piki piki,* meaning the motor cycles in the presidential escort, cross the Chania River or to enter another tribe's territory."[45]

The designs to keep the presidency out of the "West of Chania River" went so far as having Moi accused of bringing guns into the country after attending an Organization of African Unity (OAU) meeting in Kampala, Uganda in 1975, having him and his properties searched and, generally, attempting to discredit him.[46] Even after these efforts failed, Moi's first act, perhaps to mollify the Kikuyu or to *fuata nyayo* (follow the footsteps) of Kenyatta, appointed a Kikuyu. Rather interestingly, Moi, as he was approaching the constitutionally mandated two-term limit of his presidency in 2002, "anointed" Uhuru Kenyatta, a Kikuyu, as his successor. One would have imagined that the president would diversify his pool of potential successors in order to break the Kikuyu stranglehold on the republic, to include other communities in sharing "the national cake" and avoid the domination by the "larger tribes" that had led Moi, 40 years previously, to found KADU.

It was at Uhuru's coronation that Moi was reported to have claimed, "KANU iko na wenyewe" (translated to "KANU has its owners")[47] and paradoxically sought to elevate Uhuru over Kibaki, who was from Othaya/Nyeri, "West of Chania River", thus playing right into the 1969 "Kiambu Mafia" plan to keep the presidency in Gatundu. Was Moi repaying Kenyatta and Njonjo, who had helped him ascend to power? If he was, the rest of the country was missing out on the possibility of having one of their own ascend to power, and thus, Moi was inadvertently piling onto the perception that the Kikuyu were continuing with their domination of Kenya. The outcome of the 2002 election further cemented this view: whichever candidate stood a fair chance of being elected president, the top two presidential contenders were Kikuyu. The opportunities to separate the Kikuyu from presidential leadership, for the first half of Kenya's independence era were rather unsuccessful: Kikuyus held the presidency or the vice presidency.

After the introduction of multi-party politics, for the first time, Kikuyus were out of government in a significant way: they were the core of the opposition, had few ministerial or consequential appointments, and were literally "on the run" in places like the Rift Valley, Maasailand and the Coast. Yet after 10 years out of power, the presidency went back to the Kikuyus *and* west of Chania River, with Kibaki's election. Thus, the possibility of a sense of historic entitlement and/or leadership can be discerned. It is not clear that there have been significant public discussions about the "West of Chania River" inference or Kenyatta's utterance, *nĩ irue*, uttered in Kisumu in October 1969 preceding the Kisumu massacre. It is evident that the combination of historical factors, historical tragedies and external interference (colonialism and ultimately independence) and beliefs about socio-cultural practices vis-à-vis leadership, have had more than a cursory influence on Kenya.

Much of the intense ethnic conflict pitting the Kikuyu versus "other" has been against the Kalenjin, yet there have been opportunities for cooperation between the two groups. Thus, the possibilities for achieving détente, of resolving their perceived sources of conflict amicably do exist. The rapprochement between the Kikuyu and the Kalenjin, the only two societies to ever have produced a president in the history of Kenya was evident in 2013. Yet, one fears that in 2022, at the end of the second term of Uhuru Kenyatta, when the Kikuyu are expected to back William Ruto, flouting this agreement might rekindle the hostility. There are also lingering questions surrounding 2017: if the Kenyatta–Ruto ticket fails to win the presidency for a second term, would the Kikuyus still be bound by the (unwritten) agreement to support Ruto against another Kikuyu candidate in 2022? Politics, indeed, is intrigue.

Possibilities for pacific elections

The civility expected during (the run-up to) elections can often be taken for granted, yet even as the president calls for peaceful elections, rhetoric from other parts of the country can contribute to divisiveness. Perhaps the 2007 presidential election demonstrated that civility can only go so far. In Kenya, the nuance of "us" versus "them", "our people" versus "outsiders", is already manifesting itself. A year before the next scheduled general election, the concepts of "outsiders" are manifesting; "disgruntled MPs led by Starehe's Maina Kamanda confronted Ruto at his office and demanded to know why he was endorsing an 'outsider' for governor against ODM's Evans Kidero."[48] The MPs' sin was in supporting Eugene Wamalwa's bid to run for the governor's office in Kenya's most populous county, Nairobi, perceiving him to be an outsider (a Luhya, who was once a member of parliament in western Kenya). Positions such as these cement the idea of "owners" and "outsiders", complicating efforts at overcoming ethnic divisions based on ancestral community land ownership, domination of the political scene and other issues.

Actions and reactions that affirm these divisions are not helpful either; for example, MP Maina Kamanda, speaking of the Kalenjin, from whence the deputy president (DP) stems, in June 2016 raised political hackles by saying:

> even if we promised someone a seat, we will have to sit down and talk. We will not just give away the seat like that. If you think because we agreed it will go like that, we have the votes and therefore have to be respected.[49]

These remarks caused members of the ruling party, Jubilee, and specifically the Kikuyu community, to rush to condemn the statements, yet as Standard media reported, "Historical voting patterns show that Central Kenya voters are known for voting only for their own candidates, lending credence to Kabogo's views."[50] Njagi and Wainaina added that "his [Kabogo's] utterances are likely to rock Jubilee's unity as President Kenyatta's victory in 2013 was largely due to overwhelming support from Mr. Ruto's Rift Valley base."[51]

Thus, even thought the 2017 general election period did not see ethnic conflict, considering that a Kikuyu is at the top of the ticket, is head of government and his deputy is a Kalenjin, thus binding the two communities that have perpetrated – and perhaps experienced – the most ethnic conflict in independent Kenya, 2022 is a considerably different calculation. Will the Kikuyu community front a presidential candidate, or continue with the Kikuyu–Kalenjin alliance that has kept the presidency within those two communities, or will other communities unite and wrest it from their grip? More important, reinforcement of the idea that Kenya belongs to Kenyans is especially important during elections and, indeed, during the rest of the year. Paradoxically, having "outsiders" run for elective office can mitigate the notion of political seats and regions meant to exclude the "other" and serve as a unifier in that the leadership qualities, rather than ethnic origin or belongingness becomes paramount. Yet, if advanced democracies are anything to go by, calling a whole group of immigrants "rapists, drug dealers and criminals" hardly illustrates good judgment to be followed by countries in transition.

Does Kenya need to aspire to become a liberal democracy? It is useful to consider the primary tenets of liberal democracy, which is individualistic in nature, values private property and how this contrasts with the African conditions of "African socialism." Thus, rather than striving to become a liberal democracy, ethnically divided societies, which in some instances exhibit a history of community-level democracy, might do well to experiment with consociational democracy, "managed democracy". In the case of Russia, managed democracy is characterized by Skillen as "'interweaving' its well-established authoritarian traditions with democratic institutions."[52]

The ethnic angle: the two tribes thesis

Countries with fewer (rather than a plurality of) ethnic groups, when they experience conflict, do so in ways that have devastating consequences: consider, for example, Burundi's, Rwanda's and Iraq's ethnic and sectarian bloodletting. Granted, there are major outliers, for example, Somalia, whose ethnic composition is close to 99 percent homogeneously Somali. Plurality of ethnicity has been, in the history of most African – and even some now "Western" countries, such as the successor states to Yugoslavia – a spectacularly destructive force. Conversely, it can be a most constructive force, forming the basis for diversity and national cohesion, properly managed. Previously, the concept of consociational democracy in ethnically divided states was discussed, a method that might assure higher probability of peaceful coexistence between the different ethnic groups in

Kenya. Importantly, it is helpful to examine some of the benefits of multi-ethnic societies, which have been touted to include bringing a wide variety into daily life (music, culture, food, clothes), helping people of disparate backgrounds to share and enjoy other groups resources and productions, introducing new ideas and ways of doing things in the country and, as was evident in prior times, increasing economic productivity and creating new products and employment, all of which would decrease the benefits of monopolizing the so-called national cake.[53]

There has been quite a failure of imagination among the public leaders in Kenya: ethnic diversity *should* be celebrated, positively, more than it should divide Kenyans. In Pamplona, Spain, the fiestas of San Fermin, 6 to 14 July every year, about the same time that the Great Wildebeest Migration (or the Great Migration) happens across the River Mara, hundreds of thousands of spectators and participants take part in this ancient festival. In August, at the La Tomatina festival in Buñol, close to 20,000 fight with tomatoes, attendance numbers have sometimes been reported at 50,000. Kenya, a diverse land of close to 50 million people, with 42 communities, could well organize a half-day of community activities: articulation of traditions, dances, poetry, storytelling and other cultural vignettes that would be shared with the rest of the country and the world, bringing not only income but also knowledge of the heritage of the communities. The only benefit that has come of this diversity has tended to be negative.

Kenya might also benefit from looking to other countries and organizations that bear some of their characteristics, for example, Tanzania, with its emphasis on national unity through the "Ujamaa" philosophy. Also, since it appears that there continues to be an intergenerational change that facilitates greater inter-ethnic cooperation. Specifically, Gomez writes that "the emergence of inter-ethnic partnerships suggests that members of these two multi-ethnic societies, specifically those from the middle class, are comfortable and confident enough to transcend ethnic divides to establish close cooperative ties."[54] Inter-ethnic cooperation is enhanced notwithstanding the potential costs thereof, "to increase the economic pie, rather than compete for stagnant or shrinking pie slices. Such conducive *cooperation* leads to enhanced benefits for all ethnic groups, as cooperation becomes the conduit to economic growth."[55] In Kenya's case, this has been abundantly evident. The "Likoni clashes" in 1997 flatlined the tourism sector, in a way that the benefits that were envisaged in expelling "outsiders" so imperiled the local tourism sector that no foreigners were willing to come, travel advisories issued, hotels and businesses that supported the industry collapsing and thus produced unintended consequences even for those that stayed.

Two distinct trajectories in Kenya manifested during colonialism – which translated to socio-economic and political clout after independence. Some ethnic groups were indirectly affected by colonialism, but also retained (traditional economic) autonomy. Others, such as the Kikuyu, were directly impacted by colonialism, changing their lifestyles. Both groups thus have "something in common and distinct from other similar groups."[56] The Kikuyus are considered 'ethnic entrepreneurs' who "created elaborate histories or glorified aspects of 'folk culture' to justify their group's uniqueness."[57] This allowed early political organization, e.g. the KCA, and turning GEMA into a Kikuyu political lobby group. Parish, however, is not as optimistic. He writes that "there is something almost primordial in ethnic identity that mankind is unable to overcome: a preference to associate with others like oneself and to shun difference."[58] Peaceful coexistence therefore becomes a proactive activity, rather than happenstance, a goal to work towards, rather than an incidental occurrence. Compromise by the elites – the individuals who run governments – may be the next most important strand to help guide the process of pacification along. Shoup illustrates an example of this type of cooperation, writing of Malaysia, ethnically divided and rocked by sectarianism: "the Alliance model worked very well for roughly a decade because elites from the three primary parties were generally willing to compromise."[59]

The "two tribes" thesis is not an entirely new concept; it, however, manifests and is expressed in a variety of ways. Almost invariably, every society will have divisions: class, social, economic or based on some other category. Yet, increasingly, even in democratic capitalist societies, these differences are manifested in the differences in wealth. Increasingly, one hears of "the 1 percent", "the 99 percent", "the 47 percent" and so on. Around the world, the wealth inequality leads to statistics such as a billion that lives on less than US$1 a day, another billion or so on less than US$1.25 a day and so on. There are caste systems in countries such as India, yet these caste systems also underlie an economic class divide. The wealth and life opportunity differences between haves and the have-nots, even in such egalitarian societies as communist countries (or, at any rate, the perception of egalitarian societies), are quite stark. Kim Jong Un got his education in Switzerland, while most other North Koreans worked in factories in distressing conditions. Uhuru Kenyatta and Fidel Odinga were educated abroad, where perennial strikes by poorly paid teachers and lecturers in Kenya put them out of reach of the disruptions, yet they returned to occupy high positions in government. Are all animals, in the words of George Orwell, really equal?

Although Kenya is designated as a sovereign, independent country with internationally recognized boundaries, the reality is that lack of national coherence, inherent institutional weaknesses, and constant ethnic conflict; it hardly has a unitary national identity or a shared collective destiny. As such, it is a little more than an amalgamation of ethnic groups/communities with a national flag, an anthem and sporadic unity (particularly during international athletic meets, the Olympics, national tragedies with external causes) and shared documents – national identity cards and passports. Most Kenyans identify with their ethnic group; most of their formative experiences are grounded in strengths articulated better by the ethnic group than by the nation. For example, the first language they speak, all the way into about the third grade of primary (elementary) school, is their mother tongue. Ethnic identity, therefore, is much more robust and important and is the earliest identity an individual acquires.

The use of ethnic groups recognizes the contemporary literature, especially in anthropological circles, which argues that "the term 'tribe' has become as pejorative as were the terms like 'primitive', 'savage', 'rude', 'non-civilized.'"[60] Ethnic groups – in Kenya more commonly and contemporarily referred to as "communities" – are generally defined as a variation of certain features. As defined by the US Supreme

Court in *Montoya v. United States*, a tribe is defined as a body of Indians of "the same or similar race, united in a community under one leadership or government, and inhabiting a particular though sometimes ill-defined territory."[61] This definition has been periodically challenged given the racial definitions of the US government, taken against other determinations of what constitutes a race. Junger's definition is "the group of people that you would both help feed and help defend."[62] Godin's tribe develops more from association than from kinship and blood; he writes that "human beings can't help it: we need to belong. One of the most powerful of our survival mechanisms is to be part of a tribe, to contribute to (and take from) a group of *like minded* people"[63] (my italics).

Nobles introduces a rather interesting view of the tribe particularly in the case of North America as slavery intensified and more Africans were brought from Africa to North America. Hayes argues that as Africans, individuals identified themselves as "we", rather than "I", "as an Ashanti, or an Ibo rather than the person"[64] but the collection of more diverse peoples, who did not share the same background, experiences and ethnicity, led to the development of "we" – black or Africans now based on the shared experience in slavery. Wilkins argues that

> the term *tribe* can be defined from two perspectives – *ethnological* and *political-legal*. From an ethnological perspective, a tribe may be defined as a group of indigenous people connected by biology or blood; kinship, cultural and spiritual values; language; political authority; and a territorial land base.[65]

This is a more pertinent definition of the ethnic groups that can be found in Kenya, especially seen in pre-colonial times and before being amalgamated under the boundaries that define Kenya. Wilkins's definition of the political-legal is primarily based on the US's "federal recognition . . . of a tribe's legal status as a sovereign."[66]

Although the Kenyan government, scholars, elites and especially public institutions acknowledge different ethnic groups/communities, the government lacks a comprehensive philosophy on recognition of the groups or a policy on the distribution of national resources such as positions in the civil service. There is a National Cohesion and Integration Commission, whose vision is "a peaceful, united, harmonious and integrated Kenyan society"[67] based on six strategic pillars: national identity; policy, legal and institutional framework; investing in the diversity of Kenyans; reconciliation and integration; public complaints; and enforcement and institutional capacity.[68] The commission, instituted following the 2010 constitution, has sought to tamp down the rising tide of nationwide tension and ethnic violence, the distribution of ethnic composition in learning institutions' staffing.[69] More broadly, it has sought to address the causes of the hostilities between different groups, and determined from its assessment of the civil service, that "77 per cent of all public service positions are held by six communities";[70] this has been a perennial source of friction between different ethnic groups.

Rather interestingly, the percentage representation of the different ethnic groups in terms of employment in the Kenyan civil service – read government jobs – often mirrors the ethnic group's percentage in the overall population of Kenya. This is true, other than with the Kikuyu community, which accounts for 25 percent of employees of the national government, against its population percentage of around 22 percent. Other communities' representations are closer to the aggregate: for example, the representation against the population percentage (in parentheses): of the Luhya is 12.2 percent (14 percent population), the Kalenjin 11.4 percent (12 percent population), the Luo 10.4 percent (13 percent population) and the Kamba 10.3 percent (11 percent population). It has also sought to build bridges between communities, sue for peace, and bring about peace agreements in regions with perennial conflict and generally build the consensus and idea that the country is united. Yet it is not clear that its strategy of collapsing Kenya into one homogeneous (or heterogeneous but peaceful) unit is likely to work outside of major institutional reforms that begin at the very beginning: the earliest years of upbringing, which also depend on community attitudes towards other groups.

At the risk of running afoul of anthropologists by utilizing the concept of "tribe" expressing primitive attributes of a group of people or a community, it is useful to discuss the "two tribes" idea as has been done in prior literature. This is useful in attempting to illustrate the basic concept of the binary in any one society, even that of Kenya, notwithstanding its numerous ethnic groups. The complexity of the process of 42-plus (it appears that there is never consensus on how many ethnic groups there are in Kenya) – synthesizing themselves into two tribes is discussed by McLaren, quoting an unnamed Kenyan in the US, responding to the question of which of the "fifty-odd" tribes they are from:

> I could answer your question because I am not ashamed of my tribe. It is part of who I am, and I know who I am. But at the risk of sounding rude, I would rather not answer, and let me explain why. In reality, in every country, there are only two tribes: the haves and the have-nots, whatever their tribe.[71]

Kunnie reinforces this, noting that during the height of the 2007/2008 ethnic violence, one commentator responded "there are only two tribes in Kenya . . . the haves and the have-nots",[72] a position supported by Balaton-Chrimes: "It is sometimes argued that Kenya has only two tribes: the rich and the poor."[73]

Knowing this, the elites – one would generally expect the elites to know, and be, members of the "other, that is, haves" tribe – the recruitment of their tribes – and kinspeople – facilitates the elites' maintenance of the status quo. At the same time, the most populous tribe, that is, the have-nots, generally see their fate, their economic well-being, tied with the leadership of the community and the nation. Kunnie writes that

> [t]he hundreds of thousands of impoverished men and women living in Nairobi's slums like Kibera and Mbare took to the streets in angry protests when they realized that the candidate for whom they had voted and on whom they had pinned their hopes for economic change, Raila Odinga, was not going to be accorded justice in an election controlled by the ruling party.[74]

A rhetorical question that is often posed to individuals, who are die-hard believers of the 40-plus ethnic groups, rather than the two-tribe thesis, is used to illustrate the stranglehold of elites and reflecting African socialism. "If you are a Kikuyu/Luo and you run out of sugar, are you more likely to get additional sugar (immediately) from Uhuru/Raila, or from your immediate neighbor who may be of a different ethnicity?" Most individuals recognize that they are quite unlikely to ever "hang out" with the elites in their ethnic group, for whom they have fought spirited battles against the perceived "other". They also appreciate that their neighbors are more likely to come to their aid than the elites they so spiritedly support; the inconsistency between the reality and the perception regularly fails to square with electoral behavior and support of elites.

The concept of two tribes has even found its way into discussions in Kenya's National Assembly. In parliamentary proceedings on 10 September 1997, one honorable Member of Parliament (MP) articulated that

> there are two tribes nowadays in Kenya, the tribe of those who have and those who do not have. When we go to the streets, 10 o'clock in the morning, all the streets are full of people who are idle. If you ask them what they are doing, they are looking for jobs.[75]

Thus, on the one hand, the elites recognize that although they appeal to the members of their own ethnic groups in order to be elected to office, and that unemployment affects nearly all their constituents equally, they also acknowledge that there are really two tribes: them versus the citizens. In Kenya-speak, this has transformed into *wenye-nchi* (owners of the country) and *wananchi* (citizens, or children of the country). That the MP articulated this, less-than-tacit reality, such acknowledgment by a member of the elites of the economic/class division is quite rare. Yet even for all this evidence, it must be noted that Kenyans have managed to keep themselves divided based on their ethnic group, as one Facebook user articulated, including their fears: "Uhuru is President? Luos will have their private parts chopped off and Kalenjins will never be safe in their land no matter what. Pretend but this is the sad truth."[76]

In the immortal words of Reba McEntire, "Is There Life Out There", where Kenyan communities do not butcher each other with abandon after every contested election? Or is it the norm that every four to five years, hundreds of Kenyans lose their lives to ethnic bloodletting that is, and can it be avoided? Should this even be the most important question for the country, or are there more pressing issues, such as low levels of social and economic development, an unemployment rate of around 40 percent, HIV-AIDS, malaria deaths higher than the better-funded HIV-AIDS, the resurgence of polio, measles and other neglected tropical diseases? Is ethnic violence with a few hundred deaths thereafter, such a tragedy? Perhaps it is the price that democracy must pay, and Kenya loses, after all, more than 3,000 people to traffic accidents each year, close to 12,000 versus the several hundred or so every five years, both of which are perhaps equally preventable. In any event, 2017 and 2022 are years to watch for the trajectory of Kenya's nascent electoral democracy.

Notes

1 Armed Conflict Location & Event Data (ACLED). ACLED (Data) Version 6 (1997–2015). (Web). Accessed on 12/12/2016 from: www.acleddata.com/data/version-6-data-1997-2015/
2 Monty G. Marshall, Ted Robert Gurr & Keith Jaggers. "Polity IV Project: Armed Conflict and Intervention (ACI) Datasets: Dataset, User's Manual, and Country Reports." (Severn, MD: Center for Systemic Peace, 2015).
3 Michael Hardt & Antonio Negri. "Globalization and Democracy." In Paul Schumaker, Ed. *The Political Theory Reader*. (Malden, MA: Blackwell Publishing, 2010): 92.
4 ICISS. "The Responsibility to Protect: Report of the International Commission on Intervention and State Sovereignty." December 2001. (Ottawa, CA: International Development Research Centre, 2001): xi.
5 United Nations. *Rome Statute of the International Criminal Court*. (Rome, Italy, United Nations Organization, 17 July 1998): 1.
6 On the subject of sovereignty, Bliss asserts several "concerns" with the use of the concept: that the word is ambiguous, its origin (feudal) applied to a single person (one sovereign, many subjects); that it was personal rule by the king (according to Hobbes); that sovereignty is inherent in society and cannot be individualized; that it is 'the primitive absolute right of law-making" within any man or class of men; that it is omnipotence (no limitation upon the power of the state or the people; and that it is highly imprecise. See: Philemon Bliss. *Of Sovereignty*. (Clark, NJ: The Lawbook Exchange, 2005): 2–8.
7 Jean-Jacques Rousseau & Maurice Cranston. *The Social Contract*. (New York, NY: Penguin Classics, 1968): 69.
8 Rousseau & Cranston. *The Social Contract*. 69.
9 Rousseau & Cranston. *The Social Contract*. 68.
10 Cristina Gabriela Badescu. *Humanitarian Intervention and the Responsibility to Protect: Security and Human Rights*. (New York, NY: Routledge, 2011): 140.
11 Badescu. *Humanitarian Intervention and the Responsibility to Protect*. 140.
12 See Patrick S. Wegner. *The International Criminal Court in Ongoing Intrastate Conflicts: Navigating the Peace-Justice Divide*. (Cambridge, UK: Cambridge University Press, 2015) and Surabhi Ranganathan. *Strategically Created Treaty Conflicts and the Politics of International Law*. (Cambridge, UK: Cambridge University Press, 2014), among others.
13 Dawn Rothe & Christopher W. Mullins. *State Crime: Current Perspectives*. (New Brunswick, NJ: Rutgers University Press, 2011): 288.
14 Elizabeth G. Ferris. *The Politics of Protection: The Limits of Humanitarian Action*. (Washington, DC: The Brookings Institution, 2011): 169.
15 Lisa Kammerud. "In the Shadow of Violence: The Ever Project Sheds Light on the Dynamics of Violence." *Democracy at Large*, 2, No. 2 (2006): n.p. To the definition of electoral violence, Nabudere adds the following acts: hooliganism, use of force to disrupt political meetings or voting at polling stations, or the use of dangerous weapons to intimidate voters and other electoral processes or to cause bodily harm or injury to any person connected with electoral processes." D. Wadada Nabudere. *Afrikology and Transdisciplinarity: A Restorative Epistemology*. (Pretoria, South Africa: Africa Institute of South Africa, 2012): 9.
16 Emmanuel Gyimah-Boadi. "Managing Electoral Conflicts: Lessons from Ghana." In Timothy D. Sisk & Andrew Reynolds, Eds. *Elections and Conflict Management in Africa*, Vol. 31. (Washington, DC: USIP Press, 1998): 102.
17 Anna K. Jarstad. "Post-Accord Elections and Armed Conflict." In Ashok Swain, Ramses Amer & Joakim Öjendal, Eds. *The Democratization Project: Opportunities and Challenges*. (New York, NY: Anthem Press, 2011): 157.

18 Paul Tiyambe Zeleza. "The Causes & Costs of War in Africa: From Liberation Struggles to the 'War on Terror'." In Alfred G. Nhema & Paul Tiyambe Zeleza, Eds. *The Roots of African Conflicts: The Causes & Costs*. (Oxford, UK: James Currey, 2008): 2.
19 Steven I. Wilkinson. *Votes and Violence: Electoral Competition and Ethnic Riots in India*. (Cambridge, UK: Cambridge University Press, 2004): 97.
20 Marc A. Lemieux. "Iraq's Conflicted Transition to Democracy: Analyzing Elections in a Violent Society." In David Gillies, Ed. *Elections in Dangerous Places: Democracy and the Paradoxes of Peacebuilding*. (Montreal, CA: McGill-Queen's University Press, 2011): 33.
21 Sabine Höhn. "New Start of False Start? The ICC and Electoral Violence in Kenya." In Gerhard Anders & Olaf Zenker, Eds. *Transition and Justice: Negotiating the Terms of New Beginnings in Africa*. (Malden, MA: Wiley-Blackwell, 2015): 188.
22 Fondo Sikod. "Conflicts & Implications for Poverty & Food Security Policies in Africa." In Alfred G. Nhema & Paul Tiyambe Zeleza, Eds. *The Roots of African Conflicts: The Causes & Costs*. (Oxford, UK: James Currey, 2008): 199.
23 Gyimah-Boadi. "Managing Electoral Conflicts: Lessons from Ghana." 102–105.
24 See, for example, Thomas Edward Flores & Irfan Nooruddin. *Elections in Hard Times: Building Stronger Democracies in the 21st Century*. (Cambridge, UK: Cambridge University Press & The Wilson Center, 2016): 60.
25 For clarification on the INUS Condition, part of Durand's explanation is reproduced here: "INUS is an acronym coined by Mackie (1965) for 'an Insufficient but Necessary part of a condition which is itself unnecessary but sufficient for the result.' An INUS condition is an insufficient but necessary part (conjunction) of the factor that produces the effect; that factor being non-necessary but sufficient (disjunction) to produce the effect. An example helps understand this INUS condition. A house is burning. A short circuit is an unnecessary but sufficient condition that may have caused the fire: unnecessary because a fire may have other causes, and sufficient because in the presence of inflammable objects, the fire may catch. Inflammable objects are in turn necessary conditions for the fire to burn but insufficient alone to ignite. If the police officer can determine the occurrence of a short circuit and eliminate all other possible sources of fire, she can conclude that the short circuit was the cause of the fire. Finally, in this case, the short circuit is a non-sufficient and unnecessary cause of the effect (the fire)," Rodolphe Durand. "Competitive Advantages Exist: A Critique of Powell." *Strategic Management Journal*, 23 (2002): 867.
26 Edward N. Muller. "Income Inequality, Regime Repressiveness, and Political Violence." *American Sociological Review*, 50, No. 1 (February, 1985): 53.
27 Muller. "Income Inequality, Regime Repressiveness, and Political Violence." 53.
28 Nabudere. *Afrikology and Transdisciplinarity*. 9.
29 Daily Nation Staff. "President Kenyatta Warns Foreign Countries against Interfering in 2017 Elections." *Nation Newspapers* (online video). 12 December 2016.
30 Isaac Ongiri. "Uhuru Warns on Chaos as Kenya Readies for Polls." *Nation Newspapers*. Tuesday 13 December 2016. (Web).
31 In Kikuyu Ethnology, the community comes descends from Gĩkũyũ and Mũmbi, and therefore refer to themselves as the people of the House of Mũmbi, or *Nyũmba ya Mũmbi,* often shortened to *Nyũmba*.
32 James Mulli. "Kikuyu." In Melvin E. Page, Ed. *Colonialism: An International Social, Cultural, and Political Encyclopedia*. (Santa Barbara, CA: ABC-CLIO, 2003): 316.
33 Adam Hummel. *Amani Haki Yetu: Peace Is Our Right*. (Bloomington, IN: iUniverse, 2012): 25.
34 Anke Weber, Wesley Hiers & Anaïd Flesken. *Politicized Ethnicity: A Comparative Perspective*. (New York, NY: Palgrave Macmillan 2016): 30.
35 Weber. *Politicized Ethnicity*. 30.
36 Mulli. "Kikuyu." 316.

37 Mary Fitzpatrick, Tim Brewer & Matthew Firestone. *East Africa*. (Melborne, Australia: Lonely Planet, 2016) (eBook): 47.
38 Edward W. Soja. *The Geography of Modernization in Kenya: A Spatial Analysis of Social, Economic, and Political Change*. (Syracuse, NY: Syracuse University, 1968): 24.
39 Fitzpatrick, Brewer & Firestone. "East Africa." 47.
40 Adam Hummel. *Amani Haki Yetu: Peace Is Our Right*. (South Africa: Partridge, 2014): 24.
41 Hummel. *Amani Haki Yetu*. 24.
42 Karuti Kanyinga. "The Legacy of the White Highlands: Land Rights, Ethnicity and the Post-2007 Election Violence in Kenya." In Peter Kagwanja & Roger Southall, Eds. *Kenya's Uncertain Democracy: The Electoral Crisis of 2008*. (New York, NY: Routledge, 2010): 77.
43 Aspects of cultural dominance manifest themselves in the context of language; the Kikuyu language has lent words, expressions and other aspects of dominance to "Sheng" and is one of the most spoken, second ethnic languages after Swahili.
44 Most contemporary political science/international relations definitions of power define it as "the ability of A to get B to do what A wants, at an acceptable cost to B"; in this case, one might allude to getting the Kikuyus to do what the rest of the country wants, while simultaneously not alienating the Kikuyu people, as was the case during the Moi years.
45 Macharia Munene. *Historical Reflections on Kenya: Intellectual Adventurism, Politics and International Relations*. (Nairobi, Kenya: University of Nairobi Press, 2012): 136. The Chania reference is generally thought to refer to Nyeri/Murang'a areas of the traditional Kikuyu territory, as one has to cross the Chania River, especially to go to Nyeri and parts of Murang'a, thus inferring that leadership would remain with the Kiambu Kikuyu; others have asserted that this included everything west of Central Province, particularly the Rift Valley and Western/Nyanza provinces, especially given Kenyatta's fallout with Jaramogi Oginga Odinga.
46 Ephalina A. Maina, Wycliffe A. Oboka & Julius Makong'o. *History and Government Form 3*. (Nairobi, Kenya: East African Educational Publishers, 2004): 174.
47 Munene. *Historical Reflections on Kenya*. 136.
48 Star Team. "Angry MPs Meet Ruto over Eugene Bid for Governor." *The Star*. 3 August 2016. (Web).
49 Standard Team. "Kabogo Remarks on Ruto's 2022 Support for Top Seat Jolt Jubilee." *Standard Digital*. Sunday 12 June 2016. (Web).
50 Standard Team. "Kabogo Remarks on Ruto's 2022 Support for Top Seat Jolt Jubilee." n.p1.
51 John Njagi & Eric Wainaina. "Jubilee MPs Tell off Kabogo over Anti-Ruto Talk." *Daily Nation*. Thursday 9 June 2016. (Web).
52 Daphne Skillen. *Freedom of Speech in Russia: Politics and Media from Gorbachev to Putin*. (New York, NY: Routledge, 2016): 269.
53 Michael Keene. *GCSE Religious Studies: Religion in Life & Society Student Book for Edexcel/A*. (Dunstable, UK: Folens Publishers, 2002): 69.
54 Edmund Terence Gomez. "Inter-Ethnic Relations, Business and Identity: The Chinese in Britain and Malaysia." In Nicholas Tarling & Terence Gomez, Eds. *The State, Development and Identity in Multi-Ethnic Societies: Ethnicity, Equity and the Nation*. (New York, NY: Routledge, 2008): 52.
55 Milica Z. Bookman. *Ethnic Groups in Motion: Economic Competition and Migration in Multi-Ethnic States*. (London, UK: Frank Cass & Co. Ltd., 2002): 228.
56 Thomas Barfield. "Afghanistan Is Not the Balkans: Central Asian Ethnicity and Its Political Consequences." In Robert L. Canfield & Gabriele Rasuly-Paleczek, Eds. *Ethnicity, Authority and Power in Central Asia: New Games Great and Small*. (New York, NY: Routledge, 2011): 98.
57 Barfield. *Ethnicity, Authority and Power in Central Asia*. 98.
58 Matthew Parish. *Free City in the Balkans: Reconstructing a Divided Society in Bosnia*. (New York, NY: I. B. Tauris & Co., 2010): 18.

59 Brian S. Shoup. *Conflict and Cooperation in Multi-Ethnic States: Institutional Incentives, Myths and Counter-Balancing*. (New York, NY: Routledge, 2008): 114.
60 Vinay Kumar Srivastava & Sukant K. Chaudhury. "Anthropological Studies of Indian Tribes." In Yogesh Atal, Ed. *Sociology and Social Anthropology in India*. (New Delhi, India: Dorling Kindersley (India), 2009): 74.
61 See Mark Edwin Miller. *Forgotten Tribes: Unrecognized Indians and the Federal Acknowledgment Process*. (Lincoln, NE: University of Nebraska Press, 2004): 28 and Gerald Torres and Kathryn Milun. "Translating *Yonnondio* by Precedent and Evidence: The Mashpee Indian Case." In Richard Delgado & Jean Stefancic, Eds. *Critical Race Theory: The Cutting Edge*, 2nd Ed. (Philadelphia, PA: Temple University Press, 2000): 54.
62 Sebastian Junger. *Tribe: On Homecoming and Belonging*. (New York, NY: Twelve, 2016): 110. As articulated, this definition has more to do with the concept of soldiers fighting in war than in perhaps a Native American or African ethnic group or community.
63 Seth Godin. *Tribes: We Need You to Lead Us*. (New York, NY: Penguin Group, 2008): 3.
64 Wade W. Nobles. "African Philosophy: Foundations for Black Psychology." In Floyd Windom Hayes, Ed. *A Turbulent Voyage: Readings in African American Studies*, 3rd Ed. (Lanham, MD: Rowman & Littlefield Publishers, 2000): 289.
65 David Eugene Wilkins. *American Indian Politics and the American Political System*, 2nd Ed. (Lanham, MD: Rowman & Littlefield Publishers, 2007): 17.
66 Wilkins. *American Indian Politics and the American Political System*. 17.
67 NCIC. "Vision and Mission." (Web): n.p. Accessed on 12/16/2016 from: https://www.cohesion.or.ke/
68 NCIC. "Vision and Mission." n.p.
69 Ouma Wanzala. "Varsities, NCIC Clash over Report on Ethnicity." *Daily Nation*. Wednesday 7 December 2016. (Web).
70 Samwel Born Maina. "Six Tribes Take up More Than Half of All Public Sector Jobs – Report." *Daily Nation*. Saturday 5 September 2015. (Web).
71 Brian D. McLaren. *Why Did Jesus, Moses, the Buddha, and Mohammed Cross the Road? Christian Identity in a Multi-Faith World*. (New York, NY: Jericho Books, 2012): 248.
72 Julian E. Kunnie. *The Cost of Globalization: Dangers to the Earth and Its People*. (Jefferson, NC: McFarland & Company, 2015): 272.
73 Samantha Balaton-Chrimes. *Ethnicity, Democracy and Citizenship in Africa: Political Marginalisation of Kenya's Nubians (Contemporary African Politics)*. (New York, NY: Routledge, 2016): 23.
74 Kunnie. *The Cost of Globalization*. 272.
75 Kenya National Assembly. *Kenya National Assembly Official Record (Hansard) Sep 10, 1997*. (Nairobi, Kenya: Government Press, 1997): 2298.
76 Agnes Lucy Lando & Stella W. Mwangi. "Social Media and Cell Phones Are Bonding and Vilification Tools: Exposing Kenya's 2013 Postelection Violence." In Bala A. Musa & Jim Willis, Eds. *From Twitter to Tahrir Square: Ethics in Social and New Media Communication*. (Santa Barbara, CA: ABC-CLIO, 2014): 288.

References

Armed Conflict Location & Event Data (ACLED). ACLED (Data) Version 6 (1997–2015). (Web). Accessed on 12/12/2016 from: www.acleddata.com/data/version-6-data-1997-2015/

Badescu, Cristina Gabriela. *Humanitarian Intervention and the Responsibility to Protect: Security and Human Rights*. New York, NY: Routledge, 2011.

Balaton-Chrimes, Samantha. *Ethnicity, Democracy and Citizenship in Africa: Political Marginalisation of Kenya's Nubians (Contemporary African Politics)*. New York, NY: Routledge, 2016.

Barfield, Thomas. "Afghanistan Is Not the Balkans: Central Asian Ethnicity and Its Political Consequences." In Robert L. Canfield & Gabriele Rasuly-Paleczek, Eds. *Ethnicity, Authority and Power in Central Asia: New Games Great and Small*. New York, NY: Routledge, 2011. Ch. 5, pp. 95–109.

Bliss, Philemon. *Of Sovereignty*. Clark, NJ: The Lawbook Exchange, 2005.

Bookman, Milica Z. *Ethnic Groups in Motion: Economic Competition and Migration in Multi-Ethnic States*. London, UK: Frank Cass & Co. Ltd., 2002.

Daily Nation Staff. "President Kenyatta Warns Foreign Countries against Interfering in 2017 Elections." *Nation Newspapers*. 12 December 2016 (online video). Accessed on 12/13/2016 from: www.nation.co.ke/video/1951480-3484596-42p9edz/index.html

Durand, Rodolphe. "Competitive Advantages Exist: A Critique of Powell." *Strategic Management Journal*, 23 (2002): 867–872. Doi:10.1002/smj.253

Ferris, Elizabeth G. *The Politics of Protection: The Limits of Humanitarian Action*. Washington, DC: The Brookings Institution, 2011.

Fitzpatrick, Mary, Tim Bewer & Matthew Firestone. *East Africa*. Melbourne, Austrailia: Lonely Planet, 2016. (eBook).

Flores, Thomas Edward & Irfan Nooruddin. *Elections in Hard Times: Building Stronger Democracies in the 21st Century*. Cambridge, UK: Cambridge University Press & The Wilson Center, 2016.

Godin, Seth. *Tribes: We Need You to Lead Us*. New York, NY: Penguin Group, 2008.

Gomez, Edmund Terence. "Inter-Ethnic Relations, Business and Identity: The Chinese in Britain and Malaysia." In Nicholas Tarling & Terence Gomez, Eds. *The State, Development and Identity in Multi-Ethnic Societies: Ethnicity, Equity and the Nation*. New York, NY: Routledge, 2008.

Gyimah-Boadi, Emmanuel. "Managing Electoral Conflicts: Lessons from Ghana." In Timothy D. Sisk & Andrew Reynolds, Eds. *Elections and Conflict Management in Africa*, Vol. 31. Washington, DC: USIP Press, 1998. Ch. 6, pp. 101–118.

Hakimi, Monica. "Distributing the Responsibility to Protect." In André Nollkaemper & Dov Jacobs, Eds. *Distribution of Responsibilities in International Law*. Cambridge, UK: Cambridge University Press, 2015.

Hardt, Michael & Antonio Negri. "Globalization and Democracy." In Paul Schumaker, Ed. *The Political Theory Reader*. Malden, MA: Blackwell Publishing, 2010.

Höglund, Kristine. "Electoral Violence in Conflict-Ridden Societies: Concepts, Causes, and Consequences." *Terrorism & Political Violence*, 21, No. 3 (2009): 412–427. doi:10.1080/09546550902950290

Höhn, Sabine. "New Start of False Start? The ICC and Electoral Violence in Kenya." In Gerhard Anders & Olaf Zenker, Eds. *Transition and Justice: Negotiating the Terms of New Beginnings in Africa*. Malden, MA: Wiley-Blackwell, 2015. Ch. 9, pp. 175–198.

Hummel, Adam. *Amani Haki Yetu: Peace Is Our Right*. Bloomington, IN: iUniverse, 2012.

ICISS. "The Responsibility to Protect: Report of the International Commission on Intervention and State Sovereignty." December 2001. Ottawa, CA: International Development Research Centre, 2001.

Jarstad, Anna K. "Post-Accord Elections and Armed Conflict." In Ashok Swain, Ramses Amer & Joakim Öjendal, Eds. *The Democratization Project: Opportunities and Challenges*. New York, NY: Anthem Press, 2011.

Junger, Sebastian. *Tribe: On Homecoming and Belonging*. New York, NY: Twelve, 2016.

Kammerud, Lisa. "In the Shadow of Violence: The Ever Project Sheds Light on the Dynamics of Violence." *Democracy at Large*, 2, No. 2 (2006).

Kanyinga, Karuti. "The Legacy of the White Highlands: Land Rights, Ethnicity and the Post-2007 Election Violence in Kenya." In Peter Kagwanja & Roger Southall, Eds. *Kenya's Uncertain Democracy: The Electoral Crisis of 2008*. New York, NY: Routledge, 2010.

Keene, Michael. *GCSE Religious Studies: Religion in Life & Society Student Book for Edexcel/A*. Dunstable, UK: Folens Publishers, 2002.

Kenya National Assembly. *Kenya National Assembly Official Record (Hansard) Sep 10, 1997*. Nairobi, Kenya: Government Press, 1997.

Kunnie, Julian E. *The Cost of Globalization: Dangers to the Earth and Its People*. Jefferson, NC: McFarland & Company, 2015.

Lando, Agnes Lucy & Stella W. Mwangi. "Social Media and Cell Phones Are Bonding and Vilification Tools: Exposing Kenya's 2013 Postelection Violence." In Bala A. Musa & Jim Willis, Eds. *From Twitter to Tahrir Square: Ethics in Social and New Media Communication*. Santa Barbara, CA: ABC-CLIO, 2014.

Lemieux, Marc A. "Iraq's Conflicted Transition to Democracy: Analyzing Elections in a Violent Society." In David Gillies, Ed. *Elections in Dangerous Places: Democracy and the Paradoxes of Peacebuilding*. Montreal, CA: McGill-Queen's University Press, 2011. Ch. 3, pp. 32–52.

Maina, Ephalina A., Wycliffe A. Oboka & Julius Makong'o. *History and Government Form 3*. Nairobi, Kenya: East African Educational Publishers, 2004.

Maina, Samwel Born. "Six Tribes Take up More Than Half of All Public Sector Jobs – Report." *Daily Nation*. Saturday 5 September 2015. (Web). Accessed on 12/16/2016 from: www.nation.co.ke/news/Six-tribes-take-up-more-than-half-of-all-public-sector-jobs-/1056-2859898-ch02m0/index.html

Marshall, Monty G., Ted Robert Gurr & Keith Jaggers. 2015. "Polity IV Project: Armed Conflict and Intervention (ACI) Datasets: Dataset, User's Manual, and Country Reports." Severn, MD: Center for Systemic Peace. (Web). Accessed 12/12/2016 from: www.systemicpeace.org/inscrdata.html

Mcallister, Ian. "Civic Education and Political Knowledge in Australia." *Australian Journal of Political Science*, 33, No. 1 (1998): 7–23. doi:10.1080/10361149850697

McLaren, Brian D. *Why Did Jesus, Moses, the Buddha, and Mohammed Cross the Road? Christian Identity in a Multi-Faith World*. New York, NY: Jericho Books, 2012.

Miller, Mark Edwin. *Forgotten Tribes: Unrecognized Indians and the Federal Acknowledgment Process*. Lincoln, NE: University of Nebraska Press, 2004.

Muller, Edward N. "Income Inequality, Regime Repressiveness, and Political Violence." *American Sociological Review*, 50, No. 1 (February, 1985): 47–61. Accessed on 12/13/2016 from: www.jstor.org/stable/2095339

Mulli, James. "Kikuyu." In Melvin E. Page, Ed. *Colonialism: An International Social, Cultural, and Political Encyclopedia*. Santa Barbara, CA: ABC-CLIO, 2003.

Munene, Macharia. *Historical Reflections on Kenya: Intellectual Adventurism, Politics and International Relations*. Nairobi, Kenya: University of Nairobi Press, 2012.

Nabudere, D. Wadada. *Afrikology and Transdisciplinarity: A Restorative Epistemology*. Pretoria, South Africa: Africa Institute of South Africa, 2012.

NCIC. "Vision and Mission." (Web). Accessed on 12/16/2016 from: www.cohesion.or.ke/

Njagi, John & Eric Wainaina. "Jubilee MPs Tell off Kabogo over Anti-Ruto Talk." *Daily Nation*. Thursday 9 June 2016. (Web). Accessed on 12/15/2016 from: www.nation.co.ke/news/Jubilee-MPs-tell-off-Kabogo-over-anti-Ruto-talk/1056-3240896-qam642z/index.html

Nobles, Wade W. "African Philosophy: Foundations for Black Psychology." In Floyd Windom Hayes, Ed. *A Turbulent Voyage: Readings in African American Studies*, 3rd Ed. Lanham, MD: Rowman & Littlefield Publishers, 2000.

Ongiri, Isaac. "Uhuru Warns on Chaos as Kenya Readies for Polls." *Nation Newspapers*. Tuesday 13 December 2016. (Web). Accessed on 12/13/2016 from: www.nation.co.ke/news/politics/Uhuru-warns-leaders-on-2017-poll-violence/1064-3484350-po72xf/index.html

Parish, Matthew. *Free City in the Balkans: Reconstructing a Divided Society in Bosnia*. New York, NY: I. B. Tauris & Co., 2010.

Ranganathan, Surabhi. *StrategicallyCreated Treaty Conflicts and the Politics of International Law*. Cambridge, UK: Cambridge University Press, 2014.

Rothe, Dawn & Christopher W. Mullins. *State Crime: Current Perspectives*. New Brunswick, NJ: Rutgers University Press, 2011.

Rousseau, Jean-Jacques & Maurice Cranston. *The Social Contract*. New York, NY: Penguin Classics, 1968.

Shoup, Brian S. *Conflict and Cooperation in Multi-Ethnic States: Institutional Incentives, Myths and Counter-Balancing*. New York, NY: Routledge, 2008.

Sikod, Fondo. "Conflicts & Implications for Poverty & Food Security Policies in Africa." In Alfred G. Nhema & Paul Tiyambe Zeleza, Eds. *The Roots of African Conflicts: The Causes & Costs*. Oxford, UK: James Currey, 2008. Ch. 8, pp. 199–213.

Skillen, Daphne. *Freedom of Speech in Russia: Politics and Media from Gorbachev to Putin*. New York, NY: Routledge, 2016.

Srivastava, Vinay Kumar & Sukant K. Chaudhury. "Anthropological Studies of Indian Tribes." In Yogesh Atal, Ed. *Sociology and Social Anthropology in India*. New Delhi, India: Dorling Kindersley (India), 2009. Ch. 2, pp. 50–119.

Standard Team. "Kabogo Remarks on Ruto's 2022 Support for Top Seat Jolt Jubilee." *Standard Digital*. Sunday 12 June 2016. (Web). Accessed on 12/14/2016 from: www.standardmedia.co.ke/mobile/article/2000204889

Torres, Gerald & Kathryn Milun. "Translating *Yonnondio* by Precedent and Evidence: The Mashpee Indian Case." In Richard Delgado & Jean Stefancic, Eds. *Critical Race Theory: The Cutting Edge*, 2nd Ed. Philadelphia, PA: Temple University Press, 2000.

United Nations General Assembly, Sixtieth Sessions. "60/1. 2005 World Summit Outcome." A/RES/60/1. 24 October 2005. Accessed on 12/12/2016 from: www.un.org/womenwatch/ods/A-RES-60-1-E.pdf

United Nations General Assembly, Sixty-Third Session. "Implementing the Responsibility to Protect: Report of the Secretary-General." A/63/677. 12 January 2009. Accessed on 12/12/2016 from: www.un.org/en/ga/search/view_doc.asp?symbol=A/63/677

Wanzala, Ouma. "Varsities, NCIC Clash over Report on Ethnicity." *Daily Nation*. Wednesday 7 December 2016. (Web). Accessed on 12/16/2016 from: www.nation.co.ke/news/education/Varsities-NCIC-clash-over-report-on-ethnicity/2643604-3478720-h5k1jc/index.html

Weber, Anke, Wesley Hiers & Anaïd Flesken. *Politicized Ethnicity: A Comparative Perspective*. New York, NY: Palgrave Macmillan, 2016.

Wegner, Patrick S. *The International Criminal Court in Ongoing Intrastate Conflicts: Navigating the Peace-Justice Divide*. Cambridge, UK: Cambridge University Press, 2015.

Wilkins, David Eugene. *American Indian Politics and the American Political System*, 2nd Ed. Lanham, MD: Rowman & Littlefield Publishers, 2007.

Wilkinson, Steven I. *Votes and Violence: Electoral Competition and Ethnic Riots in India*. Cambridge, UK: Cambridge University Press, 2004.

Zeleza, Paul Tiyambe. "The Causes & Costs of War in Africa: From Liberation Struggles to the 'War on Terror'." In Alfred G. Nhema & Paul Tiyambe Zeleza, Eds. *The Roots of African Conflicts: The Causes & Costs*. Oxford, UK: James Currey, 2008. pp. 1–35.

Index